STUDY GUIDE

Henry Borne

SOCIOLOGY

EIGHTH EDITION

John J. Macionis

Prentice Hall, Upper Saddle River, New Jersey 07458

©2001 by PRENTICE-HALL, INC.
PEARSON EDUCATION
Upper Saddle River, New Jersey 07458

10 9 8 7 6 5 4 3

ISBN-0-13-018506-X

Printed in the United States of America

Table of Contents

Preface

This study guide has been written to enhance the foundation of sociological ideas and issues that are presented in the text, *Sociology 8/e* by John Macionis. To help you review and think about the material found in the text, the study guide has been organized into several different sections to accompany each chapter in the text.

A *Chapter Outline* provides a basis for organizing segments of information from each chapter in the text. A section on *Learning Objectives* identifies the basic knowledge, explanations, comparisons, and understandings students should have after reading and reflecting upon each chapter. This section is followed by **Key Terms** in which the important concepts from each chapter are listed, with space provided for the student to write the definition for each of the terms. *Important Researchers* cites many of the researchers cited in the text, with space provided for students to write out important ideas, findings, etc. The next section provides *Study Questions*, including true-false, multiple-choice, matching, fill-in, and short answer type questions. They are followed by *Answers to Study Questions*, which include a list of the page numbers where the answers to these questions can be found. The seventh section, *In Focus—Important Issues*, provides the student an opportunity to answer questions relating to some of the more important concepts and ideas presented in each chapter. The final section, *Comment and Analysis*, provides space for students to raise questions and make comments on the boxes in each chapter.

This study guide is intended as a learning tool to accompany the text *Sociology*. It will hopefully provide the student with the opportunity to gain more knowledge of sociology as it is presented by the author, who discusses the social issues and problems confronting us today.

On a personal note, I want to congratulate Dr. Macionis for writing such an excellent and engaging sociology text. He offers students a very meaningful perspective on many important issues confronting our society and the world. I believe students will be excited by this text, and rewarded by what it has to offer them both personally and academically. It has been a pleasure for me to write this Study Guide. I would like to thank Nancy Roberts, Publisher, Sociology/Anthropology of Prentice Hall for her giving me the opportunity to write this study guide. I would also like to thank Chris De John for all of his work on this project. I also very much appreciate the great efforts of Christina Scalia, Editorial Assistant—Sociology, and Nicole Conforti, Consulting Editor on this project. Finally, my love to my family—Cincy, Ben, and Abby—for their support and love.

HB

1 | The Sociological Perspective

PART I: CHAPTER OUTLINE

PART II: LEARNING OBJECTIVES

1. To be able to define sociology and understand the basic components of the sociological perspective.
2. To be able to provide examples of the ways in which social forces affect our everyday lives.
3. To recognize the importance of taking a global perspective in order to recognize the interdependence of our world's nations and people.
4. To begin to recognize factors in society that encourage people to perceive the world sociologically.
5. To be able to recognize the benefits of using the sociological perspective.
6. To be able to identify important historical factors in the development of the discipline of sociology as a science.
8. To be able to identify and discuss the differences between the three major theoretical paradigms used by sociologists in the analysis of society.

PART III: KEY CONCEPTS

Define each of the following concepts in the space provided or on a separate piece of paper. Check the accuracy of your answers by referring to the key concepts section at the end of the chapter in the text as well as referring to the italicized definitions located throughout the chapter. Do the same for each chapter as you read through the text during the semester.

global perspective

high-income countries

latent functions

low-income countries

macro-level orientation

manifest functions

micro-level orientation

middle-income countries

positivism

2

social-conflict paradigm

social dysfunction

social function

social marginality

social structure

sociology

stereotype

structural-functional paradigm

symbolic-interaction paradigm

theoretical paradigm

theory

PART IV: IMPORTANT RESEARCHERS

Jane Addams	Herbert Spencer
Emile Durkheim	Karl Marx
Max Weber	Robert Merton
Peter Berger	C. Wright Mills
Lenore Weitzman	W.E.B. Du Bois

Harriet Martineau   Auguste Comte

PART V: STUDY QUESTIONS

<u>True-False</u>

1.   T   F   A major component of the sociological perspective is the attempt to seek the *particular in the general*.

2.   T   F   Emile Durkheim's research on *suicide* illustrates the point that not all aspects of social life can be meaningfully studied using the sociological perspective.

3.   T   F   In 1995, most African American, Hispanic, and white high school graduates enrolled in college that same year.

4.   T   F   African Americans and females have *higher suicide rates* than whites and males.

5.   T   F   The *middle-income countries* of the world are primarily found in Latin America, Eastern Europe, and much of southern Africa.

6.   T   F   Less than ten percent of the world's population lives in *North America*.

7.   T   F   *Encountering people who are different, social marginality,* and *social disruption* are identified as factors that prompt people to view the world sociologically.

8.   T   F   Most men and women who continue beyond a bachelor's degree to earn advanced training in sociology go on to careers in *teaching* and *research*.

9.   T   F   The discipline of *sociology* first emerged in Europe during the nineteenth century.

10. T   F   Auguste Comte saw sociology as the product of a three-stage historical development, including the *theological stage,* the *metaphysical stage*, and the *scientific stage.*

11. T   F   *Positivism* is an approach to understanding the world based on metaphysics.

12. T   F   Jane Addams founded *Hull House*, a settlement house in Chicago, where she provided assistance to immigrant families.

13. T   F   A *theory* is a statement of how and why specific facts are related.

14. T   F   *Latent functions* refer to social processes which appear on the surface to be functional for society, but which are actually detrimental.

15. T   F   The *symbolic-interaction* and *social-conflict* paradigms both operate from a *micro-level orientation.*

16. T   F   The *symbolic-interactionist* paradigm presents society less in terms of abstract generalizations and more as everyday experiences.

17. T   F   The core question of the *structural-functional* paradigm is: How is society divided?

18. T   F   A *generalization* is defined as an exaggerated description that one applies to all people in some category.

1.   The *Pine Street Inn* is:

        (a)   a state prison in California.
        (b)   a homeless shelter in Boston.
        (c)   a location in New York City's Greenwich Village where sociologists meet to talk about social issues.
        (d)   a residence hall at Yale University.

2.   What is the *essential wisdom* of sociology?

        (a)   Patterns in life are predestined.
        (b)   Society is essentially nonpatterned.
        (c)   Surrounding society affects our actions, thoughts, and feelings.
        (d)   Common sense needs to guide sociological investigations.

3.   The sociological perspective involves *seeing the strange in the familiar*. Which of the following best provides the essential meaning of this phrase?

        (a)   Sociology interprets social life primarily relying on common sense.
        (b)   Sociologists believe intuition rather than logic is the preferred way to study society.
        (c)   Sociologists focus on the bizarre behaviors that occur in society.
        (d)   Sociologists work to avoid the assumption that human behavior is simply a matter of what people decide to do.

4.   Which sociologist, in a systematic empirical study, linked the incidence of *suicide* to the degree of *social integration* of different categories of people?

        (a)   Emile Durkheim
        (b)   Max Weber
        (c)   Robert Merton
        (d)   C. Wright Mills
        (e)   Karl Marx

5.   In 1995, sixty-three percent of *whites* graduating from high school went on to college that fall. For *African Americans*, the corresponding figure was _____ percent.

        (a)   12
        (b)   18
        (c)   26
        (d)   40
        (e)   51

6. *Low-income countries* are described as

   (a) nations with little industrialization and severe poverty.
   (b) nations with limited natural resources and large populations.
   (c) nations with per capita incomes of less than $15,000.
   (d) nations with no industrialization and limited natural resources.

7. Which of the following is *not* identified by the author as a reason a *global perspective* is so important?

   (a) Societies the world over are increasingly interconnected.
   (b) Many problems that we face in the United States are not found in other societies.
   (c) Thinking globally is a good way to learn more about ourselves.
   (d) All of the above are identified by our author as reasons why a global perspective is so important.

8. In the *global village* presented by the author, which of the following continents is represented by more than one-half of the village's residents?

   (a) Europe
   (b) Africa
   (c) North America
   (d) South America
   (e) Asia

9. Which of the following is/are identified as situations that simulate *sociological thinking*?

   (a) encountering people who are different from us
   (b) social marginality
   (c) social crisis
   (d) all of the above
   (e) none of the above

10. Learning to understand our individual lives in terms of the social forces that have shaped them is a state of mind that C. Wright Mills called

   (a) science.
   (b) hypothesis testing.
   (c) the sociological imagination.
   (d) perspective.
   (e) positivism.

11. The benefits of sociology go well beyond personal growth. Sociologists have helped shape public policy and law in countless ways. To illustrate this, the work by Lenore Weitzman on _____ had a real impact on public policy and resulted in the passage of several laws in California.

   (a) macro-level forces affecting suicide rates
   (b) date rape
   (c) financial hardships facing women after a divorce
   (d) standardized educational assessment measures

12. Sociology first flowered as a discipline in which countries?

   (a) the United States and Canada
   (b) France, Germany, and England
   (c) Russia and Poland
   (d) Spain and Italy
   (e) Greece and Egypt

13. The term *sociology* was coined in 1838 by

   (a) Auguste Comte.
   (b) Karl Marx.
   (c) Herbert Spencer.
   (d) Emile Durkheim.
   (e) Max Weber.

14. According to Auguste Comte, the key to understanding society was to look at it

   (a) using common sense.
   (b) using intuition.
   (c) theologically.
   (d) metaphysically.
   (e) scientifically.

15. *Positivism* is the idea that _____, rather than any other type of human understanding, is the path to knowledge.

   (a) human nature
   (b) science
   (c) faith
   (d) optimism
   (e) common sense

16.   Two *founders of sociology* who had radically different views on society--one more conservative and focused on sociology as a science, the other more critical and focused on change--were

   (a)   C. Wright Mills and Robert Merton.
   (b)   Jane Addams and Peter Blau.
   (c)   Emile Durkheim and Robert Merton.
   (d)   Auguste Comte and Karl Marx.

17.   _____ translated the works of Auguste Comte from French to English in 1853. She also was a noted scholar in her own right, revealing the evils of slavery and arguing for laws to protect factory workers.

   (a)   Jane Addams
   (b)   Lois Benjamin
   (c)   Ruth Bogda
   (d)   Irene Rappoport
   (e)   Harriet Martineau

18.   A *basic image* of society that guides thinking and research is the definition for

   (a)   a theoretical paradigm.
   (b)   manifest functions.
   (c)   social marginality.
   (d)   positivism.

19.   Any relatively stable pattern of social behavior refers to

   (a)   social functions.
   (b)   theories.
   (c)   social structure.
   (d)   positivism.

20.   Consequences of social structure which are largely *unrecognized* and *unintended* are called

   (a)   paradigms.
   (b)   manifest functions.
   (c)   latent functions.
   (d)   social integration.

21.   Sometimes social structures can have undesirable consequences for the operation of society. Robert Merton called these

   (a)   paradigms.
   (b)   social dysfunctions.
   (c)   latent functions.
   (d)   manifest functions.

22. Which of the following is a criticism of *structural-functionalism*?

   (a) This theoretical paradigm focuses too much attention on social conflict.
   (b) This theoretical paradigm attends to questions concerning how life is experienced by individuals on a day-to-day basis while ignoring larger social structures.
   (c) This theoretical paradigm tends to ignore inequalities which can generate tension and conflict.
   (d) This theoretical paradigm stresses the functional value of social change, while ignoring the integrative qualities of different social institutions.

23. Which of the following theoretical perspectives is best suited for analysis using a *macro-level* orientation?

   (a) dramaturgical analysis
   (b) social exchange theory
   (c) symbolic-interactionist paradigm
   (d) ethnomethodology
   (e) social-conflict paradigm

24. _____ did not see sociology as a dry, academic discipline. On the contrary, he wanted to apply sociology to solving the pressing problems of his time (1868-1963), especially racial inequality.

   (a) Karl Marx
   (b) Auguste Comte
   (c) Herbert Spencer
   (d) W.E.B. Du Bois

25. Which of the following aspects of social life is used by the author to illustrate the insights provided by the theoretical paradigms used by sociologists?

   (a) sports
   (b) war
   (c) bureaucracy
   (d) education
   (e) family

26. The questions "How is society experienced?" and, "How do individuals attempt to shape the reality perceived by others?" are most likely asked by a researcher using which of the following theoretical paradigms?

   (a) structural-functional
   (b) symbolic-interaction
   (c) social Darwinism
   (d) social-conflict
   (e) none of the above

9

27.   Sociology is not involved in *stereotyping* because

   (a)   sociology makes generalizations about categories of people, not stereotypes.
   (b)   sociologists base their generalizations on research.
   (c)   sociologists strive to be fair-minded.
   (d)   all of the above
   (e)   none of the above

Matching

1. ____ The study of the larger world and our society's place in it.
2. ____ Nations with limited industrialization and moderate personal income.
3. ____ Used the Great Depression to illustrate the importance of social crisis as a prompt to view the world sociologically.
4. ____ An approach to studying the world based on science.
5. ____ A statement of how and why specific facts are related.
6. ____ A framework for building theory based on the assumption that society is a complex system whose parts work together to promote solidarity and stability.
7. ____ Relatively stable patterns of social behavior.
8. ____ The largely unrecognized and unintended consequences of social structure.
9. ____ A framework for building theory that sees society as an arena of inequality that generates conflict and change.
10. ____ An exaggerated description applied to all people in some category.

   a. common sense   i. global perspective
   b. theory   j. social structure
   c. social-conflict paradigm   k. C. Wright Mills
   d. Third-World nations   l. positivism
   e. Herbert Spencer   m. structural-functional paradigm
   f. sociological imagination   n. generalization
   g. middle-income countries   o. sociology
   h. latent functions   p. stereotype

Fill-In

1. The systematic study of human society is the general definition for _____.
2. Emile Durkheim reasoned that the variation in *suicide rates* between different categories of people had to do with *social* _____.
3. A _____ _____ is a view of the larger world and our society's place in it.
4. The United States, Canada, and most of the nations of Western Europe are classified in terms of economic development as being the _____-*income countries*.
5. Three important reasons for taking a *global perspective* include: societies around the world are increasingly _____, many human problems that we face in the United States are far more _____ elsewhere, and it is a good way to learn more about _____.

10

6. According to C. Wright Mills, using the *sociological* _____ can transform individual lives as it transforms society. Further, as we see others grapple with the same problems we do enables us to join together and turn *personal* _____ into *public* _____.

7. Three changes are especially important to the development of sociology in Europe during the nineteenth century, including: a new _____ *economy*, a growth of _____, and _____ change.

8. Auguste Comte asserted that scientific sociology was a result of a progression throughout history of thought and understanding in *three stages*: the _____, _____, and _____.

9. A _____ is a statement of how and why specific facts are related.

10. A _____ _____ provides a basic image of society that guides thinking and research.

11. _____ _____ are consequences for the operation of society as a whole.

12. Talcott Parsons, Robert Merton, and Emile Durkheim are identified as helping develop the _____ *paradigm*.

13. The _____ *paradigm* is a framework for building theory that sees society as an arena of inequality that generates conflict and change.

14. Concern with small-scale patterns of social interaction, such as *symbolic-interaction theory*, operates through a _____-_____ *orientation*.

15. The *symbolic-interactionist paradigm* has its roots in the thinking of _____, a German sociologist who emphasized the need to understand the need to understand a setting from the point of view of the people in it.

16. An exaggerated description applied to all people in some category refers to _____.

Definition and Short-Answer

1. Differentiate between the concepts *manifest* and *latent functions* and provide an illustration for each.

2. Discuss Emile Durkheim's explanation of how *suicide rates* vary between different categories of people. Explain how this research demonstrates the application of the *sociological perspective*.

3. What are the three types of countries identified in the text as measured by their level of *economic development*? What are the characteristics of the countries that represent each of the three types?

4. What are the three major reasons why a *global perspective* is so important today?

5. What were three *social changes* in seventeenth and eighteenth century Europe that provided the context for the development of *sociology* as a scientific discipline?

6. What are the three major components of the *sociological perspective*? Describe and provide an illustration for each.

7. What are the three major *theoretical paradigms* used by sociologists? Identify two key questions raised by each in the analysis of society. Identify one weakness for each of these paradigms for understanding the nature of human social life.

8. How do the three paradigms help us understand the place of *spots* in our society?

9. What are three reasons why sociology is *not to be considered* nothing more than *stereotyping*?

10. What are the four *benefits* of using the sociological perspective? Provide an illustration for two of these.

11. What is the relationship between *sociology* and *social marginality*? Provide an illustration.

12. What does C. Wright Mills mean by turning *personal problems* into *public issues*? Provide an illustration.

11

PART VI: ANSWERS TO STUDY QUESTIONS

True-False

1.	F	(p. 1)	10.	T	(p. 13)
2.	F	(p. 4)	11.	F	(p. 13)
3.	T	(p. 5)	12.	T	(p. 13)
4.	F	(p. 5)	13.	T	(p. 14)
5.	T	(p. 6)	14.	F	(p. 15)
6.	T	(p. 6)	15.	F	(pp. 16-17)
7.	T	(pp. 9-10)	16.	T	(p. 17)
8.	T	(p. 10)	17.	F	(p. 19)
9.	T	(pp. 11-12)	18.	F	(p. 21)

Multiple Choice

1.	b	(p. 1)	15.	b	(p. 13)
2.	c	(p. 1)	16.	d	(p. 13)
3.	d	(pp. 2-3)	17.	e	(p. 13)
4.	a	(p. 4)	18.	a	(p. 14)
5.	e	(p. 5)	19.	c	(p. 15)
6.	a	(p. 6)	20.	c	(p. 15)
7.	b	(pp. 6-7)	21.	b	(p. 15)
8.	e	(p. 6)	22.	c	(p. 16)
9.	d	(p. 9)	23.	e	(pp. 16-17)
10.	c	(p. 10)	24.	d	(p. 17)
11.	c	(p. 10)	25.	a	(p. 19)
12.	b	(pp. 11-12)	26.	b	(p. 19)
13.	a	(p. 12)	27.	d	(p. 21)
14.	e	(p. 13)			

Matching

1.	i	(p. 5)	6.	m	(p. 14)
2.	g	(p. 6)	7.	j	(p. 15)
3.	k	(p. 10)	8.	h	(p. 15)
4.	l	(p. 13)	9.	c	(p. 16)
5.	b	(p. 14)	10.	p	(p. 21)

1. sociology (p. 1)
2. integration (p. 4)
3. global perspective (p. 5)
4. high (p. 6)
5. interconnected, serious, ourselves (pp. 6-7)
6. imagination, problems, issues (p. 10)
7. industrial, cities, political (p. 11)
8. theological, metaphysical, scientific (p. 13)
9. theory (p. 14)
10. theoretical paradigm (p. 14)
11. Social functions (p. 15)
12. structural-functionalism (p. 15)
13. social-conflict (p. 16)
14. micro-level (p. 17)
15. Max Weber (p. 18)
16. stereotypes (p. 21)

PART VII: IN FOCUS--IMPORTANT ISSUES

- The Sociological Perspective

    Define and illustrate each of the three *components of the sociological perspective*:

    seeing the general in the particular

    seeing the strange in the familiar

    seeing individuality in social context

- The Importance of Global Perspective

    What are the three reasons why a *global perspective* is so important?

- Applying the Sociological Perspective

  Provide an example of how each of the following encourages the application of the sociological perspective:

    encountering people who are different from us

    social marginality

    social crisis

  What are the four *benefits* of using the sociological perspective?

- The Origins of Sociology

  What were the three striking *transformations* in Europe during the eighteenth and nineteenth centuries that were especially important for the emergence of sociology?

  Auguste Comte saw sociology as the product of a three-stage historical development. Define each of them:

    theological stage

    metaphysical stage

    scientific stage

- Sociological Theory

  Define each of the following *theoretical paradigms*:

  structural-functionalism

  social-conflict

  symbolic-interactionism

  Identify one *strength* and one *weakness* for each of the following theoretical paradigms:

  structural-functionalism

  strength

  weakness

  social-conflict

  strength

  weakness

  symbolic-interactionism

  strength

  weakness

15

What do structural-functionalists mean by the *functions of sports*?

What do social-conflict theorists mean by stating that sports is closely linked to *social inequality*?

What points are being made by symbolic-interactionists about sports as *interaction*?

Provide an example from this chapter illustrating the point that sociological thinking involves *generalizations*, not stereotypes:

PART VIII: ANALYSIS AND COMMENT

Go back through the chapter and write down key points from each of the following boxes. Then, for each of the boxes identified, write out three questions concerning the issues raised which you feel would be valuable to discuss in class. Do the same for each chapter as you read through the text.

Applying Sociology

"What's in a Name? How Social Forces Affect Personal Choices"

Key Points: Questions:

"The Sociological Imagination: Turning Personal Problems into Public Issues"

Key Points: Questions:

"Sociology at Work: Understanding the Issue of Race"

Key Points: Questions:

Global Sociology

"The Global Village: A Social Snapshot of Our World"

Key Points: Questions:

Controversy and Debate

"Is Sociology Nothing More than Stereotypes?"

Key Points: Questions:

Window on the World--Global Map 1-1

"Economic Development in Global Perspective"

Key Points: Questions:

Seeing Ourselves--National Map 1-1

"Suicide Rates across the United States"

Key Points: Questions:

2 Sociological Investigation

PART I: CHAPTER OUTLINE

I. The Basics of Sociological Investigation
    A.   Science As One Form of "Truth"
    B.   Common Sense Versus Scientific Evidence
II. Science: Basic Elements and Limitations
    A.   Concepts, Variables, and Measurement
        1.   Defining Concepts
        2.   Reliability and Validity
        3.   Relationships among Variables
    B.   The Ideal of Objectivity
        1.   Max Weber: Value-Free Research
    C.   Some Limitations of Scientific Sociology
    D.   A Second Framework: Interpretive Sociology
    E.   A Third Framework: Critical Sociology
    F.   Gender and Research
    G.   Research Ethics
V. The Methods of Sociological Research
    A.   Testing a Hypothesis: The Experiment
        1.   The Hawthorne Effect
        2.   An Illustration: The Stanford County Prison
    B.   Asking Questions: Survey Research
        1.   Population and Sample
        2.   Questionnaires and Interviews
        3.   An Illustration: Studying the African American Elite
    C.   In the Field: Participant Observation
        1.   An Illustration: Street Corner Society
    D.   Using Available Data: Secondary and Historical Analysis
        1.   An Illustration: A Tale of Two Cities
    E.   The Interplay of Theory and Method
    F.   Putting It All Together: Ten Steps in Sociological Investigation
VI. Summary
VII. Key Concepts
VIII. Critical-Thinking Questions
IX. Applications and Exercises
X. Sites to See

PART II: LEARNING OBJECTIVES

1. To review the fundamental requirements for engaging in scientific investigation using the sociological perspective.
2. To become familiar with the basic elements of science and how they are used in sociological investigation.
3. To see how research is affected by politics and gender.
4. To begin to view ethical considerations involved in studying people.
5. To become familiar with research methods used by sociologists in the investigation of society.
6. To begin to understand the interplay of theory and method.
7. To be able to identify and describe each of the ten steps in sociological research.

PART III: KEY CONCEPTS

androcentricity

cause and effect

concept

control

correlation

critical sociology

dependent variable

deductive logical thought

empirical evidence

experiment

gender

gynocentricity

hypothesis

independent variable

inductive logical thought

interpretive sociology

interview

mean

measurement

median

mode

objectivity

operationalizing a variable

participant observation

population

questionnaire

reliability

replication

research method

sample

science

scientific sociology

secondary analysis

spurious correlation

survey

validity

variable

Verstehen

PART IV: IMPORTANT RESEARCHERS

Max Weber   Alvin Gouldner

Philip Zimbardo   Lois Benjamin

William F. White   E. Digby Baltzell

PART V: STUDY QUESTIONS

True-False

1.   T   F   Research by Lois Benjamin focused on *uneducated, lower-class* African Americans and how they deal with racism.

2.   T   F   *Science* is defined as a logical system that bases knowledge on direct, systematic observation.

3.   T   F   Our author argues that a major strength of sociology is that it is basically just using *common sense*.

4.   T   F   A *concept* is defined as the process of determining the value of a variable in a specific case.

5.   T   F   The *mode* is the statistical term referring to the value which occurs most often in a series of numbers.

6.   T   F   *Reliability* refers to consistency in measurement.

7.   T   F   If two variables are *correlated*, by definition one is an *independent variable* and one is a *dependent variable*.

8.   T   F   Max Weber argued that people involved in scientific research must strive to be *value-free*.

9.	T	F	*Interpretation* is rarely beneficial in sociological investigation.
10.	T	F	*Androcentricity* refers to approaching an issue from a male perspective.
11.	T	F	A *hypothesis* is an unverified statement of a relationship between variables.
12.	T	F	The *Hawthorne Effect* refers to a change in a subject's behavior caused simply by the awareness of being studied.
13.	T	F	A *sample* refers to a research method in which subjects respond to a series of items in a questionnaire or an interview.
14.	T	F	*Snowball sampling* is an example of a representative random sampling strategy.
15.	T	F	Most field research is *exploratory* and *descriptive*.
16.	T	F	Unlike experiments or surveys, participant observation usually involves little *qualitative research*.
17.	T	F	*Secondary research* refers to a research model in which a researcher uses data collected by others.
18.	T	F	E. Digby Baltzell's historical study of Boston and Philadelphia supports research linking attitudes toward *achievement* and *equality* with religious doctrine.
19.	T	F	*Inductive logical thought* is reasoning that transforms general theory into specific hypotheses suitable for testing.
20.	T	F	The first step in the scientific research process should always be to determine what research design will be used to obtain the data.

Multiple Choice

1. _____ *evidence* is information we can verify with our senses.

   (a) consensual
   (b) common sense
   (c) intrapsychic
   (d) holistic
   (e) empirical

2. _____ is a logical system that bases knowledge on direct, systematic observation.

   (a) A research method
   (b) Sociological investigation
   (c) A hypothesis
   (d) Science
   (e) A theory

3. *Sociological investigation* starts with the simple requirements of

   (a) belief and common sense.
   (b) spuriousness and logical deduction.
   (c) use of the sociological perspective, being curious, and asking questions.
   (d) sampling and replication.
   (e) expertise and validity.

4.   Which of the following common sense statements are *false* according to empirical evidence?

        (a)   Poor people are far more likely than rich people to break the law.
        (b)   Most poor people do not want to work.
        (c)   Most people marry because they are in love.
        (d)   People change as they grow old, losing many interests as they increasingly focus on their health.
        (e)   all of the above

5.   A _____ is a mental construct that represents some part of the world, inevitably in a simplified form.

        (a)   variable
        (b)   concept
        (c)   hypothesis
        (d)   research design
        (e)   measurement

6.   Specifying exactly what is to be measured in assigning a value to a variable is called

        (a)   validity.
        (b)   objectivity.
        (c)   operationalizing a variable.
        (d)   reliability.
        (e)   control.

7.   The *arithmetic average* in a series of numbers is the

        (a)   control.
        (b)   median.
        (c)   mode.
        (d)   mean.
        (e)   conceptualization.

8.   The *descriptive statistic* that represents the value that occurs *midway* in a series of numbers is called the

        (a)   median.
        (b)   correlation.
        (c)   mode.
        (d)   norm.
        (e)   mean.

9.   The quality of *consistency* in measurement is known as

      (a)   spuriousness.
      (b)   reliability.
      (c)   empirical evidence.
      (d)   objectivity.
      (e)   validity.

10.   Measuring what one *intends* to measure is the quality of measurement known as

      (a)   reliability.
      (b)   operationalization.
      (c)   validity.
      (d)   control.
      (e)   objectivity.

11.   A higher level of education causes greater earnings over one's lifetime. In this case, *higher level of education* is

      (a)   a spurious variable.
      (b)   a dependent variable.
      (c)   an independent variable.
      (d)   the median.
      (e)   the control variable.

12.   An apparent, although false, relationship between two (or more) variable caused by some other variable refers to

      (a)   deductive correlation.
      (b)   inductive correlation.
      (c)   replicated correlation.
      (d)   operationalized correlation
      (e)   spurious correlation.

13.   A state of personal neutrality in conducting research is known as

      (a)   subjective interpretation.
      (b)   objectivity.
      (c)   control variable.
      (d)   spurious relationship.
      (e)   validity.

14. According to Max Weber, it is essential that researchers be _____ in their investigations.

    (a)   value-free
    (b)   subjective
    (c)   spurious
    (d)   selective in their reporting of facts
    (e)   concerned about social welfare

15. The study of society that focuses on the meanings people attach to their social word refers to

    (a)   critical sociology.
    (b)   quantitative sociology.
    (c)   residual sociology.
    (d)   interpretive sociology.

16. _____ is the study of society that focuses on the need for social change

    (a)   Androcentricity
    (b)   Qualitative research
    (c)   Critical sociology
    (d)   Interpretive sociology

17. The issue of *androcentricity* relates to

    (a)   over-generalization.
    (b)   social activism.
    (c)   economic elitism.
    (d)   gender bias.
    (e)   political correctness.

18. A _____ is a systematic plan for conducting research.

    (a)   hypothesis
    (b)   research design
    (c)   sample
    (d)   replication

19. An unverified statement of a relationship between variables is a(n)

    (a)   correlation.
    (b)   logical deduction.
    (c)   hypothesis.
    (d)   logical induction.
    (e)   theory.

20.   Which *research method* is explanatory and is usually used to test hypotheses?

    (a)   the survey
    (b)   participant observation
    (c)   the experiment
    (d)   the use of existing sources
    (e)   the interview

21.   A change in a subject's behavior caused simply by the awareness of being studied refers to

    (a)   the Hawthorne effect.
    (b)   androcentricity.
    (c)   replication.
    (d)   objectivity.
    (e)   control.

22.   Phillip Zimbardo's *prison study* is used in the text to illustrate what research design?

    (a)   participant observation
    (b)   survey--using questionnaires
    (c)   survey--using interviews
    (d)   the experiment
    (e)   secondary analysis

23.   A _____ refers to the people who are the focus of research.

    (a)   research design
    (b)   variable
    (c)   sample
    (d)   population
    (e)   concept

24.   A disadvantage of the *interview* type of survey is that

    (a)   it does not permit follow-up questions.
    (b)   the subjects' answers cannot be clarified.
    (c)   a person is less likely to complete a survey if contacted personally.
    (d)   the researcher may inadvertently influence the subject.

25.   A type of sampling in which the researcher starts out with people she knows and asks them to suggest others is know as

    (a)   residual sampling.
    (b)   snowball sampling.
    (c)   consensus sampling.
    (d)   contact sampling.

26.   Which sociological method (sometimes referred to as the *case study*) is primarily used for *exploration* and *description*?

    (a)   the interview
    (b)   the questionnaire
    (c)   the experiment
    (d)   the use of existing sources
    (e)   participant observation

27.   People who introduce field researchers to the community and remain a source of information and help are referred to as

    (a)   stooges.
    (b)   stoolies.
    (c)   key informants.
    (d)   bookbinders.
    (e)   participant observers.

28.   _____ *analysis* is a research method in which a researcher uses data collected by others.

    (a)   Secondary
    (b)   Residual
    (c)   Marginal
    (d)   Ethnographic

29.   E. Digby Baltzell's study of important and successful Americans, comparing Puritans and Quakers, is an example of which research method?

    (a)   experiment
    (b)   participant observation
    (c)   secondary analysis
    (d)   survey--questionnaire
    (e)   survey--interview

30.   If a researcher begins a sociological investigation with general ideas about the world which then are used to produce specific hypotheses suited for scientific testing, the process is known as

    (a)   inductive logical thought.
    (b)   a qualitative methodology.
    (c)   empirical analysis.
    (d)   deductive logical thought.
    (e)   speculative reasoning.

31. The question representing the *fifth step* in the sociological research process is

    (a)   How will you record the data?
    (b)   Are there ethical concerns?
    (c)   What have others already learned?
    (d)   What do the data tell you?
    (e)   What are your conclusions?

32. How can people *lie* with statistics?

    (a)   People select their data.
    (b)   People interpret their data.
    (c)   People use graphs to "spin" the truth.
    (d)   All of the above.

Matching

1. ____ A logical system that bases knowledge on direct, systematic observation.
2. ____ A mental construct that represents an aspect of the world, inevitably in a somewhat simplified way.
3. ____ The quality of measurement gained by measuring precisely what one intends to measure.
4. ____ A relationship in which two (or more) variables change together.
5. ____ An apparent, although false, relationship between two (or more) variables caused by some other variable.
6. ____ A state of personal neutrality in conducting research.
7. ____ The study of society that focuses on the meanings people attach to their social world.
8. ____ The study of society that focuses on the need for social change.
9. ____ A systematic plan for conducting research.
10. ____ A part of a population that represents the whole.
11. ____ A research method in which subjects respond to a series of statements and questions in a questionnaire or interview.
12. ____ A series of written questions a researcher presents to subjects.
13. ____ The study entitled *Street Corner Society* by William Foote Whyte is an example of this type of research method.
14. ____ A research method in which a researcher uses data collected by others.

    a.   interpretive sociology   h.   science
    b.   correlation   i.   sample
    c.   research method   j.   spurious correlation
    d.   survey   k.   questionnaire
    e.   participant observation   l.   validity
    f.   concept   m.   critical sociology
    g.   objectivity   n.   secondary analysis

Fill-In

1. Sociological investigation begins with two basic *requirements*: Looking at the world using the _____ _____, and being _____ and _____ _____.

2. _____ _____ is the study of society based on systematic observation of social behavior.

3. _____ *evidence* refers to evidence we can verify with our senses.

4. Four *ways of knowing* include _____, _____, _____, and _____.

5. A _____ is a *mental construct* that represents an aspect of the world, inevitably in a somewhat simplified way.

6. _____ is the process of determining the value of a variable in a specific case.

7. A statistical measure referring to the arithmetic average of a series of numbers is called the _____.

8. _____ refers to two variables that *vary together*, such as the extent of crowding and juvenile delinquency.

9. The state of complete personal *neutrality* in conducting research is referred to as _____.

10. The German sociologist _____ _____ distinguished between *value-relevant* choice of research topics and *value-free* conduct of sociological investigation.

11. _____ refers to *repetition of research* by other researchers.

12. _____ *sociology* is the study of society that focuses on the meanings people attach to their social world.

13. Five ways in which *gender* can jeopardize good research include: _____, _____, _____, gender _____, _____ standards, and _____.

14. In an *experiment*, controlling outside influences often involves dividing subjects into an _____ *group* and a _____ *group*.

15. A _____ refers to the people who are the focus of research.

16. The _____ is a *research method* in which subjects respond to a series of statements or questions in a *questionnaire* or an *interview*.

17. A _____ is a part of a population that represents the whole.

18. Two types of surveys include _____ and _____.

19. _____ percent of the respondents in Lois Benjamin's study on *talented African Americans* were *female*.

20. *Fieldwork, ethnographies*, and *case studies* are all examples of _____ _____ research.

21. _____ *research* involves an investigation in which a researcher gathers impressionistic, not numerical, data.

22. William Foote Whyte's relationship with *Doc* in his study *Street Corner Society* illustrates the importance of a _____ _____ in participant observation research.

23. E. Digsby Baltzell's research using secondary analysis focused on the *Puritans* of the Boston area and the *Quakers* of the Philadelphia area. He argues that the former group respected _____ and the latter group believed in _____, which he argued explained in part why the number of "famous people" from each group is so different.

24. _____ _____ _____ is reasoning that transforms specific observations into general theory. Baltzell's research using secondary analysis is an example of this type of reasoning.

25. In contrast to E. Digsby Baltzell, Phillip Zimbardo used _____ logical thought in his prison research.

Definition and Short-Answer

1. What are the two *requirements* which underlie the process of sociological investigation?
2. What are the four *ways of knowing the "truth?"* Describe and illustrate each of these.
3. What are the three factors which must be determined to conclude that a *cause and effect* relationship between two variables may exist?
4. Margaret Eichler points out five dangers to sound research that involves *gender*. Identify and define each.
5. Define the concept *hypothesis*. Further, write your own hypothesis and operationalize the variables identified.
6. Identify two advantages and two disadvantages for each of the four major *research methods* used by sociologists.
7. What are the basic steps of the sociological *research process*? Briefly describe each.
8. Three illustrations are provided to show that *common sense* does not always guide us to a meaningful sense of reality. What two examples can you give concerning common sense not paving the way toward our understanding of what is really happening in social life?
9. Identify and define the *major elements* of scientific investigation.
10. Using standardized high school achievements tests as an example, illustrate the difference between *reliability* and *validity*.
11. Differentiate between the viewpoints of Max Weber and Alvin Gouldner concerning *objectivity* in social science research.
12. Identify four *limitations* of scientific sociology.
13. What are the basic guidelines for *research ethics* in sociological research?
14. What can *interpretive sociology* tell us about society that pure quantitative sociological research cannot?
15. What sorts of questions about society are being asked by researchers using *critical sociology*?
16. Explain why Phillip Zimabardo's prison research is an example of *deductive logical thought*.
17. What are three ways in which people can *lie with statistics*? Find an example of one of these ways in a popular magazine or newspaper.

PART VI: ANSWERS TO STUDY QUESTIONS

True-False

1.	F	(p. 25)		11.	T	(p. 37)
2.	T	(p. 26)		12.	T	(p. 38)
3.	F	(p. 27)		13.	F	(p. 39)
4.	F	(p. 28)		14.	F	(p. 41)
5.	T	(p. 29)		15.	T	(p. 43)
6.	T	(p. 29)		16.	F	(p. 43)
7.	F	(p. 30)		17.	T	(p. 45)
8.	T	(p. 32)		18.	T	(p. 47)
9.	F	(p. 34)		19.	F	(p. 48)
10.	T	(p. 35)		20.	F	(p. 49)

Multiple Choice

1.	e	(p. 26)		17.	d	(p. 35)
2.	d	(p. 26)		18.	b	(p. 36)
3.	c	(p. 26)		19.	c	(p. 37)
4.	e	(p. 27)		20.	c	(p. 37)
5.	b	(p. 28)		21.	a	(p. 38)
6.	c	(p. 29)		22.	d	(p. 38)
7.	d	(p. 29)		23.	d	(p. 39)
8.	a	(p. 29)		24.	d	(p. 41)
9.	b	(p. 29)		25.	b	(p. 41)
10.	c	(p. 29)		26.	e	(p. 43)
11.	c	(p. 30)		27.	c	(p. 44)
12.	e	(p. 31)		28.	a	(p. 45)
13.	b	(p. 32)		29.	c	(p. 46)
14.	a	(p. 32)		30.	d	(p. 48)
15.	d	(p. 34)		31.	b	(p. 49)
16.	c	(p. 34)		32.	d	(pp. 50-51)

Matching

1.	h	(p. 26)		8.	m	(p. 34)
2.	f	(p. 28)		9.	c	(p. 36)
3.	l	(p. 29)		10.	i	(p. 39)
4.	b	(p. 30)		11.	d	(p. 39)
5.	j	(p. 31)		12.	k	(p. 40)
6.	g	(p. 32)		13.	e	(p. 43)
7.	a	(p. 34)		14.	n	(p. 45)

<u>Fill-In</u>

1. sociological perspective, curious, asking questions (p.26)
2. Scientific sociology (p. 26)
3. empirical (p. 26)
4. faith, expertise, consensus, science (p. 26)
5. concept (p. 28)
6. measurement (p. 28)
7. mean (p. 29)
8. Correlation (p. 30)
9. objectivity (p. 32)
10. Max Weber (p. 32)
11. Replication (p. 33)
12. Interpretive (p. 34)
13. androcentricity, overgeneralizing, blindness, double, interference (pp. 35-36)
14. experimental, control (p. 38)
15. population (39)
16. survey (p. 39)
17. sample (p. 39)
18. questionnaires, interviews (pp. 40-41)
19. 37 (p. 42)
20. participant observation (pp. 42-43)
21. qualitative (p. 43)
22. key informant (p. 44)
23. achievement, equality (p. 47)
24. Inductive logical thought (p. 48)
25. deductive (p. 48)

PART VII: IN FOCUS—IMPORTANT ISSUES

- The Basics of Sociological Investigation

Sociological investigation starts with two simple *requirements*. What are these?

Provide two examples of why *common sense* is challenged by scientific evidence.

- Science: Basic Elements and Limitations

  Define and illustrate each of the following *elements of science:*

  concept

  variable

  measurement

  reliability

  validity

  correlation

  cause and effect

  objectivity

What are the four *limitations* of scientific sociology?

What are five important *ethical considerations* involved in sociological research?

- The Methods of Sociological Research

What is a *research method*?

Describe each of the following research methods:

experiment

survey

participant observation

secondary analysis

Explain why Phillip Zimbardo's experiment on prisons is an example of *deductive logical thought*.

List the ten basic steps in *sociological investigation*:

PART VIII: ANALYSIS AND COMMENT

Applying Sociology

"Three Useful (and Simple) Statistical Measures"

Key Points: Questions:

"Survey Questions: A Word or Two Makes All the Difference"

Key Points: Questions:

"Reading Tables: An Important Skill"

Key Points: Questions:

Social Diversity

"Conducting Research With Hispanics"

Key Points   Questions:

Controversy and Debate

"Can People Lie with Statistics?"

Key Points: Questions:

Seeing Ourselves

"National Map 2-1: Affluent Minorities Across the United States"

Key Points: Questions:

39

3 Culture

PART I: CHAPTER OUTLINE

I.   What is Culture?
   A.   Culture and Human Intelligence
   B.   Culture, Nation, and Society
II. The Components of Culture
   A.   Symbols
   B.   Language
      1.   Language: Only for Humans?
      2.   Does Language Shape Reality?
   C.   Values and Beliefs
      1.   Key Values of U.S. Culture
      2.   Values: Sometimes in Conflict
   D.   Norms
      1.   Mores and Folkways
      2.   Social Control
   E.   "Ideal" and "Real" Culture
   F.   Material Culture and Technology
   G.   New Information Technology and Culture
III. Cultural Diversity: Many Ways of Life In One World
   A.   High Culture and Popular Culture
   B.   Subculture
   C.   Multiculturalism
   D.   Counterculture
   E.   Cultural Change
      1.   Cultural Lag
      2.   Causes of Cultural Change
   F.   Ethnocentrism and Cultural Relativity
   G.   A Global Culture?
IV. Theoretical Analysis of Culture
   A.   Structural-Functional Analysis
   B.   Social-Conflict Analysis
   C.   Sociobiology
V.   Culture and Human Freedom
   A.   Culture As Constraint
   B.   Culture As Freedom

40

PART II: LEARNING OBJECTIVES

1.   To begin to understand the sociological meaning of the concept of culture.

2.   To consider the relationship between human intelligence and culture.

3.   To know the components of culture and to be able to provide examples of each.

4.   To consider the current state of knowledge about whether language is uniquely human.

5.   To consider the significance of symbols in the construction and maintenance of social reality.

6.   To identify the dominant values in our society and to recognize their interrelationships with one another and with other aspects of our culture.

7.   To be able to provide examples of the different types of norms operative in a culture, and how these are related to the process of social control.

8.   To be able to explain how subcultures and countercultures contribute to cultural diversity.

9.   To begin to develop your understanding of multiculturalism.

10.   To be able to differentiate between ethnocentrism and cultural relativism.

11.   To be able to compare and contrast analyses of culture using structural-functional, social-conflict, and sociobiological paradigms.

12.   To be able to identify the consequences of culture for human freedom and constraint.

PART III: KEY CONCEPTS

Afrocentrism

beliefs

counterculture

cultural conflict

cultural integration

cultural lag

cultural relativism

cultural transmission

cultural universals

culture

culture shock

discovery

diffusion

ethnocentrism

Eurocentrism

folkways

high culture

ideal culture

idealism

instincts

invention

language

material culture

materialism

multiculturalism

natural selection

nonmaterial culture

norms

prescriptive norms

proscriptive norms

real culture

sanctions

Sapir-Whorf thesis

social control

society

sociobiology

subculture

symbol

technology

values

PART IV: IMPORTANT RESEARCHERS

Napoleon Chagnon   Edward Sapir and Benjamin Whorf

Charles Darwin   George Peter Murdock

Marvin Harris   Robin Williams

PART V: STUDY QUESTIONS

True-False

1.   T   F   *Individualism* is even more valued in Japan than in the United States.
2.   T   F   *Nonmaterial culture* refers to the intangible world of ideas created by members of a society.
3.   T   F   No way of life is "natural" to humanity, even though most people around the world view their own behavior that way.
4.   T   F   According to the evolutionary record, the human line diverged from our closest primate relative, the great apes, some *12 millions years ago*.
5.   T   F   In 1999 there were 191 politically independent *nations* in the world.
6.   T   F   Cultural *symbols* often change over time, and even vary within a single society.
7.   T   F   The term *society* refers to a shared way of life.
8.   T   F   *Cultural transmission* is defined as the process by which culture is passed from one generation to the next.
9.   T   F   Helen Keller, who became blind and deaf during infancy, was introduced to the symbolic world of language with the word "hot."
10. T   F   The *Sapir-Whorf thesis* concerns the extent to which the dominant values of a culture are affected by its level of technological development.
11. T   F   *Values* are defined as rules and expectations by which society guides the behavior of its members.
12. T   F   *Mores* are norms which have little moral significance within a culture.
13. T   F   Social *sanctions*, operating as a system of social control, can involve rewards or punishments.
14. T   F   *Technology* is defined as the knowledge that people apply to the task of living in their surroundings.
15. T   F   Compared to Japan, the United States is a very *monocultural* nation.
16. T   F   *Virtual culture* refers to the gap between "ideal" and "real" culture.
17. T   F   During the last decade, most *immigrants* to the United States have come from Asia and Latin America.
18. T   F   *Multiculturalism* refers to an educational program recognizing the cultural diversity of the United States and promoting the equality of all cultural traditions.
19. T   F   Three major sources of cultural change are *invention, discovery,* and *diffusion*.
20. T   F   The practice of judging any culture by its own standards is referred to as *ethnocentrism*.
21. T   F   *Structural-functionalists* argue that there are no *cultural universals*.
22. T   F   *Sociobiology* rests on the theory of evolution proposed by Charles Darwin.
23. T   F   According to the author of our text, culture has diminished human autonomy to the point where we are *culturally programmed* much like other animals are *genetically programmed*.
24. T   F   Sociologist James Hunter claims that the *culture wars* in our society are tied to the fact that most individuals in our society fall into one of two major camps: "traditionalists" and "progressives."

44

1.   The most popular music in the U.S. in 1998 (based on record sales) was

      (a)   country.
      (b)   rap.
      (c)   rock and roll.
      (d)   heavy metal.

2.   *Culture* is

      (a)   the process by which members of a culture encourage conformity to social norms.
      (b)   the beliefs, values, behavior, and material objects that constitute a people's way of life.
      (c)   the practice of judging another society's norms.
      (d)   a group of people who engage in interaction with one another on a continuous basis.

3.   The personal disorientation that accompanies exposure to an unfamiliar way of life is termed

      (a)   anomie.
      (b)   alienation.
      (c)   cultural relativism.
      (d)   culture shock.
      (e)   cultural transmission.

4.   The *Yanomamo* are

      (a)   a small tribal group of herders living in Eastern Africa.
      (b)   a technologically primitive horticultural society living in South America.
      (c)   a nomadic culture living above the Arctic circle as hunters.
      (d)   a small, dying society living as farmers in a mountainous region of western Africa.
      (e)   a people who until very recently were living in complete isolation from the rest of the world in a tropical rain forest in Malaysia.

5.   Studying *fossil records*, scientists have concluded that the first creatures with clearly human characteristics existed about _____ years ago.

      (a)   2 million
      (b)   12 thousand
      (c)   40 million
      (d)   60 thousand
      (e)   12 million

6. *Homo sapiens* is a Latin term that means

   (a) thinking person.
   (b) to walk upright.
   (c) evolving life form.
   (d) dependent person.

7. Homo sapiens continued to evolve so that, about _____ years ago, humans who looked more or less like ourselves roamed the earth.

   (a) 3,000,000
   (b) 1,000,000
   (c) 40,000
   (d) 200,000
   (e) 10,000

8. The road to "civilization," based on permanent settlements and specialized occupations, began in the Middle East about _____ years ago.

   (a) 40,000
   (b) 22,000
   (c) 12,000
   (d) 4,000

9. The organized interaction of people in a nation or within some other boundary is the definition for

   (a) culture.
   (b) social structure.
   (c) enculturation.
   (d) socialization.
   (e) society.

10. In 1999, how many politically independent nations were there in the world?

    (a) 2004
    (b) 456
    (c) 283
    (d) 191

11. Which of the following identifies two of the *components of culture*?

    (a) values and norms
    (b) social change and social statics
    (c) social structure and social function
    (d) people and the natural environment

12. *Symbols*, a component of culture, can

(a) vary from culture to culture.
(b) provide a foundation for the reality we experience.
(c) vary within a given culture.
(d) all of the above.

13. A system of *symbols* that allows members of a society to communicate with one other is the definition of

(a) language.
(b) cultural relativity.
(c) cultural transmission.
(d) values.
(e) norms.

14. The *language* that is the native tongue of twenty percent of the world's population (more than any other language) is

(a) English.
(b) Chinese.
(c) Spanish.
(d) Arabic.

15. Culturally defined *standards* of desirability, goodness, and beauty, which serve as broad guidelines for social living, is the definition for

(a) norms.
(b) mores.
(c) beliefs.
(d) sanctions.
(e) values.

16. The *Sapir-Whorf thesis* relates to

(a) human evolution.
(b) language and cultural relativity.
(c) social sanctions.
(d) victimization patterns.

17. Progress and freedom are examples of U.S.

(a) norms.
(b) sanctions.
(c) values.
(d) beliefs.

18. Specific statements that people hold to be true refer to

    (a) norms.
    (b) values.
    (c) sanctions.
    (d) technology.
    (e) beliefs.

19. According to the research cited in the text, which of the following is *not* a central cultural value in U.S. society?

    (a) equal opportunity
    (b) science
    (c) racism and superiority
    (d) friendship

20. Rules and expectations by which a society guides the behavior of is members refers to

    (a) norms.
    (b) values.
    (c) sanctions.
    (d) beliefs.

21. The old adage "Do as I say, not as I do" illustrates the distinction between

    (a) ideal and real culture.
    (b) the Sapir-Whorf hypothesis and "real" culture.
    (c) cultural integration and cultural lag.
    (d) folkways and mores.
    (e) subcultures and countercultures.

22. *Tangible* human creations are called

    (a) technology.
    (b) values.
    (c) artifacts.
    (d) real culture.

23. Knowledge that people apply to the task of living in their surroundings refers to

    (a) social control.
    (b) technology.
    (c) real culture.
    (d) ideal culture.

24.   Cultural patterns that distinguish a society's *elite* are referred to as

    (a)   popular culture.
    (b)   high culture.
    (c)   affluent culture.
    (d)   prestige culture.
    (e)   counterculture.

25.   Cultural patterns that set apart some segment of a society's population is termed

    (a)   social stratification.
    (b)   social differentiation.
    (c)   counterculture.
    (d)   cultural lag.
    (e)   subculture.

26.   Inconsistencies within a cultural system resulting from the unequal rates at which different cultural elements change is termed

    (a)   cultural lag.
    (b)   counterculture.
    (c)   culture shock.
    (d)   cultural relativity.
    (e)   ethnocentrism.

27.   The spread of cultural elements from one society to another is called

    (a)   invention.
    (b)   integration.
    (c)   diffusion.
    (d)   discovery.

28.   *Ethnocentrism* is

    (a)   an educational program recognizing past and present cultural diversity.
    (b)   cultural patterns that set apart some segment of society's population.
    (c)   cultural patterns that strongly oppose those widely accepted within a society.
    (d)   the practice of judging another culture by the standards of one's own culture.
    (e)   the practice of judging another culture by its own standards.

29.   The theoretical paradigm that focuses upon *universal cultural traits* is

    (a)   cultural ecology.
    (b)   structural-functionalism.
    (c)   cultural materialism.
    (d)   social-conflict.

30. The philosophical doctrine of *materialism* is utilized in the analysis of culture by proponents of which theoretical paradigm?

    (a) sociobiologists
    (b) cultural ecology
    (c) social-conflict
    (d) structural-functionalism
    (e) symbolic-interaction

31. Political opposition, often accompanied by social hostility, rooted in different cultural values refers to

    (a) cultural conflict.
    (b) social chaos.
    (c) cultural materialism.
    (d) cultural shock.

32. In studying *cultural conflict* in our society, sociologist John Hunter has identified two competing categories of people in our society, including

    (a) consensualists and subconsensualists.
    (b) instrumentalists and moralists.
    (c) conventionalists and postcoventionalists.
    (d) traditionalists and progressives.
    (e) rationalists and traditionalists.

Matching

1. ___ The intangible world of ideas created by members of society.
2. ___ Anything that carries a particular meaning recognized by people who share a culture.
3. ___ The official language of twenty percent of the world's population.
4. ___ States that people perceive the world through the cultural lens of language.
5. ___ Rules and expectations by which a society guides the behavior of its members.
6. ___ Takes the form of rewards and punishments.
7. ___ Knowledge that a society applies to the task of living in a physical environment.
8. ___ An educational program recognizing past and present diversity in U.S. society and promoting the equality of all cultural traditions.
9. ___ Cultural patterns that strongly oppose those widely accepted within a society.
10. ___ The fact that cultural elements change at different rates, which may disrupt a cultural system.
11. ___ The practice of judging another culture by the standards of one's own culture.
12. ___ A theoretical paradigm that explores ways in which biology affects how humans create culture.

a.	sanctions	i.	Chinese
b.	sociobiology	j.	technology
c.	counterculture	k.	norms
d.	cultural lag	l.	symbol
e.	Sapir-Whorf thesis	m.	ethnocentrism
f.	ethnocentrism	n.	English
g.	nonmaterial culture	o.	Arabic
h.	multiculturalism		

Fill-In

1. The 6.1 billion people on earth today are members of a single biological species: _____.
2. _____ are the biological programming over which animals have no control.
3. The *tangible things* created by members of society are referred to as _____ _____.
4. The concept _____ _____ is derived from the Latin meaning *thinking person*.
5. Worldwide, experts have documented the existence of over _____ languages.
6. Five key *components of culture* are: _____, _____, _____, _____, and _____ _____.
7. A _____ is anything that carries a particular meaning recognized by people who share a culture.
8. Culture shock is both _____ and _____ by the traveler.
9. *Cultural* _____ refers to the process by which one generation passes culture to the next.
10. The most widely spoken languages in the world today, spoken by 20, 10, and 6 percent of the world's population respectively are _____, _____, and _____.
11. While _____ are broad guidelines for social living, _____ are statements that people hold to be true.

12. _____ *norms* tell us what we *should do*, while _____ *norms* tell us what we *should not do*.

13. _____ refer to rules and expectations by which a society guides the behavior of its members.

14. _____ _____ refers to the various means by which members of a society encourage conformity to norms.

15. Knowledge that people apply to the task of living in their surroundings refers to _____.

16. Members of our society, especially youngsters, are fed a steady diet of _____ *culture*, images that spring from the minds of contemporary culture-makers and that reach us via a screen: on television, in the movies, or through computer cyber-space.

17. Sociologists use the term _____ *culture* to refer to cultural patterns that distinguish a society's elite; _____ *culture* designates cultural patterns that are widespread among a society's population.

18. Historically, we have viewed the United States as a "melting pot" where many nationalities blend into a single "American" culture. But, given our cultural diversity, how accurate is the "melting pot" image? For one thing, subcultures involve not just _____ but _____.

19. _____ refers to an educational program recognizing the cultural diversity of the United States and promoting the equality of all cultural traditions.

20. Women's increased participation in the labor force parallels many changing family patterns, including first marriages at a later age and a rising divorce rate. Such patterns illustrate _____ _____, the close relationship among various elements of a cultural system.

21. The fact that some cultural elements change more quickly than others, which may disrupt a cultural system, is known as _____ _____.

22. _____ refers to the practice of judging another culture by the standards of one's own culture.

23. Today, more than ever before, we can observe many of the same cultural practices the world over. This *global culture* is evidenced by the presence of a global _____, global _____, and global _____.

24. The *social-conflict paradigm* is rooted in the philosophical doctrine of _____.

25. _____ is a theoretical paradigm that explores ways in which human biology affects how we create culture.

Definition and Short-Answer

1. Three *causes of cultural change* are identified in the text. Identify these and provide an illustration of each.

2. Discuss the research presented in the text concerning the uniqueness of *language* to humans. What are your opinions on this issue?

3. Describe the process of *natural selection*.

4. Review the statistics presented in *Table 3-1* concerning changing values among college students. What have been the most significant changes? In which areas have values remained consistent? To what extent do your values fit the picture of contemporary college students? Explain.

5. What are the basic qualities of the *Yanomamo* culture? What factors do you think may explain why they are so aggressive? To what extent are you able to view these people from a *cultural relativistic* perspective?

6.   What is the basic position being taken by *sociobiologists* concerning the nature of culture? What are three examples used by sociobiologists to argue that human culture is determined by biology? To what extent do you agree or disagree with their position? Explain.

7.   Define the philosophical doctrine of *idealism.*

8.   What is the *Sapir-Whorf thesis*? What evidence supports it? What evidence is inconsistent with this hypothesis?

9.   In what ways are we *globally connected?*. Illustrate two of these.

10. Write a paragraph in which you express your opinions about the issue of multiculturalism in our society. Address the benefits of this perspective being suggested by proponents of multiculturalism, as well as the potential problems with this perspective suggested by its critics.

11. Provide two examples of how culture *constrains* us (limits our freedom).

12. What conclusions do you make about immigration concerning the data presented in *Figure 3-2.*?

13. Differentiate between *values* and *norms*, providing two illustrations for each.

14. Review the list of *core values* of our culture in the United States. Rank order the ten identified in the text in terms of how important they are in our society from your point of view. What values, if any, do you believe should be included in the "top ten" list? Do you feel any of those listed should not be on the list?

PART VI: ANSWERS TO STUDY QUESTIONS

True-False

1.	F	(p. 60)		13.	T	(p. 70)
2.	T	(p. 60)		14.	T	(p. 71)
3.	T	(p. 61)		15.	F	(p. 72)
4.	T	(p. 62)		16.	F	(p. 71)
5.	T	(p. 63)		17.	T	(p. 72)
6.	T	(p. 63)		18.	T	(p. 75)
7.	F	(p. 63)		19.	T	(p. 77)
8.	T	(p. 64)		20.	F	(p. 79)
9.	F	(p. 64)		21.	F	(p. 81)
10.	F	(p. 67)		22.	T	(p. 83)
11.	F	(p. 67)		23.	F	(p. 85)
12.	F	(p. 70)		24.	T	(p. 84)

Multiple Choice

1.	b	(p. 59)	17.	c	(p. 67)
2.	b	(p. 60)	18.	e	(p. 67)
3.	d	(p. 60)	19.	d	(pp. 67-68)
4.	b	(p. 62)	20.	a	(p. 69)
5.	e	(p. 62)	21.	a	(p. 70)
6.	a	(p. 63)	22.	c	(p. 70)
7.	c	(p. 63)	23.	b	(p. 71)
8.	c	(p. 63)	24.	b	(p. 73)
9.	e	(p. 63)	25.	e	(p. 74)
10.	d	(p. 63)	26.	a	(pp. 77)
11.	a	(p. 63)	27.	c	(p. 87)
12.	d	(pp. 63-64)	28.	d	(p. 79)
13.	a	(p. 64)	29.	b	(p. 81)
14.	b	(p. 66)	30.	c	(p. 82)
15.	e	(p. 67)	31.	a	(p. 84)
16.	b	(p. 67)	32.	d	(p. 84)

Matching

1.	g	(p. 60)	7.	j	(p. 71)
2.	l	(p. 63)	8.	h	(p. 75)
3.	i	(p. 66)	9.	c	(p. 77)
4.	e	(p. 67)	10.	d	(p. 77)
5.	k	(p. 69)	11.	f	(p. 79)
6.	a	(p. 70)	12.	b	(p. 83)

Fill-In

1. homo sapiens (p. 59)
2. instincts (p. 60)
3. material culture (p. 60)
4. homo sapiens (p. 63)
5. 5,000 (p. 63)
6. symbols, language, values, norms, material objects (p. 63)
7. symbol (p. 63)
8. experienced, inflicted (p. 64)
9. transmission (p. 64)
10. Chinese, English, Spanish (p. 66)
11. values, beliefs (p. 67)
12. prescriptive, proscriptive (pp. 69)
13. Norms (p. 69)
14. Social control (p. 70)
15. technology (p. 71)
16. virtual (p. 71)
17. high, popular (p. 73)
18. difference, hierarchy (p. 74)
19. Multiculturalism (p. 75)
20. cultural integration (p. 77)
21. cultural lag (p. 77)
22. Ethnocentrism (p. 79)
23. economy, communications, migration (p. 80)
24. materialism (p. 83)
25. Sociobiology (p. 83)

PART VII: IN FOCUS--IMPORTANT ISSUES

- What is Culture?

    Illustrate each of the following:

    nonmaterial culture

    material culture

    What is meant by the author that no way of life is "natural" to humanity?

    Briefly recount the evolutionary background of human beings:

    Differentiate between the following terms:

    culture

    nation

    society

- The Components of Culture

    Define and illustrate each of the following *components of culture*

        symbols

        language

        values

        beliefs

        norms

        social control

    List the ten *key values of U.S. culture* as identified in the text:

    Provide an illustration of *values in conflict*:

- Cultural Diversity: Many Ways of Life In One World

  Identify and describe an example for each of the following terms:

  counterculture

  subculture

  multiculturalism

  cultural lag

  ethnocentrism

  cultural relativism

  What are three reasons given in the text for the existence of a *global culture*?

- Theoretical Analysis of Culture

    Briefly describe each how each of the following *theoretical approaches* helps us understand cultural uniformity and diversity:

    structural-functionalism

    social-conflict analysis

    sociobiology

- Culture and Human Freedom

    In what ways does culture *constrain* us?

    In what ways does culture offer us *freedom*?

PART VIII: ANALYSIS AND COMMENT

Global Sociology

"Confronting the Yanomamo: The Experience of Culture Shock"

Key Points: Questions:

Critical Thinking

"Don't Blame Me! The New "Culture of Victimization""

Key Points: Questions:

"Virtual Culture: Is It Good for Us?"

Key Points: Questions:

Controversy and Debate

"What Are the "Culture Wars?""

Key Points: Questions:

Window on the World--Global Map 3-1

"Language in Global Perspective"

Key Points: Questions:

Seeing Ourselves--National Map 3-1

"What'll Ya Have? Popular Beverages across the United States"

Key Points: Questions:

Seeing Ourselves--National Map 3-2

"Language Diversity across the United States"

Key Points: Questions:

4 Society

PART II: LEARNING OBJECTIVES

1.   To be able to differentiate between the four "visions" of society offered by sociologists.

2.   To learn about the ideas of Gerhard and Jean Lenski, Karl Marx, Max Weber, and Emile Durkheim concerning the structure of society and social change.

3.   To be able to identify and describe the different types of society as distinguished by their level of technology.

PART III: KEY CONCEPTS

agriculture

alienation

anomie

bourgeoisie

bureaucracy

capitalists

class consciousness

class conflict

collective consciousness

division of labor

false consciousness

horticulture

hunting and gathering

idealism

ideal-type

industrialism

infrastructure

materialism

material surplus

mechanical solidarity

organic solidarity

pastoralism

postindustrialism

proletarians

rationality

rationalization of society

social conflict

social fact

social institutions

society

sociocultural evolution

superstructure

tradition

PART IV: IMPORTANT RESEARCHERS

Gerhard and Jean Lenski   Max Weber

PART V: STUDY QUESTIONS

True-False

1.	T	F	According to Karl Marx, the story of society spins around *social conflict*.
2.	T	F	As used sociologically, the concept of *society* refers to people who interact in a defined territory and share a culture.
3.	T	F	Max Weber believed that *rational* thinking dominates modern society.
4.	T	F	A criticism of the Lenskis' concept of *sociocultural evolution* is that it doesn't take technology into account when being used to explain social change.
5.	T	F	Hunting and gathering societies are typically *nomadic*.
6.	T	F	Technologically simple societies change very *slowly*.
7.	T	F	*Horticulture* refers to the use of hand tools to raise crops.
8.	T	F	*Hunting and gathering* societies tend to be characterized by more social inequality than horticultural or agrarian societies.
9.	T	F	*Agrarian* societies emerged about 5,000 years ago.
10.	T	F	As societies developed from hunting and gathering to horticultural and agrarian societies, the status of women relative to men *increased*.
11.	T	F	*Postindustrialism* is a process in which the importance of technology is declining relative to previous historical periods.
12.	T	F	For Karl Marx, the most significant form of *social conflict* arises from the way society produces material goods.
13.	T	F	According to the theory of Karl Marx, social institutions like the family and religion comprise an important component of society's *infrastructure*.
14.	T	F	According to Karl Marx, the *capitalists* are people who sell their productive labor for wages.
15.	T	F	According to Karl Marx, *class consciousness* refers to explanations of social problems as the shortcomings of individuals rather than the flaws of society.
16.	T	F	Karl Marx condemned capitalism for producing *alienation*, or the experience of isolation and misery resulting from powerlessness.
17.	T	F	In line with the philosophical doctrine of *idealism*, Max Weber emphasized how human ideas shape society.
18.	T	F	An *ideal type* is defined as an abstract statement of the essential characteristics of any social phenomenon.
19.	T	F	Max Weber's study of *Calvinism* provides striking evidence of the power of ideas to shape society.

64

20.	T	F	According to Max Weber, among other things, *rational social organization* is characterized by specialized tasks, impersonality, and an awareness of time.
21.	T	F	According to Emile Durkheim, a *social fact* is an objective reality beyond the lives of individuals.
22.	T	F	*Anomie* is the experience of isolation and misery resulting from powerlessness.
23.	T	F	According to Emile Durkheim, *organic solidarity* characterizes preindustrial societies.
24.	T	F	For Emile Durkheim, the key to change in a society is the expanding *division of labor*.
25.	T	F	According to Emile Durkheim, modernity rests far less on *functional interdependence* and far more on *moral consensus*.
26.	T	F	Unlike Karl Marx and Max Weber, Emile Durkheim was *relatively optimistic* about industrialization and the development of modern society.

Multiple-Choice

1. The _____ nomads who wander the vastness of the Sahara in western Africa, north of the city of Timbuktu in the nation of Mali, are known as the "blue men of the desert."

    (a) Tasaday
    (b) !Kung
    (c) BaMbuti
    (d) Tuaregs

2. People who interact in a defined territory and share a culture refers to the concept of

    (a) culture.
    (b) social organization.
    (c) social structure.
    (d) society.

3. Gerhard and Jean Lenski focus on which factor as a major determinant of social change?

    (a) human ideas
    (b) technology
    (c) social conflict
    (d) social solidarity
    (e) religious doctrine

4. The concept of *sociocultural evolution* focuses our attention on _____ as a key force in cultural change.

    (a) technology
    (b) values
    (c) beliefs
    (d) sanctions

65

5. The key organizational principle of *hunting and gathering* societies is

   (a) politics.
   (b) religion.
   (c) health.
   (d) kinship.

6. A settlement of several hundred people who use hand tools to cultivate plants, is family-centered, and came into existence 10-12,000 years ago is a(n)

   (a) hunting and gathering society.
   (b) horticultural society.
   (c) pastoral society.
   (d) agrarian society.

7. Which of the following is/are characteristic of *hunting and gathering societies*?

   (a) Hunters and gatherers have little control over their environment.
   (b) Hunting and gathering societies are built on kinship.
   (c) Hunting and gathering societies are nomadic.
   (d) Hunting and gathering societies have few formal leaders and are egalitarian.
   (e) all of the above

8. Which of the following qualities is/are more characteristic of *horticultural* and *agrarian* societies as compared to hunting and gathering societies?

   (a) greater social inequality
   (b) greater material surplus
   (c) greater specialization
   (d) all of the above

9. *Agrarian* societies first emerged about _____ years ago.

   (a) 1,000
   (b) 12,000
   (c) 25,000
   (d) 50,000
   (e) 5,000

10. The development of metal for use in agrarian societies

   (a) increased the status of women in society.
   (b) lowered the status of males in society.
   (c) had little effect on the status of either men or women.
   (d) lowered the status of females in society.

11. Which of the following is/are accurate statements concerning *industrial society*?

    (a) The industrial era began about 1750.
    (b) With industrial technology, societies began to change faster than ever before.
    (c) Occupational specialization became more pronounced than ever in industrial society.
    (d) Industrial technology recast the family, lessening its traditional significance as the center of social life.
    (e) all of the above

12. *Postindustrial* society is _____-based.

    (a) family
    (b) labor
    (c) gender
    (d) leisure
    (e) information

13. For Karl Marx, ideas, values, and social institutions like *religion, education,* and the *family* are part of the _____ of society.

    (a) superstructure
    (b) predestination
    (c) rationality
    (d) infrastructure
    (e) ideal type

14. _____ refer(s) to the major spheres of social life, or societal subsystems, organized to meet human needs.

    (a) Social structure
    (b) Social organization
    (c) Social institutions
    (d) Social change
    (e) Culture

15. Which social institution did Karl Marx argue dominated all the others?

    (a) family
    (b) economy
    (c) politics
    (d) religion

16. According to Karl Marx, the *capitalists* controlled the means of production in society. As new productive forces eroded the feudal order, a new class of merchants and skilled craftsworkers emerged, known as the *bourgeioise*. This terms means:

   (a) "the exploited."
   (b) "the workers."
   (c) "of the town."
   (d) "the tyrannical."

17. In order for exploited classes to take political action to improve their situation, Karl Marx proposed they must:

   (a) become aware of their shared oppression.
   (b) organize to take collective action.
   (c) replace false consciousness with class consciousness.
   (d) all of the above

18. *Alienation* is defined as

   (a) the experience of isolation and misery resulting from powerlessness.
   (b) deliberate, matter-of-fact calculation of the most efficient means to accomplish a particular goal.
   (c) predestination.
   (d) social bonds, based on specialization, that unite members of a society.
   (e) a condition in which society provides little moral guidance to individuals.

19. Max Weber's analysis of society reflects the *philosophical approach* known as

   (a) materialism.
   (b) idealism.
   (c) cultural ecology.
   (d) egalitarianism.
   (e) radicalism.

20. Max Weber argued that *modern society* was characterized by

   (a) conflict.
   (b) harmony.
   (c) indecision.
   (d) ambiguity.
   (e) rationality.

21. Max Weber's "great thesis" concerned the relationship between:

    (a)   conflict and change.
    (b)   technology and ideas.
    (c)   Protestantism and capitalism.
    (d)   alienation and powerlessness.
    (e)   social order and social facts.

22. The concepts of *social fact, anomie,* and *mechanical solidarity* are most associated with which theorist?

    (a)   Max Weber
    (b)   Jean Lenski
    (c)   Herbert Spencer
    (d)   Karl Marx
    (e)   Emile Durkheim

23. A condition in which society provides little moral guidance to individuals is the definition for

    (a)   anomie.
    (b)   alienation.
    (c)   mechanical solidarity.
    (d)   infrastructure.
    (e)   rationality.

24. For Emile Durkheim, the key dimension of cultural change is society's expanding

    (a)   mechanical solidarity.
    (b)   false consciousness.
    (c)   division of labor.
    (d)   infrastructure.
    (e)   class conflict.

Matching

1. ____ The aspect of society focused on by Max Weber.
2. ____ The aspect of society focused on by Gerhard and Jean Lenski.
3. ____ The technology of using hand tools to cultivate plants.
4. ____ Technology that supports an information-based economy.
5. ____ Major spheres of social life, or society's subsystems, organized to meet basic human needs.
6. ____ According to Karl Marx, the economic system represents a society's _____.
7. ____ The experience of isolation and misery resulting from powerlessness.
8. ____ An abstract statement of the essential characteristics of any social phenomenon.
9. ____ A condition in which society provides little moral guidance to individuals.
10. ____ Social bonds, based on shared morality, that unites members of preindustrial societies.
11. ____ Social bonds, based on specialization, that unites members of industrial societies.
12. ____ Specialized economic activity.

a. postindustrialism
b. ideal type
c. division of labor
d. ideas
e. alienation
f. social institutions
g. anomie
h. horticulture
i. mechanical solidarity
j. technology
k. organic solidarity
l. infrastructure

Fill-In

1. While Gerhard and Jean Lenski focused on how _____ shapes society, Max Weber investigated the influence of _____ on society.
2. _____ *evolution* refers to the changes that occur as a society gains new technology.
3. A _____ society is one whose members use hand tools to raise crops.
4. Domesticating plants and animals generate a _____ _____.
5. _____ refers to technology that supports an information-based economy.
6. The key to Marx's thinking is the idea of _____ _____, or the struggle between segments of society over valued resources.
7. Karl Marx referred to those who *own* the means of production as the _____, and those who provide the *labor* for its operation as the _____.
8. Karl Marx viewed the *economic system* as the social _____ and other social institutions as society's _____.
9. _____ _____ refers to explanations of social problems grounded in the shortcomings of individuals rather than the flaws of society.
10. In Karl Marx's theory, _____ is the experience of isolation and misery resulting from powerlessness.
11. Karl Marx cited four ways in which capitalism *alienates* workers, including alienation from the act of _____, from the _____ of work, from other _____, and from _____ potential.

12. The only way out of the trap of capitalism, argued Marx, is to remake society. He envisioned a more humane productive system, one where people would be equals. He called this system _____.

13. Max Weber demonstrated the importance of _____ in shaping social change.

14. An _____ _____ is an abstract statement of the essential characteristics of any social phenomenon.

15. By _____ Max Weber meant sentiments and beliefs passed from generation to generation.

16. Max Weber argued that people in modern societies favor _____, or deliberate, matter-of-fact calculation of the most efficient means to accomplish a particular task.

17. According to Max Weber, *rational social organization* has seven distinctive characteristics, including: distinctive _____ _____, _____ organizations, _____ tasks, _____ discipline, awareness of _____, _____ competence, and _____.

18. The kind of organization Max Weber termed _____ arose along with capitalism as an expression of the *rationality* that shapes modern society.

19. Any part of society that is argued to have an objective existence apart from the individual Emile Durkheim called a _____ _____.

20. Emile Durkheim acknowledged he advantages of modern-day freedom, but he warned of increased _____, or a condition in which society provides little moral guidance to individuals.

21. Social bonds, common in industrial society, based on specialization, were what Emile Durkheim called _____ _____.

Definition and Short-Answer

1. How do the Lenskis define *sociocultural evolution*?
2. What are the basic *types of societies* identified by the Gerhard and Jean Lenski? What are three general characteristics of each?
3. What is meant by the term *material surplus*? What are its effects on society?
4. What does our author mean by the *limits of technology*?
5. What is the meaning of the philosophy of *idealism*? *Materialism*?
6. According to Karl Marx, what are the four ways in which industrial capitalism *alienates* workers? Provide an illustration for each.
7. Differentiate between Karl Marx's concepts *infrastructure* and *superstructure*.
8. According to Max Weber, what are the roots of *rationality* in modern society?
9. For Max Weber, what are the characteristics of *rational social organization*? Provide an illustration for three of these.
10. What concerned Max Weber about *rationality*? Provide an illustration.
11. What does Emile Durkheim mean by suggesting that society has an *objective existence* apart from individuals? Provide an illustration.
12. Summarize the basic similarities and differences between the views of Gerhard and Jean Lenski, Karl Marx, Max Weber, and Emile Durkheim on modern society. Which theorist most impresses you in terms of explaining what holds a society together? What about how a society changes?

PART VI: ANSWERS TO STUDY QUESTIONS

True-False

1.	T	(p. 89)	14.	F	(p. 97)
2.	T	(p. 89)	15.	F	(pp. 99-100)
3.	T	(p. 89)	16.	T	(p. 100)
4.	F	(p. 90)	17.	T	(p. 102)
5.	T	(p. 90)	18.	T	(p. 102)
6.	T	(p. 90)	19.	T	(p. 104)
7.	T	(p. 91)	20.	T	(p. 105)
8.	F	(p. 92)	21.	T	(p. 107)
9.	T	(p. 92)	22.	T	(p. 108)
10.	F	(p. 93)	23.	F	(p. 109)
11.	F	(p. 95)	24.	T	(p. 109)
12.	T	(p. 97)	25.	F	(p. 109)
13.	F	(p. 98)	26.	T	(p. 109)

Multiple-Choice

1.	d	(p. 89)	13.	a	(p. 98)
2.	d	(p. 89)	14.	c	(p. 98)
3.	b	(p. 90)	15.	b	(p. 98)
4.	a	(p. 90)	16.	c	(p. 99)
5.	d	(p. 90)	17.	b	(pp. 99-100)
6.	b	(p. 91)	18.	a	(p. 100)
7.	e	(pp. 91-92)	19.	b	(pp. 102)
8.	d	(pp. 91-92)	20.	e	(p. 103)
9.	e	(p. 92)	21.	c	(p. 104)
10.	d	(p. 93)	22.	e	(pp. 107-108)
11.	e	(p. 94)	23.	a	(p. 108)
12.	e	(p. 95)	24.	c	(p. 109)

Matching

1.	d	(p. 89)	7.	e	(p. 100)
2.	j	(p. 89)	8.	b	(p. 102)
3.	h	(p. 91)	9.	g	(p. 109)
4.	a	(p. 95)	10.	i	(p. 109)
5.	f	(p. 98)	11.	k	(p. 109)
6.	l	(p. 98)	12.	c	(p. 109)

Fill-In

1. technology, ideas (p. 89)
2. sociocultural (p. 90)
3. horticultural (p. 91)
4. material surplus (p. 92)
5. Postindustrialism (p. 95)
6. social conflict (p. 97)
7. capitalists, proletariat (p. 97)
8. infrastructure, superstructure (p. 98)
9. false consciousness (p. 98)
10. alienation (p. 100)
11. working, products, workers, human (p. 100)
12. socialism (p. 101)
13. ideas (p. 102)
14. ideal type (p. 102)
15. tradition (p. 102)
16. rationality (p. 102)
17. Social institutions, large-scale, specialized, personal, time, technical, impersonality (pp. 105)
18. bureaucracy (p. 106)
19. social facts (p. 107)
20. anomie (p. 108)
21. organic solidarity (p. 109)

PART VII: IN FOCUS--IMPORTANT ISSUES

- Gerhard Lenski and Jean Lenski: Society and Technology

Describe each of the following types of societies based on their respective *level of technological development*:

hunting and gathering societies

horticultural societies

agrarian societies

pastoral societies

industrial societies

postindustrial societies

What are the benefits of the advancements in *technology* in industrial and postindustrial societies? What are the problems caused by these advancements?

- Karl Marx: Society and Conflict

Summarize one important point concerning Karl Marx's views on each of the following:

society and production

conflict and history

capitalism and class conflict

capitalism and alienation

revolution

- Max Weber: The Rationalization of Society

Differentiate between the two following world views:

tradition

rationality

Summarize Max Weber's great thesis.

Describe each of the following characteristics of *rational social organization*:

distinctive social institutions

large-scale organizations

specialized tasks

personal discipline

awareness of time

technical competence

impersonality

According to Max Weber, what is the relationship between *rationality* and *alienation*?

- Emile Durkheim: Society and Function

What did Emile Durkheim mean by saying society exists beyond ourselves (society as structure)?

Why did Emile Durkheim suggest *crime* is not "pathological" (function: society as system)?

What evidence was used by Emile Durkheim to suggest that society is not merely "beyond ourselves," but also "in ourselves?"

Describe the following two forms of the *division of labor*:

mechanical solidarity

organic solidarity

- Critical Evaluation: Four Visions of Society

What holds society together?

    According to Gerhard Lenski and Jean Lenski:

    According to Karl Marx:

    According to Max Weber:

    According to Emile Durkheim:

How and why have societies changed?

    According to Gerhard Lenski and Jean Lenski:

    According to Karl Marx:

    According to Max Weber:

    According to Emile Durkheim:

PART VIII: ANALYSIS AND COMMENT

Social Diversity

"Technology and the Changing Status of Women"

Key Points: Questions:

Applying Sociology

"Alienation and Industrial Capitalism"

Key Points: Questions:

"The Information Revolution: What Would Durkheim (and Others) Have Thought?"

Key Points: Questions:

Controversy and Debate

"Is Society Getting Better or Worse?"

Key Points: Questions:

Window on the World

"Global Map 4-1: High Technology in Global Perspective"

Key Points: Questions:

5 | Socialization

PART I: CHAPTER OUTLINE

I.   Social Experience: The Key to Our Humanity
    A.   Human Development: Nature and Nurture
          1.   Charles Darwin: The Role of Nature
          2.   The Social Sciences: The Role of Nurture
    B.   Social Isolation
          1.   Studies of Nonhuman Primates
          2.   Studies of Isolated Children
II.   Understanding The Socialization Process
    A.   Sigmund Freud: The Elements of Personality
          1.   Basic Human Needs
          2.   Freud's Model of Personality
          3.   Personality Development
    B.   Jean Piaget: Cognitive Development
          1.   The Sensorimotor Stage
          2.   The Preoperational Stage
          3.   The Concrete Operational Stage
          4.   The Formal Operational Stage
    C.   Lawrence Kohlberg: Moral Development
    D.   Carol Gilligan: Bringing In Gender
    E.   George Herbert Mead: The Social Self
          1.   The Self
          2.   The Looking-Glass Self
          3.   The I and the Me
          4.   Development of the Self
    F.   Erik H. Erikson: Eight Stages of Development

PART II: LEARNING OBJECTIVES

1.   To understand the "nature-nurture" debate regarding socialization and personality development.
2.   To become aware of the effects of social isolation on humans and other primates.
3.   To become aware of the key components of Sigmund Freud's model of personality.
4.   To be able to identify and describe the four stages of Jean Piaget's cognitive development theory.
5.   To be able to identify and describe the stages of moral development as identified by Lawrence Kohlberg.
6.   To analyze Carol Gilligan's critique of Kohlberg's moral development model.
7.   To be able to identify and describe the stages of personality development as outlined by Erik H. Erikson.
8.   To consider the contributions of George Herbert Mead to the understanding of personality development.
9.   To be able to compare the spheres of socialization (family, school, etc.) in terms of their effects on an individual's socialization experiences.
10.   To develop a life-course perspective of the socialization experience.
11.   To begin to understand the cross-cultural and historical patterns of death and dying as part of the life course.
12.   To be able to discuss the sociological perspective on socialization as a constraint to freedom.

PART III: KEY CONCEPTS

adolescence

adulthood

ageism

anticipatory socialization

behaviorism

childhood

cognition

cohort

concrete operational stage

ego

eros

formal operations stage

game stage

generalized other

I

id

looking-glass self

hidden curriculum

hurried child syndrome

institutionalized

mass media

me

old age

peer group

personality

preoperational stage

resocialization

repression

self

sensorimotor stage

significant other

social behaviorism

socialization

sublimation

superego

taking the role of the other

thanatos

total institution

PART IV: IMPORTANT RESEARCHERS

Kingsley Davis   John Watson

Harry and Margaret Harlow   Sigmund Freud

Jean Piaget   Lawrence Kohlberg

Carol Gilligan   Erik H. Erikson

Charles Horton Cooley   George Herbert Mead

Elizabeth Kubler-Ross

True-False

1.	T	F	As defined by our author, the concept of *personality* does not concern actual behavior.
2.	T	F	John Watson was a nineteenth-century psychologist who argued that human behavior was largely determined by *heredity*.
3.	T	F	The Harlows' research on rhesus monkeys concerning *social isolation* illustrates that while short-term isolation can be overcome, long-term isolation appears to cause irreversible emotional and behavioral damage to monkeys.
4.	T	F	The cases of *Isabelle, Anna,* and *Genie* support the arguments made by naturalists that certain personality characteristics are determined by heredity.
5.	T	F	*Socialization* is a complex, lifelong process.
6.	T	F	Sigmund Freud envisioned *biological factors* as having little or no influence on personality development.
7.	T	F	The *id* in Freud's psychoanalytic theory represents the human being's basic needs which are unconscious and demand immediate satisfaction.
8.	T	F	The first stage in Jean Piaget's *cognitive development* theory is referred to as the *preoperational stage*.
9.	T	F	According to Jean Piaget, language and other symbols are first used in the *preoperational stage*.
10.	T	F	While Sigmund Freud saw human beings torn by opposing forces of biology and culture, Jean Piaget saw the mind as active and creative.
11.	T	F	According to Lawrence Kohlberg, during the *conventional stage* of moral development, a person takes behavior at face value rather than trying to infer a person's intention in making a moral judgement.
12.	T	F	Carol Gilligan's research focuses on how *gender* affects *moral reasoning*.
13.	T	F	According to Carol Gilligan, taking a *rule-based* approach to moral reasoning is superior to taking a *person-based* approach.
14.	T	F	George Herbert Mead argued that *biological factors* played *little or no* role in the development of the self.
15.	T	F	George Herbert Mead refers to *taking the role of the other* as the interplay between the *I* and *me*.
16.	T	F	George Herbert Mead's concept of the *generalized other* refers to general cultural norms and values shared by us and others that we use as a reference point to evaluate ourselves.
17.	T	F	According to Erik H. Erikson's theory of personality development, the first challenge faced in life is *intimacy* versus *isolation*.
18.	T	F	Erik H. Erikson's theory views personality formation as a *lifelong process*.
19.	T	F	The concept *hidden curriculum* relates to the important cultural values being transmitted to children in school.
20.	T	F	*Peer group* is a social group whose members have interests, social positions, and age in common.
21.	T	F	Children in the United States spend as much time watching television as they do going to school.

22.	T	F	Two major criticisms of the U.S. mass media are that *minorities* are either portrayed in films and television in stereotypical fashion or are ignored altogether.
23.	T	F	Looking back in time and around the world shows that *childhood* is grounded in culture.
24.	T	F	A *cohort* is a setting in which people are isolated from the rest of society and manipulated by an administrative staff.

Multiple Choice

1. _____ holds that behavior is not instinctual but learned.

   (a) The theory of natural selection
   (b) Behaviorism
   (c) Sociobiology
   (d) Evolutionary theory

2. The story of *Anna* illustrates the significance of _____ in personality development.

   (a) heredity
   (b) social interaction
   (c) physical conditions
   (d) ecology
   (e) history

3. What did the experiments on social isolation among rhesus monkeys show?

   (a) Artificial wire monkeys provided sufficient contact for young monkeys to develop normally.
   (b) The behavior of rhesus monkey infants is totally dissimilar to human infants.
   (c) Deprivation of social experience, rather than the absence of a specific parent, has devastating effects.
   (d) Biological forces in rhesus monkeys cushions them from the negative effects of social isolation.

4. Which of the following is representative of *Sigmund Freud's* analysis of personality?

   . (a) Biological forces play only a small role in personality development.
   (b) The term instinct is understood as very general human needs in the form of urges and drives.
   (c) The most significant period for personality development is adolescence.
   (d) Personality is best studied as a process of externalizing social forces.

5.   Sigmund Freud theorized that humans have two basic needs. First is the need for bonding, which Freud called the life instinct, or *eros*. Second, we also have an aggressive drive he called the *death instinct*, or

(a)   storge
(b)   philos
(c)   agape
(d)   the superego
(e)   thanatos

6.   *Sigmund Freud's* model of personality does *not* include which of the following elements?

(a)   superego
(b)   id
(c)   self
(d)   ego

7.   Culture existing within the individual was what *Sigmund Freud* called

(a)   thanatos.
(b)   eros.
(c)   the ego.
(d)   the id.
(e)   the superego.

8.   In Sigmund Freud's model of personality, what balances the innate pleasure-seeking drive with the demands of society?

(a)   id
(b)   ego
(c)   superego
(d)   thanatos

9.   Jean Piaget's focus was on

(a)   how children develop fine motor skills.
(b)   how children are stimulated by their environment.
(c)   cognition--how people think and understand.
(d)   the role of heredity in determining human behavior.

10.   The first stage in Jean Piaget's *cognitive development theory* is

(a)   the preoperational stage.
(b)   the preconventional stage.
(c)   the concrete operations stage.
(d)   the sensorimotor stage.

11. According to *Jean Piaget*, which of the following best describes the *preoperational stage* of cognitive development?

    (a)   the level of human development in which the world is experienced only through sensory contact
    (b)   the level of human development characterized by the use of logic to understand objects and events
    (c)   the level of human development in which language and other symbols are first used
    (d)   the level of human development characterized by highly abstract thought

12. For a person operating at the *conventional stage* of Lawrence Kohberg's moral development theory

    (a)   "rightness" amounts to "what feels good to me."
    (b)   an attempt is made to assess the intention in reaching moral judgements instead of simply observing what others do.
    (c)   abstract ethical principles are applied, instead of just using her or his culture's norms to make moral judgements.
    (d)   moral decisions are based on avoidance of punishment.

13. According to research by Carol Gilligan, *males* use a _____ perspective concerning moral reasoning.

    (a)   justice
    (b)   independent
    (c)   visual
    (d)   mechanical

14. According to Carol Gilligan, *females* use a _____ perspective concerning moral reasoning.

    (a)   loving
    (b)   liking
    (c)   irrational
    (d)   care and responsibility
    (e)   social behaviorist

15. *George Herbert Mead's* perspective has often been described as

    (a)   psychological pragmatism.
    (b)   behaviorism.
    (c)   social behaviorism.
    (d)   psychoanalysis.
    (e)   naturalism.

16. The concept of the *looking-glass self* refers to

   (a) Freud's argument that through psychoanalysis a person can uncover the unconscious.
   (b) Piaget's view that through biological maturation and social experience individuals become able to logically hypothesize about thoughts without relying on concrete reality.
   (c) Watson's behaviorist notion that one can see through to a person's mind only by observing the person's behavior.
   (d) Cooley's idea that the self-image we have is based on how we suppose others perceive us.

17. George Herbert Mead used the term _____ to describe the widespread cultural norms and values shared by us and others that we use as a point of reference in evaluating ourselves.

   (a) looking-glass self
   (b) socialization
   (c) significant other
   (d) generalized other

18. According to Erik H. Erikson, what is the challenge of *middle adulthood*?

   (a) integration versus despair
   (b) initiative versus guilt
   (c) industry versus inferiority
   (d) making a difference versus self-absorption

19. A national sample of *adolescents* in the U.S. were asked: Whom do you trust? The category of people receiving the great percentage of "yes" for an answer (83 percent) was

   (a) peers.
   (b) parents.
   (c) teachers.
   (d) friends.
   (e) the internet.

20. The process of social learning directed toward assuming a desired status and role in the future is called

   (a) resocialization.
   (b) socialization.
   (c) looking-glass self.
   (d) anticipatory socialization.

21. _____ of U.S. adults reported having walked out of a movie or having turned off a television show due to *high levels of violence*.

   (a) Three-fourths
   (b) One-half
   (c) One-fifth
   (d) Three-eighths

22. According to Elisabeth Kubler-Ross, *dying* is a process involving several stages. The first stage in her developmental model is:

   (a) anger.
   (b) hatred.
   (c) denial.
   (d) resignation.

23. Which of the following is *not* one of the three distinctive characteristics of a *total institution*?

   (a) staff members supervise all spheres of daily life
   (b) staff members encourage the maintenance of individuality, and encourage creativity
   (c) food, sleeping quarters and activities are standardized
   (d) formal rules dictate how virtually every moment is spent

24. _____ refers to a process of radically altering the personality through deliberate manipulation of the environment.

   (a) Anticipatory socialization
   (b) Resocialization
   (c) Primary socialization
   (d) Degradation

Matching

1. ____ A person's fairly consistent patterns of acting, thinking, and feeling.
2. ____ A theory developed by John Watson that holds that behavior patterns are not instinctive but learned.
3. ____ According to Sigmund Freud, the presence of culture within the individual.
4. ____ In Piaget's theory, the level of development at which individuals perceive causal connections in their surroundings.
5. ____ The self-image we have based on how we suppose others perceive us.
6. ____ According to George Herbert Mead, the subjective side of the self.
7. ____ A group whose members have interests, social position, and age in common.
8. ____ Impersonal communications directed to a vast audience.
9. ____ According to Elisabeth Kubler-Ross, a person's first reaction to the prospect of dying.
10. ____ A category of people with a common characteristic, usually their age.
11. ____ Deliberate socialization intended to radically alter the individual's personality.
12. ____ A setting in which individuals are isolated from the rest of society and manipulated by an administrative staff.

a.	looking-glass self	g.	cohort
b.	behaviorism	h.	peer group
c.	mass media	i.	personality
d.	concrete operational stage	j.	total institution
e.	resocialization	k.	I
f.	superego	l.	denial

Fill-In

1. A _____ is defined as a person's fairly consistent pattern of acting, thinking, and feeling.
2. The approach called _____ developed by *John Watson* in the early twentieth century provided a perspective that stressed learning rather than instincts as the key to personality development.
3. According to *Sigmund Freud*, the _____ represents a person's conscious efforts to balance the innate pleasure-seeking drives of the human organism and the demands of society.
4. The Harlow's research using rhesus monkeys confirmed how important it is that adults cradle infants _____.
5. *Sigmund Freud* termed society's controlling influence on the drives of each individual as _____, whereas he called the process of transforming fundamentally selfish drives into more socially acceptable objectives _____.
6. *Jean Piaget's* work centered on human _____.
7. According to Jean Piaget's theory of *cognitive development*, the level of human development at which individuals think abstractly and critically is known as the _____ _____ *stage*.
8. *Lawrence Kohlberg* identifies three stages in moral development, these include the _____, the _____, and the _____.

92

9. Carol Gilligan suggests that boys tend to use a *justice perspective* in moral reasoning, relying on formal rules in reaching a judgement about right and wrong. On the other hand, says Gilligan, girls tend to use a _____ and _____ *perspective* in moral reasoning, which leads them to judge a situation with an eye toward personal relationships.

10. According to George Herbert Mead, the _____ refers to that part of an individual's personality composed of sef-awareness and self-image.

11. *George Herbert Mead* explained that infants with limited social experience respond to others only in terms of _____.

12. According to Erik H. Erikson's developmental theory, the *challenge of adolescence* involves gaining _____ versus _____.

13. Erik H. Erikson's theory views personality formation as a _____ *process*.

14. The process of social learning directed toward gaining a desired position is called _____ *socialization*.

15. Impersonal communications directed to a vast audience refers to the _____ _____.

16. The _____ _____ *syndrome* refers to the phenomenon today where children have to grapple with sex, drugs, and violence as well as fend more and more for themselves.

17. Elisabeth Kubler-Ross has described *death* as an orderly transition, involving five distinct responses. These include, in order of occurrence: _____, _____, _____, _____, and _____.

18. Prisons and mental hospitals are examples of _____ _____.

Definition and Short-Answer

1. How did the work of *Charles Darwin* influence the understanding of personality development in the last nineteenth century?

2. What was *John Watson's* view concerning personality development?

3. Review the research by *Harry* and *Margaret Harlow* on social isolation. What were the important discoveries they made?

4. Discuss the cases of *childhood isolation* presented in the text. What are the important conclusions being drawn from these cases?

5. Identify and define the parts of personality as seen by *Sigmund Freud*.

6. What are the four stages of cognitive development according to *Jean Piaget*? Briefly describe the qualities of each stage. What is one major criticism of his theory?

7. What are the stages of personality development according to Erik H. Erikson? In what two important ways does his theory differ from Sigmund Freud's?

8. Define the concept *looking-glass self*. Provide an illustration from your own personal experience.

9. Define and differentiate between the terms *generalized other* and *significant other*. Further, what are the four basic arguments being made by *George Herbert Mead* concerning personality development?

10. According to the text, what are the four important *agents of socialization*? Provide an illustration of how each is involved in the socialization process.

11. What are the stages of *adulthood* and the qualities of each?

12. What is a *total institution*? What are the typical experiences of a person who is living within a total institution? How do these experiences affect personality development?

13. Based on the sociological research cited in this chapter, to what extent can it be argued that humans are like "puppets" in society?

14. What conclusions are being made by the author concerning the *life course*?

PART VI: ANSWERS TO STUDY QUESTIONS

True-False

1.	F	(p. 115)		13.	F	(p. 122)
2.	F	(p. 116)		14.	T	(p. 122)
3.	T	(p. 117)		15.	T	(p. 127)
4.	F	(p. 117)		16.	T	(p. 123)
5.	T	(p. 118)		17.	F	(p. 124)
6.	T	(p. 118)		18.	T	(p. 125)
7.	T	(p. 119)		19.	T	(p. 126)
8.	F	(p. 119)		20.	F	(p. 126)
9.	T	(p. 120)		21.	T	(p. 127)
10.	T	(p. 120)		22.	T	(p. 129)
11.	F	(p. 121)		23.	T	(p. 131)
12.	T	(p. 121)		24.	F	(p. 133)

Multiple Choice

1.	b	(p. 116)		13.	a	(p. 122)
2.	b	(p. 117)		14.	c	(p. 122)
3.	c	(p. 117)		15.	c	(p. 122)
4.	b	(p. 118)		16.	d	(p. 123)
5.	e	(p. 118)		17.	d	(p. 123)
6.	c	(p. 119)		18.	d	(p. 124)
7.	e	(p. 119)		19.	b	(p. 126)
8.	b	(p. 119)		20	d	(p. 126)
9.	c	(p. 119)		21.	a	(p. 127)
10.	d	(p. 119)		22.	c	(p. 132)
11.	c	(p. 120)		23.	b	(p. 133)
12.	b	(p. 121)		24.	b	(p. 133)

Matching

1.	i	(p. 115)		7.	h	(p. 126)
2.	b	(p. 116)		8.	c	(p. 126)
3.	f	(p. 119)		9.	l	(p. 132)
4.	d	(p. 120)		10.	g	(p. 133)
5.	a	(p. 123)		11.	e	(p. 133)
6.	k	(p. 123)		12.	j	(p. 133)

Fill-In

1. personality (p. 115)
2. behaviorism (p. 116)
3. affectionately (p. 117)
4. ego (p. 119)

94

5. repression, sublimation (p. 119)
6. cognition (p. 119)
7. formal operations (p. 120)
8. preconventional, conventional, postconventional (pp. 120-121)
9. care, responsibility (p. 122)
10. self (p. 122)
11. imitation (p. 123)
12. identity, confusion (p. 125)
13. lifelong (p. 125)
14. anticipitory (p. 126)
15. mass media (p. 126)
16. hurried child (p. 131)
17. denial, anger, negotiation, resignation, acceptance (p. 132)
18. total institutions (p. 133)

PART VII: IN FOCUS: IMPORTANT POINTS

- Social Experience: The Key To Our Humanity

According to Charles Darwin, what role does *nature* play in human personality development?

Review the conclusions being made by social scientists concerning the role of *nurture* in human personality development, focusing on each of the following:

Studies of nonhuman primates

Studies of isolated children

- Understanding Socialization

Briefly review the major points being made by the following theorists concerning personality development. Identify and describe/define the stages of development for each theory discussed.

Sigmund Freud

Jean Piaget

Lawrence Kohlberg

Carol Gilligan

George Herbert Mead

Erik H. Erikson

- Agents of Socialization

  Briefly describe the significance for each of the following major agents of socialization on personality development:

  the family

  the school

  peer groups

  the mass media

- Socialization and the Life Course

Identify two major points being made in the text concerning each of the following stages of the human life course:

childhood

adolescence

adulthood

old age

dying

- Resocialization: Total Institutions

   What are the three major qualities of a *total institution*?

   What does the author mean by saying that *resocialization* is a two-part process?

PART VIII: ANALYSIS AND COMMENT

Critical Thinking

"The Importance of Gender in Research"

Key Points: Questions:

Social Diversity

"How Should the Media Portray Minorities?"

Key Points: Questions:

Controversy and Debate

"Are We Free within Society?"

Key Points: Questions:

Window on the World--Global Map 5-1

"Child Labor in Global Perspective"

Key Points: Questions:

Seeing Ourselves--National Map 5-1

"Television Viewing and Newspaper Reading across the United States"

Key Points: Questions:

6

Social Interaction In Everyday Life

PART I: CHAPTER OUTLINE

PART II: LEARNING OBJECTIVES

1. To be able to identify the characteristics of social structure.
2. To be able to discuss the relationship between social structure and individuality.
3. To be able to distinguish between the different types of statuses and roles.
4. To be able to describe and illustrate the social construction of reality.
5. To begin to see how the technological capacity of a society influences the social construction of reality.
6. To be able to describe and illustrate the approach known as ethnomethodology.
7. To see the importance of performance, nonverbal communication, idealization, and embarrassment to the "presentation of the self."
8. To be able to describe and illustrate dramaturgical analysis.
9. To be able to use gender and humor as illustrations of how people construct meaning in everyday life.

PART III: KEY CONCEPTS

achieved status

ascribed status

demeanor

dramaturgical analysis

ethnomethodology

humor

idealization

master status

nonverbal communication

performance

personal space

presentation of self

role

role conflict

role exit

role expectations

role performance

role set

role strain

social interaction

status

status set

social construction of reality

Thomas theorem

PART IV: IMPORTANT RESEARCHERS

Robert Merton   Harold Garfinkel

Erving Goffman   Paul Ekman

PART V: STUDY QUESTIONS

True-False

1.   T   F   A *status* refers to a pattern of expected behavior for individual members of society.
2.   T   F   Status is not related to social identity.
3.   T   F   A *status set* refers to all statuses a person holds during his or her lifetime.
4.   T   F   Both *statuses* and *roles* vary by culture.
5.   T   F   Being an honors student, being a spouse, and being a computer programmer re examples of *ascribed statuses*.
6.   T   F   *Role strain* refers to the incompatibility among roles corresponding to a single status.
7.   T   F   A physical disability can become a *master status*.
8.   T   F   The phrase *the social construction of reality* relates to the sociologist's view that statuses and roles structure our lives along narrowly delineated paths.
9.   T   F   For the *ethnomethodologist*, a deliberate lack of social cooperation may lead the researcher to see more clearly the unspoken rules of everyday life.
10.   T   F   According to *Erving Goffman, performances* are very rigidly scripted, leaving virtually no room for individual adaptation.
11.   T   F   According to research on gender and personal performances, men use significantly more space than women.
12.   T   F   Cross-cultural research suggests virtually all *nonverbal communication* is universally understood.
13.   T   F   According to *Erving Goffman's* research, *tact* is relatively uncommon in our society.
14.   T   F   According to dramaturgical analysis, *embarrassment* causes discomfort for both the presenter and the audience.
15.   T   F   An important foundation of *humor* lies in the contrast between two incongruous realities--the *conventional* and *unconventional*.
16.   T   F   One trait of humorous material which appears to be universal is *controversy*.

Multiple-Choice

1.   What is the term for a recognized social position that an individual occupies?

     (a)   prestige
     (b)   status
     (c)   social power
     (d)   role
     (e)   dramaturgy

2.   Which of the following is *not* a structural component of social interaction?

(a)   master status
(b)   role
(c)   value
(d)   role set
(e)   ascribed status

3.   *Ralph Linton* described _____ as the dynamic expression of a status.

(a)   master status
(b)   nonverbal communication
(c)   performance
(d)   dramaturgy
(e)   role

4.   What is the term for a status that has exceptional importance for social identity, often shaping a person's entire life?

(a)   role
(b)   ascribed status
(c)   achieved status
(d)   master status
(e)   role set

5.   What is the term for patterns of expected behavior attached to a particular status?

(a)   role
(b)   master status
(c)   achieved status
(d)   ascribed status

6.   A number of roles attached to a single status refers to:

(a)   a role set.
(b)   a status set.
(c)   a master status.
(d)   role conflict.

7.   The incompatibility among the roles corresponding to two or more statuses refers to:

(a)   role conflict.
(b)   role strain.
(c)   status overload.
(d)   status inconsistency.
(e)   role set.

8.   Methods of reducing *role strain* include which of the following?

(a)   discarding one or more roles
(b)   compartmentalizing roles
(c)   emphasizing some roles more than others
(d)   all of the above
(e)   none of the above

9.   The *Thomas theorem* states:

(a)   roles are only as important as the statuses to which they are attached.
(b)   statuses are only as important as the roles on which they are dependent.
(c)   the basis of humanity is built upon the dual existence of creativity and conformity.
(d)   common sense is only as good as the social structure within which it is embedded.
(e)   situations defined as real become real in their consequences.

10.   What is the term for the study of the way people make sense of their everyday lives?

(a)   naturalism
(b)   phenomenology
(c)   ethnomethodology
(d)   social psychology

11.   The approach used by *ethnomethodologists* to study everyday interaction involves:

(a)   conducting surveys.
(b)   unobtrusive observation.
(c)   secondary analysis.
(d)   breaking rules.
(e)   laboratory experiment.

12.   The investigation of social interaction in terms of *theatrical performance* is referred to as:

(a)   ethnomethodology.
(b)   dramaturgical analysis.
(c)   theatrical analysis.
(d)   phenomenology.

13. The process of the *presentation of the self* is also known as:

    (a)   ethnomethodology
    (b)   achieved status
    (c)   idealization
    (d)   ascribed status
    (e)   impression management

14. *Mr. Preedy*, the fictional character introduced in the text, provides an example of:

    (a)   role conflict.
    (b)   role strain.
    (c)   nonverbal communication.
    (d)   status inconsistency.

15. According Paul Ekman, there are several *universal emotions*. Which of the following is not one he has identified ?

    (a)   hope
    (b)   fear
    (c)   sadness
    (d)   happiness

16. What is *demeanor*?

    (a)   general conduct and deportment
    (b)   a non-felony crime
    (c)   a form of mental illness
    (d)   gender-specific activity

17. Trying to convince others (and perhaps ourselves) that what we do reflects ideal cultural standards rather than selfish motives refers to:

    (a)   backstaging.
    (b)   idealization
    (c)   ethnomethodology
    (d)   tact

18. Helping a person to "save face," or avoid embarrassment, is called:

    (a)   diplomacy.
    (b)   generosity.
    (c)   altruism.
    (d)   tact.

19.	Which of the following is *not* an example provided in the text to illustrate how *language* functions to define the sexes?

(a)	the attention function
(b)	the power function
(c)	the value function
(d)	the affective function

20.	Research by Deborah Tannen concerning communication problems between women and men focusing on the issue of:

(a)	power.
(b)	humor.
(c)	language.
(d)	tact.
(e)	personal space.

21.	Which of the following in *inaccurate* concerning humor?

(a)	Humor is a universal human trait.
(b)	Humor deals with topics that lend themselves to double meanings or controversy.
(c)	Humor and health have always been related.
(d)	Every social group considers topics too sensitive for humorous treatment.
(e)	What is humorous in one society is virtually always humorous in other societies.

22.	Which of the following is *not a function of humor*?

(a)	Humor can be a stimulant to social change.
(b)	Humor limits racism and sexism.
(c)	Humor can be a safety valve.
(d)	Humor can be used as a form of tact.

Matching

1. ____ The process by which people act and react in relation to others.
2. ____ A recognized social position that an individual occupies.
3. ____ A social position a person receives at birth or assumes involuntarily later in life.
4. ____ Expected behavior of someone who holds a particular status.
5. ____ Incompatibility among roles corresponding to a single status.
6. ____ Incompatibility among roles corresponding to two or more statuses.
7. ____ Situations defined as real become real in their consequences.
8. ____ The study of the way people make sense of their everyday lives.
9. ____ The investigation of social interaction in terms of theatrical performance.
10. ____ General conduct or deportment.

a.	ascribed status	f.	role
b.	ethnomethodology	g.	demeanor
c.	Thomas theorem	h.	status
d.	role strain	i.	dramaturgical analysis
e.	social interaction	j.	role conflict

Fill-In

1. _____ _____ refers to the process by which people act and react in relation to others.
2. _____ refers to a recognized social position that an individual occupies in society, while _____ refers to patterns of expected behaviors attached to a particular status.
3. _____ refers to the incompatibility among the roles corresponding to two or more statuses.
4. The _____ _____ *of reality* describes the process by which people creatively shape reality through social interaction.
5. The _____ _____ suggests that situations that are defined as real are real in their consequences.
6. The study of everyday, common-sense understandings that people within a culture have of the world around them is known as _____.
7. _____ *analysis* is the investigation of social interaction in terms of theatrical performance.
8. _____ refers to ways in which individuals, in various settings, attempt to create specific impressions in the minds of others.
9. Props in a doctor's office, like books and framed diplomas, are examples of the _____ *region* of the setting.
10. According to *Erving Goffman*, _____ refers to general conduct or deportment.
11. When people try to convince others that what they are doing reflects ideal cultural standards rather than less virtuous motives, *Erving Goffman* said they are involved in _____.
12. According to Paul Ekman there are four *elements of a performance* that can be used to detect deception. These include: _____, _____, _____ _____, and _____ _____.

13. According to Erving Goffman, as carefully as individuals may craft their performances, slip-ups of all kinds occur. The result is _____, or discomfort following a spoiled performance (or "losing face").

14. Language defines men and women differently in t least three ways--in terms of _____, _____, and _____.

15. *Humor* stems from the contrast between two incongruous realities, the _____ and the _____.

16. According to *Deborah Tannen*, women and men us language differently. The problems couples face in communicating is that what one partner _____ by a comment is not always what the other _____.

Definition and Short-Answer

1. Review the story of the physician's office and *performances* in the text. Using this account as an example, select a social situation you have been involved in and do a dramaturgical analysis to describe its context.

2. Provide an illustration of *nonverbal communication* using the story of *Mr. Preedy* as a model.

3. What are some different types of information provided by a *performer* in terms of nonverbal communication which can be used to determine whether or not a person is telling the truth? Provide an illustration.

4. Refer to *Figure 6-1* (p. 143) and using it as a model, diagram your own status and role sets. Identify points of *role conflict* and *role strain*.

5. What are three ways in which language functions to define the sexes differently? Provide an illustration for each.

6. What is *ethnomethodology*?

7. Define the concept *idealization*. Provide an illustration using the doctor's office account as a model.

8. Provide an illustration of the *Thomas theorem* from experiences you have had either at home or in school.

9. What are the basic characteristics of *humor*? Write out a joke and analyze how it manifests the characteristics discussed in the text.

PART VI: ANSWERS TO STUDY QUESTIONS

True-False

1.	F	(p. 140)	9.	T	(p. 145)
2.	F	(p. 140)	10.	F	(p. 147)
3.	F	(p. 140)	11.	T	(p. 151)
4.	T	(pp. 140-141)	12.	F	(pp. 152-153)
5.	F	(pp. 140-141)	13.	F	(pp. 152-153)
6.	T	(pp. 142-143)	14.	T	(pp. 152-153)
7.	T	(pp. 142-143)	15.	T	(pp. 165-156)
8.	F	(p. 143)	16.	T	(p. 158)

Multiple Choice

1.	b	(p. 140)	12.	b	(p. 147)
2.	c	(pp. 140-141)	13.	e	(p. 147)
3.	e	(p. 141)	14.	c	(p. 148)
4.	d	(p. 141)	15.	a	(p. 148)
5.	a	(p. 141)	16.	a	(p. 151)
6.	a	(p. 142)	17.	d	(p. 152)
7.	a	(p. 143)	18.	d	(pp. 152-153)
8.	d	(p. 145)	19.	d	(pp. 153-154)
9.	e	(p. 145)	20.	c	(p. 154)
10.	c	(p. 145)	21.	e	(p. 156)
11.	d	(p. 145)	22.	b	(pp. 158-159)

Matching

1.	e	(p. 139)	6.	j	(p. 142)
2.	h	(p. 140)	7.	c	(p. 145)
3.	a	(p. 140)	8.	b	(p. 145)
4.	f	(p. 141)	9.	i	(p. 147)
5.	d	(p. 143)	10.	g	(p. 151)

Fill-In

1. social interaction (p. 139)
2. status, role (pp. 140-141)
3. role conflict (p. 142)
4. social construction (p. 143)
5. Thomas theorem (p. 145)
6. ethnomethodology (p. 145)
7. dramaturgical (p. 147)
8. presentation of self (p. 147)
9. back (p. 147)
10. demeanor (p. 151)
11. idealizatoin (p. 152)
12. words, voice, body language, facial expressions (p. 150)
13. embarrassment (p. 152)
14. power, vlue, attention (pp. 153-155)
15. conventional, unconventional (pp. 155-156)
16. intends, hears (p. 154)

PART VII: IN FOCUS—IMPORTANT ISSUES

- Social Structure: A Guide To Everyday Living

   Provide an illustration to support the point being made by the author that members of every society rely on social structure to make sense out of everyday situations.

- Status

   Outline your current *status set*.

   Outline your *status set* as you believe it will look ten years from now.

- Role

   Provide an example for each of the following from your own life:

      role strain

      role conflict

      role exit

112

- The Social Construction of Reality

  Provide an illustration (from your own experience) of the of the *Thomas theorem*:

  Using the illustration given in the text, make up an example of how *ethnomethodology* can be used to explore the process of how people make sense of social encounters.

- Dramaturgical Analysis: "The Presentation of Self"

  Define and illustrate each of the following:

  performance

  nonverbal communication

  gender and personal performances (demeanor, use of space, staring, smiling, and touching

  idealization

  embarrassment and tact

- Interaction In Everyday Life: Two Applications

Language defines men and women differently. Illustrate how for each of the following ways this is true:

    power

    value

    attention

Identify and describe the three *foundations of humor*:

Identify and illustrate three major *topics of humor:*

Identify and illustrate three major *functions of humor:*

What is the relationship between *humor and conflict?* Provide two illustrations.

PART VIII: ANALYSIS AND COMMENT

Social Diversity

"Physical Disability as Master Status"

Key Points: Questions:

"Gender and Language: You Just Don't Understand!"

Key Points: Questions:

Applying Sociology

"Hide Those Lyin' Eyes: Can You Do It?"

Key Points: Questions:

"The "Spin" Game: Choosing Our Words Carefully"

Key Points: Questions:

Critical Thinking

"Double Take: Real Headlines That Make People Laugh"

Key Points: Questions:

Global Sociology

"The Sociology of Emotions: Do We All Feel the Same?"

Key Points: Questions:

Seeing Ourselves--National Map 6-1

"Baseball Fans Across the United States"

Key Points: Questions

7   Groups and
     Organizations

PART I: CHAPTER OUTLINE

I.   Social Groups
      A.   Primary and Secondary Groups
      B.   Group Leadership
            1.   Two Leadership Roles
            2.   Three Leadership Styles
      C.   Group Conformity
            1.   Asch's Research
            2.   Milgram's Research
            3.   Janis's Research
      D.   Reference Groups
            1.   Stouffer's Research
      E.   Ingroups and Outgroups
      F.   Group Size
            1.   The Dyad
            2.   The Triad
      G.   Social Diversity
      H.   Networks
II.   Formal Organizations
      A.   Types of Formal Organizations
            1.   Utilitarian Organizations
            2.   Normative Organizations
            3.   Coercive Organizations
      B.   Origins of Bureaucracy
      C.   Characteristics of Bureaucracy
      D.   Organizational Environment
      E.   The Informal Side of Bureaucracy
      F.   Problems of Bureaucracy
            1.   Bureaucratic Alienation
            2.   Bureaucratic Inefficiency and Ritualism
            3.   Bureaucratic Inertia
      G.   Oligarchy

III. The Evolution of Formal Organizations
    A. Scientific Management
    B. The First Challenge: Race and Gender
        1. Patterns of Exclusion
        2. The "Female Advantage:
    C. The Second Challenge: The Japanese Organization
    D. The Third Challenge: The Changing Nature of Work
    E. The McDonaldization of Society
        1. McDonaldization: Four Principles
        2. Can Rationality Be Irrational?
IV. The Future of Organizations: Opposing Trends
V. Summary
VI. Key Concepts
VII. Critical-Thinking Questions
VIII. Applications and Exercises
IX. Sites to See

PART II: LEARNING OBJECTIVES

1. To be able to identify the differences between primary groups, secondary groups, aggregates, and categories.
2. To be able to identify the various types of leaders associated with social groups.
3. To be able to compare and contrast the research of several different social scientists on group conformity.
4. To be able to recognize the importance of reference groups to group dynamics.
5. To be able to distinguish between ingroups and outgroups.
6. To understand the relevance of group size to the dynamics of social groups.
7. To be able to identify the types of formal organizations.
8. To be able to identify and describe the basic characteristics of bureaucracy.
9. To become aware of both the limitations and informal side of bureaucracy.
10. To be able to identify and discuss three important challenges of the scientific management organizational model.
11. To consider the issue of the McDonaldization of society.
12. To become aware of ways in which today's organizations differ from those of a century ago.
13. To analyze the two opposing trends concerning the future of organizations.

PART III: KEY CONCEPTS

aggregates

authoritarian leadership

bureaucracy

bureaucratic inertia

bureaucratic ritualism

category

coercive organization

crowd

democratic leadership

dyad

expressive leadership

formal organizations

groupthink

humanizing organizations

ingroup

instrumental leadership

laissez-faire leadership

McDonaldization

network

normative organization

oligarchy

organizational environment

outgroup

primary group

rationality

rationalization

reference group

scientific management

secondary group

social group

tradition

triad

utilitarian organization

PART IV: IMPORTANT RESEARCHERS

Max Weber   Georg Simmel

Charles Horton Cooley   Amitai Etzioni

Stanley Milgram   Solomon Asch

Irving Janis   Samuel Stouffer

Rosabeth Moss Kanter   Robert Michels

William Ouchi   Deborah Tannen

Sally Helgesen   George Ritzer

Frederick Winslow Taylor

PART V: STUDY QUESTIONS

True-False

1.	T	F	Any collection of individuals can be called a *group*.
2.	T	F	While members of *categories* could potentially become transformed into a social group, by definition members of *crowds* cannot be transformed into social groups.
3.	T	F	*Secondary groups* tend to be smaller than *primary groups*.
4.	T	F	*Expressive leadership* emphasizes the completion of tasks.
5.	T	F	The *Democratic leadership style* is more expressive than the *authoritarian leadership style*.
6.	T	F	*Stanley Milgram's* research on group conformity patterns illustrated that most individuals are skeptical about the legitimacy of authority for people in positions of power.

7.   T   F   *Samuel Stouffer's* research on soldiers' attitudes toward their own promotions during World War II demonstrates the significance of reference groups in making judgements about ourselves.

8.   T   F   According to research by *Georg Simmel*, large groups tend to be more stable than small groups, such as dyads.

9.   T   F   *Networks* tend to be more enduring and provide a greater sense of identity than most other types of social groups.

10.   T   F   *Normative organizations* are defined as those which impose restrictions on people who have been labeled as deviant.

11.   T   F   A voluntary organization is an example of a *utilitarian organization*.

12.   T   F   Max Weber argued that that the organizational structure concerned with efficiency was called *bureaucracy*.

13.   T   F   The *organizational environment* includes economic and political trends.

14.   T   F   *Bureaucratic inertia* refers to a preoccupation with rules and regulations to the point of thwarting an organization's goals.

15.   T   F   According to research by Deborah Tannen, a "female advantage" for organizations is that women have a greater *information focus* than men.

16.   T   F   According to research by William Ouchi, formal organizations in Japan tend to be characterized by greater *holistic involvement* than formal organizations in the United States.

17.   T   F   Worker participation programs, like those traditionally found in *Japan*, have been openly accepted by union leaders and workers here in the United States.

18.   T   F   A basic organizational principle involved in the *McDonaldization of society* is efficiency.

Multiple Choice

1. People who have some status in common, such as teachers, exemplify a

     (a)   social group
     (b)   category
     (c)   crowd
     (d)   status set

2. A social group characterized by long-term personal relationships usually involving many activities is a

     (a)   primary group.
     (b)   secondary group.
     (c)   category.
     (d)   aggregate.
     (e)   normative organization.

3. Temporary, loosely formed collections of anonymous people are referred to as

    (a)   crowds.
    (b)   groups.
    (c)   categories.
    (d)   populations.
    (e)   social organizations.

4. Which of the following is *not* true of *primary groups*?

    (a)   they provide security for their members
    (b)   they are focused around specific activities
    (c)   they are valued in and of themselves
    (d)   they are viewed as ends in themselves

5. Which of the following theorists differentiated between *primary* and *secondary* groups?

    (a)   Max Weber
    (b)   Amitai Etzioni
    (c)   Emile Durkheim
    (d)   Charles Horton Cooley
    (e)   George Herbert Mead

6. Which of the following is *not* a characteristic of a *secondary group*?

    (a)   large size
    (b)   weak emotional ties
    (c)   personal orientation
    (d)   variable, often short duration

7. Members of *secondary groups* display what type of orientation?

    (a)   personal
    (b)   residual
    (c)   natural
    (d)   closed
    (e)   goal

8. What is the term for a *group leadership* that emphasizes the completion of tasks?

    (a)   task group leadership
    (b)   secondary group leadership
    (c)   expressive leadership
    (d)   instrumental leadership
    (e)   laissez-faire leadership

9. Which of the following is *not* identified in the text as a *leadership style*?

    (a) laissez-faire
    (b) democratic
    (c) authoritarian
    (d) utilitarian

10. Crisis situations in social groups are most likely to be quickly resolved when the *leader* is

    (a) instrumental
    (b) laissez-faire
    (c) authoritarian
    (d) democratic

11. What *style of leader* tends to downplay their position and power, allowing the group to function more of less on its own?

    (a) authoritarian.
    (b) democratic.
    (c) laissez-faire.
    (d) bureaucratic.
    (e) instrumental.

12. Solomn Asch's classic investigation of group dynamics revealed the dramatic effects of

    (a) leadership styles.
    (b) leadership types.
    (c) groupthink.
    (d) group conformity.
    (e) reference groups.

13. Which researcher concluded that people are not likely to question authority figures even though common sense dictates that they should?

    (a) Solomon Asch
    (b) Irving Janis
    (c) Stanley Milgram
    (d) Charles Horton Cooley

14. The Kennedy administration's decision to invade Cuba is used as an example of

    (a) ingroups and outgroups.
    (b) reference groups.
    (c) bureaucracy.
    (d) oligarchy.
    (e) groupthink.

15. What is the sociological term for a limited understanding of some issue due to group conformity?

    (a) conformist cognizance
    (b) groupthink
    (c) doublethink
    (d) red tape

16. The term for a social group that serves as a point of reference in making evaluations or decisions is

    (a) a control group.
    (b) a reference group.
    (c) an externalized group.
    (d) an internalized group.

17. A social group commanding a member's esteem and loyalty is a(n)

    (a) ingroup.
    (b) outgroup.
    (c) reference group.
    (d) subculture.
    (e) residual group.

18. Which of the following is *not* one of the four ways in which *socia diversity* influences intergroup contact?

    (a) Large groups turn outward.
    (b) Heterogeneous groups turn outward.
    (c) Social equality promotes contact.
    (d) Physical boundaries create social boundaries.

19. Large secondary groups that are organized to achieve their goals efficiently are referred to as

    (a) social organizations.
    (b) bureaucracies.
    (c) formal organizations.
    (d) businesses.
    (e) aggregates.

20. *Amitai Etzioni* constructed a typology of *formal organizations*. Organizations such as the PTA, the Red Cross, and United Way illustrate the type of organization he called

    (a) utilitarian.
    (b) coercive.
    (c) normative.
    (d) institutional.

21. What types of *formal organizations* bestow material benefits on their members?

    (a) normative organizations
    (b) coercive organizations
    (c) social organizations
    (d) utilitarian organizations

22. Which of the following is *not* a type of formal organization as identified by *Amitai Etzioni*?

    (a) coercive
    (b) normative
    (c) hierarchial
    (d) utilitarian

23. What term refers to an *organizational model* rationally designed to perform complex tasks efficiently?

    (a) bureaucracy
    (b) complex organization
    (c) humanized organization
    (d) social organization
    (e) formal organization

24. Which of the following is not part of the *organizational environment*?

    (a) economic trends
    (b) political trends
    (c) population patterns
    (d) other organizations
    (e) company employees

25. *Bureaucratic ritualism* is

    (a) the process of promoting people to their level of incompetence.
    (b) the tendency of bureaucratic organizations to persist over time.
    (c) the rule of the many by the few.
    (d) a preoccupation with rules and regulations to the point of thwarting an organizations goals.

26. *Robert Michels* identified one of the limitations of bureaucracy to be one which involves the tendency of bureaucracy to become dominated by *oligarchy* because

    (a) technical competence cannot be maintained.
    (b) bureaucrats abuse organizational power.
    (c) bureaucrats get caught up in rule-making.
    (d) specialization gives way to generalist orientations.

27. According to *Rosabeth Moss Kanter's* research

(a) proper application of technology in bureaucracy is critical for success.
(b) oligarchy is effective in bureaucratic structures during times of rapid change.
(c) race and gender issues must be addressed as they relate to organizational hierarchies.
(d) humanizing bureaucracies would diminish productivity.
(e) none of the above

28. Research by Deborah Tannen on gender and management styles has found that *men* tend to have a(n)

(a) image focus.
(b) information focus.
(c) flexibility focus.
(d) developmental focus.

29. Which of the following is *not* identified by *Sally Helgesen* as a gender-linked issue in organizations?

(a) attentiveness to interconnections
(b) flexibility
(c) worker productivity
(d) communication skills

30. According to *William Ouchi* which of the following highlights the distinctions between formal organizations in Japan and the United States?

(a) hiring and advancement, lifetime security, holistic involvement, nonspecialized training, and collective decision making
(b) predictability, calculability, control through automation, and efficiency
(c) oligarchy, ritualism, privacy, and alienation
(d) competence, tasks, inertia, and networks

31. Which of the following is *not* a way in which today's organizations are different from those of a century ago?

(a) They are represented by competitive work teams.
(b) They allow for more creative autonomy.
(c) They are represented by more levels in the chain of command.
(d) They have greater flexibility.

32.   According to *George Ritzer*, which of the following is/are characteristic of the *McDonaldization* of society?

    (a)   efficiency
    (b)   calculability
    (c)   predictability
    (d)   control through automation
    (e)   all of the above

Matching

1. ___ Two or more people who identify and interact with one another.
2. ___ People who share a status in common.
3. ___ A small social group in which relationships are personal and enduring.
4. ___ Large and impersonal groups based on a specific interest or activity.
5. ___ Group leaders who emphasize the completion of tasks.
6. ___ The tendency of group members to conform by adopting a narrow view of some issue.
7. ___ A social group that serves as a point of reference in making evaluations or decisions.
8. ___ A social group with two members.
9. ___ Large, secondary groups that are organized to achieve their goals efficiently.
10. ___ An organizational model rationally designed to perform complex tasks efficiently.

    a.   secondary   f.   reference group
    b.   formal organization   g.   dyad
    c.   groupthink   h.   bureaucracy
    d.   instrumental leadership   i.   primary group
    e.   social group   j.   category

Fill-In

1. A _____ _____ is defined as two or more people who identify and interact with one another.
2. Political organizations and college classes are examples of _____ *groups*.
3. While *primary* relationships have a _____ orientation, *secondary* relationships have a _____ orientation.
4. _____ *leadership* refers to group leadership that emphasizes the completion of tasks.
5. _____ *leaders* focus on instrumental concerns, make decisions on their own, and demand strict compliance from subordinates.
6. According to the research by Stanley Milgram on *conformity*, people are likely to follow directions from not only *legitimate* _____ *figures* but also from groups of ordinary individuals, even when it means inflicting harm on another person.
7. *Irving Janis* studies the process he called _____ that reduces a group's capacity for critical reflection.

8. Samuel A. Stouffer's research during World War II in which he found that soldiers in army units with low *promotion rates* were actually more optimistic about their chances of being promoted than soldiers in units with high promotion rates illustrates the importance of _____ _____ for establishing a person's own sense of well-being.

9. A social group which consists of *two* members is known as a _____.

10. Peter Blau points out four ways in which the *composition of social groups* affects intergroup association, including: Group _____, _____, social _____, and physical _____.

11. A _____ is a web of social ties that links people who identify and interact little with one another.

12. Amitai Etzioni has identified three *type of formal organizations*, distinguished by why people participate in them. Ones that pay their members are called _____ organizations. People become members of _____ organizations to pursue goals they consider morally worthwhile. Finally, _____ organizations are distinguished by involuntary membership.

13. A _____ is an organizational model rationally designed to perform complex tasks efficiently.

14. The _____ _____ refers to a range of factors outside the organization that affects its operation.

15. Preoccupation with rules and regulations to the point of thwarting an organization's goals is called *bureaucratic* _____.

16. *Bureaucratic* _____ is the term used to describe the tendency of bureaucratic organizations to perpetuate themselves.

17. The *problems of bureaucracy,* especially the alienation it produces and its tendency toward oligrachy, stem from two organizational traits: _____ and _____.

18. *White men* represent 42 percent of the working-age population in the United States and hold _____ percent of management jobs. *White women* represent about the same share of the population and hold _____ percent of managerial jobs.

19. *Deborah Tannen's* research on management styles suggests that women have a greater _____ *focus* and men have greater _____ focus.

20. In terms of formal organizational philosophies, Japanese _____ is the cultural equivilent to our society's emphasis on *individual achievement*.

21. Several ways in which today's *organizations* differ from those of a century ago are identified in the text, including: greater creative _____ for skilled workers, more use of _____ work teams, a _____ organizational structure, and greater _____.

22. The four characteristics of the *McDonaldization of society* include _____, _____, _____ and _____, and _____ *through automation.*

Definition and Short-Answer

1. Differentiate between the qualities of *bureaucracies* and *small groups*. In what ways are they similar?
2. What are the three factors in decision-making processes in groups that lead to *groupthink*?
3. What are three major *limitations* of bureaucracy? Define and provide an illustration for each.

4. In what ways do bureaucratic organizations in *Japan* differ from those in the *U.S*? What are the consequences of these differences? Relate this comparison to the issue of *humanizing* organizations.
5. Differentiate between the concepts of *aggregate* and *category*.
6. Identify the basic *types of leadership* in groups and provide examples of the relative advantages and disadvantage for each type.
7. What are the general characteristics of the *McDonaldization* of society? Provide an illustration of this phenomenon in our society based on your own experience.
8. What are Peter Blau's points concerning how the structure of social groups regulates intergroup association?
9. What are the three *types of organizations* identified by Amitai Etzioni? Describe and provide an illustration for each.
10. What is meant by questioning "is rationality can be *irrational*?"
11. What are the three steps involved in *scientific management*? How might this approach work against employees?
12. From your own experience, illustrate two of the *characteristics of bureaucracy*.

PART VI: ANSWERS TO STUDY QUESTIONS

True-False

1.	F	(p. 163)	10.	F	(p. 173)
2.	F	(p. 164)	11.	F	(p. 173)
3.	F	(pp. 164-165)	12.	T	(p. 174)
4.	F	(p. 165)	13.	T	(pp. 175-276)
5.	T	(p. 166)	14.	F	(p. 177)
6.	F	(p. 167)	15.	T	(p. 180)
7.	T	(p. 168)	16.	T	(pp. 181-182)
8.	T	(p. 169)	17.	F	(p. 181)
9.	F	(p. 170)	18.	T	(p. 185)

Multiple Choice

1.	b	(p. 163)	17.	a	(p. 169)
2.	a	(p. 164)	18.	a	(p . 170)
3.	a	(p. 164)	19.	c	(p. 173)
4.	b	(p. 164)	20.	c	(p. 173)
5.	d	(p. 164)	21.	d	(p. 173)
6.	c	(p. 165)	22.	c	(p. 173)
7.	e	(p. 165)	23.	a	(p. 173)
8.	d	(p. 165)	24.	e	(pp. 175-176)
9.	d	(p. 165)	25.	d	(p. 177)
10.	c	(p. 166)	26.	b	(p. 178)
11.	c	(p. 166)	27.	c	(p. 179)
12.	d	(p. 166)	28.	a	(p. 180)
13.	c	(p. 167)	29.	c	(p. 180)
14.	e	(p. 168)	30.	a	(pp. 180-181)
15.	b	(p. 168)	31.	c	(p. 183)
16.	b	(p. 168)	32.	e	(p. 185)

Matching

1.	e	(p. 163)	6.	c	(p. 168)
2.	j	(p. 163)	7.	f	(p. 168)
3.	i	(p. 164)	8.	g	(p. 169)
4.	a	(p. 164)	9.	b	(p. 173)
5.	d	(p. 165)	10.	h	(p. 174)

Fill-In

1. social group (p. 163)
2. secondary (p. 164)
3. personal, instrumental (p. 165)
4. instrumental (p. 165)
5. authoritarian (p. 166)
6. authority (p. 167)
7. groupthink (p. 168)
8. reference groups (p. 168)
9. dyad (p. 169)
10. size, heterogeneity, equality, boundaries (p. 170)
11. network (p. 170)
12. utilitarian, normative, coercive (p. 173)
13. bureaucracy (p. 174)
14. organizational environment (p. 175)
15. ritualism (p. 177)

16. inertia (p. 177)
17. hierarchy, rigidity (p. 179)
18. 62, 27 (p. 179)
19. information, image (p. 180)
20. groupism (p. 181)
21. autonomy, competitive, flatter, flexibility (p. 183)
22. efficiency, calculability, uniformity, predictability, control (p. 185)

PART VII: IN FOCUS--IMPORTANT ISSUES

- Social Groups

    Define and illustrate each of the following:

    category

    crowd

    primary group

    secondary group

    Define and provide an example for each of the following *types of leadership:*

    instrumental leadership

    expressive leadership

    Describe each of the following *leadership styles:*

    authoritarian leadership

    democratic leadership

    laissez-faire leadership

Describe the research procedures and findings/conclusions for each of the following researcher's work on *group conformity*.

Asch's research

Milgram's research

Janis's research

Identify three *ingroups* of yours:

Identify three *outgroups* of yours:

What are the patterns you see in the above two lists?

According to Georg Simmel, how does *group size* affect group dynamics and group stability?

Identify and describe the four ways in which *social diversity* influences intergroup contact as outlined by Peter Blau.

What is a *network*? How do they differ for men and women?

- Formal Organizations

What is a *formal organization*?

Define and illustrate each of the following *types* of formal organizations

utilitarian

normative

coercive

What is meant by the term *bureaucracy?*

Max Weber identified six *key elements* of the ideal bureaucratic organization. Define and illustrate each of these:

specialization

hierarchy of offices

rules and regulations

technical competence

impersonality

formal, written communications

Identify three examples of the *informal side of bureaucracy*:

Identify and describe three major *problems of bureaucracy*:

136

- The Evolution of Formal Organizations

What are the three steps involved in *scientific management*?

Describe the nature of the *three challenges* facing formal organizations in our society today:

    race and gender

    Japanese organization

    the changing nature of work

What are the major characteristics of the *McDonaldization of society?*

- The Future of Organizations: Opposing Trends

What are the two *opposing tendencies* identified by the author?

PART VIII: ANALYSIS AND COMMENT

Global Sociology

"The Japanese Model: Will It Work in the United States?"

Key Points: Questions:

"The Internet: A Global Network"

Key Points: Questions:

138

Controversy and Debate

"Are Large Corporations a Threat to Personal Privacy?"

Key Points: Questions:

Seeing Ourselves--National Map 7-1

"The Quality of Relationships: Lawsuits across the United States"

Key Points: Questions:

Window on the World--Global Map 7-1

"Cyberspace: A Global Network"

Key Points: Questions:

8 Deviance

PART I: CHAPTER OUTLINE

I. What is Deviance?
   A. Social Control
   B. The Biological Context
   C. Personality Factors
   D. The Social Foundations of Deviance
II. Structural-Functional Analysis
   A. Emile Durkheim: The Functions of Deviance
      1. An Illustration: The Puritans of Massachusetts Bay
   B. Merton's Strain Theory
   C. Deviant Subcultures
III. Symbolic-Interaction Analysis
   A. Labeling Theory
      1. Primary and Secondary Deviance
      2. Stigma
      3. Retrospective and Projective Labeling
      4. Labeling and Mental Illness
   B. The Medicalization of Deviance
      1. The Difference Labels Make
   C. Sutherland's Differential Association Theory
   D. Hirschi's Control Theory
IV. Social Conflict Analysis
   A. Deviance and Power
   B. Deviance and Capitalism
   C. White-Collar Crime
   D. Corporate Crime
   E. Organized Crime
V. Deviance and Social Diversity
   A. Deviance and Gender
VI. Hate Crimes
VII. Crime
   A. Types of Crime
   B. Criminal Statistics

C.   The "Street" Criminal: A Profile
         1.   Age
         2.   Gender
         3.   Social Class
         4.   Race and Ethnicity
    E.   Crime in Global Perspective
VII.   The Criminal Justice System
    A.   Police
    B.   Courts
    C.   Punishment
         1.   Retribution
         2.   Deterrence
         3.   Rehabilitation
         4.   Societal Protection
VIII.   Summary
 IX.   Key Concepts
  X.   Critical-Thinking Questions
 XI.   Applications and Exercises
XII.   Sites to See

PART II: LEARNING OBJECTIVES

1.   To be able to explain how deviance is interpreted as a product of society.
2.   To be able to identify and evaluate the biological explanation of deviance.
3.   To be able to identify and evaluate the psychological explanation of deviance.
4.   To be able to identify and evaluate the sociological explanations of deviance.
5.   To be able to compare and contrast different theories representative of the three major sociological paradigms.
6.   To be able to evaluate empirical evidence used to support these different sociological theories of deviance.
7.   To be able to distinguish among the types of crime.
8.   To become more aware of the demographic patterns of crime in our society.
9.   To evaluate deviance in global context.
10.   To be able to identify and describe the elements of our criminal justice system.

PART III: KEY CONCEPTS

civil law

containment theory

conflict subculture

conformity

control theory

corporate crime

crime

crimes against property

crimes against the person

criminal justice system

criminal law

criminal recidivism

criminal subculture

deterrence

deviance

differential association

ectomorph

endomorph

hate crime

index crime

juvenile delinquency

labeling theory

medicalization of deviance

mesomorph

organized crime

plea bargaining

primary deviance

rebellion

rehabilitation

retreatism

retreatist subculture

retribution

retrospective labeling

secondary deviance

social control

social protection

stigma

white-collar crime

victimless crime

victimization survey

PART IV: IMPORTANT RESEARCHERS

Caesare Lombroso   William Sheldon

Steven Spitzer   Richard Cloward and Lloyd Ohlin

Charles Goring   Albert Cohen and Walter Miller

Walter Reckless and Simon Dintz   Edwin Sutherland

Thomas Szasz   Emile Durkheim

Robert Merton   Travis Hirschi

Howard Becker   Erving Goffman

PART V: STUDY QUESTIONS

<u>True-False</u>

1.   T   F   Using the sociological perspective, *social control* is broadly understood, including the criminal justice system as well as the general socialization process.
2.   T   F   What deviant actions or attitudes have in common is some element of *difference*.
3.   T   F   Scientific research clearly concludes that there is absolutely no relationship between *biology* and crime.

4.	T	F	*Containment theory* focuses our attention on how certain behaviors are linked to, or contained by, our genes.
5.	T	F	One of the *social foundations of deviance* is that deviance exists only in relation to cultural norms.
6.	T	F	According to Emile Durkheim, deviance affirms cultural values and norms.
7.	T	F	In Robert Merton's *strain theory,* the concept of deviance is applied by linking deviance to certain social imbalances between *goals* and *means.*
8.	T	F	Walter Miller's *subcultural theory* of deviance points out that deviant subcultures have *no focal concerns,* and therefore have no social norms to guide the behavior of their members.
9.	T	F	*Primary deviance* tends to be more harmful to society than *secondary deviance.*
10.	T	F	Thomas Szasz argues that *mental illness* is a *myth* and is a label used by the powerful in society to force people to follow dominant cultural norms.
11.	T	F	Our author suggests that during the last fifty years there has been a trend away from what is known as the *medicalization of deviance.*
12.	T	F	Edwin Sutherland's *differential association theory* suggests that certain individuals are incapable of learning from experience and therefore are more likely to become deviant.
13.	T	F	Travis Hirschi's *control theory* is states that social control depends on imagining the consequences of one's behavior.
14.	T	F	The *social-conflict* perspective links deviance to social inequality and power in society.
15.	T	F	*White-collar crime* is defined as crime committed by people of high social position in the course of their occupations.
16.	T	F	While *civil law* regulates business dealings between private parties, *criminal law* defines the individual's moral responsibilities to society.
17.	T	F	Almost every society in the world applies more stringent normative controls on *men* than to *women.*
18.	T	F	What qualifies an offense as a *hate crime* is not so much a matter of the race or ancestry of the victim as the *motivation* of the offender.
19.	T	F	Most *index crimes* in the United States are committed by white people.
20.	T	F	Using *index crimes,* the crime rate in the United States is relatively high compared to European societies.
21.	T	F	*Plea bargaining* accounts for about forty percent of criminal cases resolved by the courts.
22.	T	F	*Criminal recidivism,* while relatively high historically in the United States, has in recent years shown a significant decline.

Multiple Choice

1. _____ refers to the recognized violation of cultural norms.

   (a)   Crime
   (b)   Deviance
   (c)   Residual behavior
   (d)   Social control

2. *Containment theory* is an example of a(n) _____ explanation of deviance.

    (a) biological
    (b) economic
    (c) anthropological
    (d) sociological
    (e) psychological

3. Which of the following is *not a social foundation* of deviance?

    (a) Deviance exists in relation to cultural norms.
    (b) People become deviant in that others define them that way.
    (c) Both norms and the way people define social situations involve social power.
    (d) All are identified as foundations of deviance.

4. *Emile Durkheim* theorized that all but which of the following are *functions of deviance*?

    (a) It clarifies moral boundaries.
    (b) It affirms cultural values and norms.
    (c) It encourages social stability.
    (d) It promotes social unity.

5. Kai Erikson's investigation of the early Puritans of Massachusetts Bay is a good illusttration of whose *theory of deviance*?

    (a) Durkheim's functional theory
    (b) Merton's strain theory
    (c) Sutherland's differential association theory
    (d) Hirchi's control theory

6. *Robert Merton's strain theory* is a component of which broad theoretical paradigm?

    (a) social-conflict
    (b) symbolic-interactionism
    (c) social-exchange
    (d) human ecology
    (e) structural-functional

7. According to Robert Merton's *strain theory*, one response to the inability to succeed is _____, or the rejection of both cultural goals and means--so one, in effect, "drops out."

    (a) innovation
    (b) retreatism
    (c) interia
    (d) ritualism

8.   Which of the following is *not* an example of a *deviant subculture* identified in *Richard Cloward* and *Lloyd Olhin's* research on delinquents.

    (a)   criminal
    (b)   retreatist
    (c)   conflict
    (d)   residual

9.   Which of the following theories is *not derived* from the *structural-functional paradigm*?

    (a)   labeling theory
    (b)   strain theory
    (c)   deviant subculture theory
    (d)   control theory

10.   Which of the following is an appropriate criticism of *structural-functional theories* of deviance?

    (a)   The theories assume a diversity of cultural standards.
    (b)   The theories seem to imply that everyone who breaks the rules is labeled at deviant.
    (c)   The theories focus on the lower-class.
    (d)   The theories cannot explain very well certain types of crime.

11.   Which theory asserts that deviance and conformity result from the responses of others?

    (a)   differential association
    (b)   social conflict
    (c)   labeling
    (d)   structural-functionalism

12.   Skipping school for the first time as an eighth grader is an example of

    (a)   recidivism
    (b)   primary deviance
    (c)   a degradation ceremony
    (d)   secondary deviance

13.   What is Erving Goffman's term for a powerful negative social label that radically changes a person's self-concept and social identity?

    (a)   anomie
    (b)   secondary deviance
    (c)   medicalization of deviance
    (d)   retribution
    (e)   stigma

14. Sometimes an entire community formally stigmatizes an individual through what *Harold Garfinkel* called a

   (a)   hate crime.
   (b)   retrospective label
   (c)   recidivism process.
   (d)   degradation ceremony.
   (e)   conflict subculture.

15. What is the *medicalization of deviance*?

   (a)   the recognition of the true source of deviance
   (b)   the objective, clinical approach to deviant behavior
   (c)   the transformation of moral and legal issues into medical models
   (d)   the discovery of the links between biochemical properties and deviance

16. Once people stigmatize an individual, they may engage in _____, or interpreting someone's past in light of some present deviance.

   (a)   retrospective labeling
   (b)   projective labeling
   (c)   residual labeling
   (d)   ad hoc labeling
   (e)   labeling inertia

17. *Attachment, involvement, commitment,* and *belief* are all types of social control in

   (a)   Sutherland's differential association theory.
   (b)   Durkheim's functional theory.
   (c)   Goffman's labeling theory.
   (d)   Cohen's subcultural theory.
   (e)   Hirschi's control theory.

18. According to the *social-conflict paradigm*, who and what is labeled deviant is based primarily on

   (a)   the severity of the deviant act.
   (b)   psychological profile.
   (c)   the functions being served.
   (d)   relative power.
   (e)   the location of the deviant act.

19. What is the term for crime committed by persons of high social position in the course of their occupations.

    (a) occupational crimes
    (b) status offenses
    (c) white-collar crime
    (d) residual crime

20. _____ defines the individual's moral responsibility to society.

    (a) Civil law
    (b) Criminal law
    (c) Medicalization
    (d) Stigma
    (e) Attachment

21. _____ *crime* is a business supplying illegal goods or services.

    (a) Victimless
    (b) Residual
    (c) Corporate
    (d) Organized

22. The statements: "While what is deviant may vary, deviance itself is found in all societies;"" Deviance and the social response it provokes serve to maintain the moral foundation of society;"" Deviance can direct social change." All help to summarize which sociological explanation of deviance?

    (a) structural-functional
    (b) social-conflict
    (c) symbolic-interaction
    (d) labeling
    (e) social exchange

23. Which of the following are criticism of *social-conflict theory*?

    (a) It is an oversimplification to imply that all the laws and other cultural norms are created directly by the rich and powerful.
    (b) It implies that criminality springs up only to the extent that a society treats its members unequally.
    (c) Both (a) and (b) are criticisms of social-conflict theory.
    (d) Neither (a) nor (b) are criticisms of social-conflict theory.

24. Which contribution below is attributed to the *structural-functional theory* of deviance?

    (a)   Nothing is inherently deviant.
    (b)   Deviance is found in all societies.
    (c)   The reactions of others to deviance are highly variable.
    (d)   Laws and other norms reflect the interests of the powerful in society.

25. Which of the following are included as part of the FBI *index crimes*?

    (a)   white-collar crime and property crime
    (b)   victimless crime and federal crime
    (c)   crime against the state and civil crime
    (d)   crimes against the person and crimes against property
    (e)   violent crime and white-collar crime

26. Which of the following is *not* a type of *victimless crime*?

    (a)   gambling
    (b)   prostitution
    (c)   arson
    (d)   illegal drug use

27. In the case of *violent crimes*, eighty-four percent of the people arrested are men. For *property crimes*, of all those arrested, _____ percent are men.

    (a)   fifty
    (b)   forty-six
    (c)   seventy-one
    (d)   ninety-three

28. The U.S. *property crime rate* is twice as high as that found in Europe. The U.S. *violent crime rate* is _____ times higher that Europe's.

    (a)   1.5
    (b)   3.5
    (c)   8.0
    (d)   5.0
    (e)   2.0

29. The *criminal justice system* includes

    (a)   the police.
    (b)   the courts.
    (c)   Punishment.
    (d)   all of the above.

30. Which of the following is *not listed* as a *justification for punishment* in our criminal justice system?

    (a)   retribution
    (b)   societal protection
    (c)   deterrence
    (d)   rehabilitation
    (e)   All of the above are justifications.

Matching

1. ___ The recognized violation of cultural norms.
2. ___ Attempts by members of society to influence each other's behavior.
3. ___ According to Robert Merton's *strain theory*, these are different ways of responding to the inability to succeed through conformity.
4. ___ Types of *deviant subcultures* identified by Richard Cloward and Lloyd Ohlin's theory of relative opportunity structure.
5. ___ The assertion that deviance and conformity result, not so much from what people do, as from how others respond to those actions.
6. ___ A powerfully negative label that radically changes a person's self-concept and social identity.
7. ___ Types of *social controls* according to Travis Hirschi.
8. ___ Crime in the *suites*.
9. ___ Violations of law in which there are no apparent victims.
10. ___ A legal negotiation in which the prosecution reduces a charge in exchange for a defendant's guilty plea.

a.	criminal, conflict, retreatist	f.	attachment, involvement, belief, commitment
b.	victimless crime	g.	stigma
c.	plea bargaining	h.	social control
d.	labeling theory	i.	retreatism, rebellion, ritualism, innovation
e.	deviance	j.	white-collar crime

Fill-In

1. _____ is the violation of norms a society formally enacts into criminal law.
2. The _____ _____ _____ is the formal response to alleged violations of law on the part of police, courts, and prison officials.
3. *William Sheldon* argued that _____ might predict criminality.
4. A *psychological explanation* of deviance that posits the view that if boys have developed strong moral values and a positive self-image they will not become delinquents is called _____ theory.
5. The *social foundations of deviance* include: Deviance varies according to _____ _____, people become deviant as others _____ them that way, both rule-making and rule-breaking involve social _____.

6. According to Emile Durkheim, deviance fulfills four *essential functions*, including: _____ cultural values and norms, _____ moral boundaries, _____ social unity, and _____ social change.

7. The *strain theory* of deviance is based on the _____ *paradigm*.

8. *Richard Cloward* and *Lloyd Ohlin* explain deviance and conformity in terms of the _____ _____ structure young people face in their lives.

9. Activity that is initially defined as deviant is called _____ *deviance*. On the other hand, a person who accepts the label of deviant may then engage in _____ *deviance*, or behavior caused by the person's incorporating the deviant label into their self-concept.

10. Psychiatrist Thomas Szasz argues that *mental illness* is a _____.

11. Whether we define deviance as a *moral* or *medical* issue has three consequences. First, it affects who _____ to the deviance. Second, it affects _____ people will respond to deviance. And third, the two labels differ on the personal _____ of the deviant person.

12. Travis Hirschi links *conformity* to four types of social control, including _____, _____, _____, and _____.

13. *Social-conflict theory* demonstrates that deviance reflects *social* _____. This approach suggests that *who* or *what* is labeled as deviant is based largely on the relative _____ of categories of people.

14. _____ *crime* is defined as crimes committed by persons of high social position in the course of their occupations.

15. _____ *law* refers to general regulations involving economic affairs between private parties.

16. _____ *surveys* show that the actual level of crime is three times as great as that indicated by official reports.

17. Elliot Currie suggests that crime stems from our culture's emphasis on *individual* _____ _____.

18. The *criminal justice system* in the U.S. consists of three elements: _____, _____, and _____.

19. The four basic *justifications for punishment* include: _____, _____, _____, and _____ _____.

20. Subsequent offenses by people previously convicted of crimes is termed *criminal* _____.

21. Approximately _____ people in the U.S. are incarcerated.

22. *Violent crime rates* have declined in recent years for several reasons, including changes in _____, more _____, a better _____, and the _____ drug trade.

Definition and Short-Answer

1. According to *Travis Hirschi's control theory* there are four types of social controls. What are these? Provide an example of each.

2. According to *Robert Merton's strain theory*, what are the four deviant responses by individuals to dominant cultural patterns when there is a gap between *means* and *goals*? Provide an illustration of each.

3. According to *Emile Durkheim*, what are the *functions of deviance*?
4. *Social-conflict* theorist *Steven Spitzer* argues that deviant labels are applied to people who impede the operation of *capitalism*. What are the four reasons he gives for this phenomenon?
5. How do researchers using *differential association theory* explain deviance?
6. What is meant by the term *medicalization of deviance*? Provide two illustrations.
7. According to *Elliott Currie*, what factors are responsible for the relatively high crime rates in the United States?
8. What are the four *justifications* for the use of punishment against criminals? What evidence exists for their relative effectiveness?
9. *Richard Cloward* and *Lloyd Ohlin* investigated delinquent youth and explain deviance and conformity in terms of the *relative opportunity structure* young people face in their lives. Identify and define the three types of *subcultures* these researchers have identified as representing the criminal lifestyles of delinquent youth.
10. Describe *Thomas Szasz's* view of mental illness and deviance. What are your opinions of his arguments?
11. Briefly review the demographic *profile* of the *street criminal*.
12. Critique the official statistics of crime in the United States. What are the weaknesses of the measures used in the identification of *crime rates*?
13. What are the three consequences for the deviant person depending on whether a *moral model* or *medical model* is applied?
14. Differentiate between *organized crime* and *corporate crime*. Provide an example of each.

PART VI: ANSWERS TO STUDY QUESTIONS

True-False

1.	T	(p. 192)	12.	F	(p. 201)
2.	T	(p. 192)	13.	T	(p. 201)
3.	F	(p. 193)	14.	T	(p. 203)
4.	F	(p. 193)	15.	T	(p. 203)
5.	T	(p. 193)	16.	T	(p. 204)
6.	T	(p. 194)	17.	F	(p. 205)
7.	T	(p. 196)	18.	T	(p. 206)
8.	F	(p. 197)	19.	T	(p. 211)
9.	F	(pp. 198-199)	20.	T	(p. 211)
10.	T	(p. 200)	21.	F	(p. 214)
11.	F	(p. 200)	22.	F	(p. 216)

Multiple Choice

1.	b	(p. 191)	16.	a	(p. 200)
2.	e	(p. 193)	17.	e	(pp. 201-202)
3.	d	(pp. 193-194)	18.	d	(p. 202)
4.	c	(pp. 194-195)	19.	c	(p. 203)
5.	a	(p. 195)	20.	b	(p. 204)
6.	e	(pp. 195-196)	21.	d	(p. 204)
7.	b	(p. 196)	22.	a	(p. 205)
8.	d	(p. 197)	23.	c	(p. 205)
9.	a	(p. 198)	24.	b	(p. 205)
10.	a	(p. 198)	25.	d	(p. 206)
11.	c	(p. 198)	26.	c	(p. 206)
12.	b	(p. 199)	27.	c	(p. 208)
13.	e	(p. 200)	28.	d	(p. 211)
14.	d	(p. 200)	29.	d	(pp. 213-214)
15.	c	(p. 200)	30.	e	(pp. 214-215)

Matching

1.	e	(p. 191)	6.	g	(p. 199)
2.	h	(p. 192)	7.	f	(pp. 201-202)
3.	i	(p. 196)	8.	j	(p. 203)
4.	a	(p. 197)	9.	b	(p. 206)
5.	d	(p. 198)	10.	c	(p. 214)

Fill-In

1. Crime (p. 191)
2. criminal justice system (p. 192)
3. body structure (p. 192)
4. containment (p. 193)
5. cultural norms, define, power (pp. 193-194)
6. affirming, clarifying, promoting, encouraging (pp. 194-195)
7. structural-functional (p. 195)
8. relative opportunity (p. 196)
9. primary, secondary (pp. 198-199)
10. myth (p. 200)
11. responds, how, competence (p. 200)
12. attachment, commitment, involvement, belief (pp. 201-202)
13. inequality, power (p. 203)
14. white-collar (p. 203)
15. civil (p. 204)
16. victimization (p. 208)
17. economic success (p. 211)

18.   police, courts, punishment (pp. 213-214)
19.   retribution, deterrence, rehabilitation, societal protection (pp. 214-215)
20.   recidivism (p. 216)
21.   2 million (p. 217)
22.   policing, prisons, economy, declining (p. 217)

PART VII: IN FOCUS--IMPORTANT ISSUES

* What is Deviance?

What role does *biology* play in helping us explain deviance?

Using *containment theory*, how did Walter Reckless and Simon Dinitz explain delinquency among young boys?

Illustrate each of the following *social foundations of deviance*:

Deviance varies according to cultural norms.

People become deviant as others define them that way.

Both rule-making and rule-breaking involve social power.

155

- Structural-Functional Analysis

According to Emile Durkheim, what are the four *functions of deviance*?

In Robert Merton's *strain theory,* four adaptations to conformity are identified. List, define, and illustrate each of these.

Define and illustrate each of the following types of *deviant subcultures* as identified by Richard Cloward and Lloyd Ohlin.

What are two *criticisms* of the structural-functional analysis of deviance*?*

- Symbolic-Interaction Analysis

How is deviance explained using *labeling theory*?

What is meant by the *medicalization of deviance*? Provide an illustration of this phenomenon.

How is deviance explained using Edwin Sutherland's *differential association theory*?

Using Travis Hirschi's *control theory*, four types of social control are identified. Illustrate each of these:

attachment

commitment

involvement

belief

- Social-Conflict Analysis

  Social-conflict theory explains the relationship between *deviance and power* in three ways. Identify each of these ways.

  Steven Spitzer suggests that deviant labels are applied to people who interfere with the operation of *capitalism*. Identify the four ways he says this is the case:

- Deviance and Social Diversity

  Differentiate between the following *types of crime*:

  crimes against the person

  crimes against property

  Using the following categories, describe the demographic patterns of *street crime* in our society:

  age

  gender

  social class

  race and ethnicity

158

What are five explanations given by the text as to why African American males are overrepresented among those who are arrested in our society?

Describe how *crime rates* in the U.S. have changed over the last forty years. Make reference to specific types of violent and property crimes.

How does the crime rate in the U.S. compare to other *industrialized societies*? Why do you think these differences exist?

- The Criminal Justice System

    Identify two important points being made by the author about each of the follwing *components of the criminal justice system*:

    police

    courts

    punishment

PART VIII: ANALYSIS AND COMMENT

Global Sociology

"Cockfighting: Cultural Ritual or Abuse of Animals?"

Key Points: Questions:

Critical Thinking

"Hate-Crime Laws: Do They Punish Actions or Attitudes?"

Key Points: Questions:

Applying Sociology

"Violent Crime Is Down--But Why?"

Key Points: Questions:

160

Window on the World--Global Map 8-1

"Prostitution in Global Perspective"

Key Points: Questions:

Seeing Ourselves--National Map 8-1

"Where Psychiatrists Practice across the United States"

Key Points: Questions:

Seeing Ourselves--National Map 8-2

"Capital Punishment across the United States"

Key Points: Questions:

9 Sexuality

V. Theoretical Analysis of Sexuality
    A. Structural-Functional Analysis
        1. The Need to Regulate Sexuality
        2. Latent Functions: The Case of Prostitution
    B. Symbolic-Interaction Analysis
        1. The Social Construction of Sexuality
        2. Global Comparisons
    C. Social-Conflict Analysis
        1. Sexuality: Reflecting Social Inequality
        2. Sexuality: Creating Social Inequality
           a. Queer Theory
VI. Summary
VII. Key Concepts
VIII. Critical-Thinking Questions
IX. Applications and Exercises
X. Sites to See

PART II: LEARNING OBJECTIVES

1. To gain a sociological understanding of human sexuality focusing on both biological and cultural factors.
2. To become more aware of the sexual attitudes found in the United States today.
3. To be able to describe both the sexual revolution and sexual counter-revolution that occurred during the last half century in the United States.
4. To be able to discuss human sexuality as it is experienced across different stages of the human life course.
5. To be able to discuss issues relating to the biological and social causes of sexual orientation.
6. To be able to describe the demographics of sexual orientation in our society, including the research methods used to obtain such information about our population.
7. To gain a sociological perspective on several sexual controversies, including teen pregnancy, pornography, prostitution, and sexual violence and abuse.
8. To be able to discuss issues relating to human sexuality from the viewpoints offered by structural-functional, symbolic-interactionist, and social-conflict analyses.

PART III: KEY CONCEPTS

abortion

asexuality

bisexuality

double standard

hermaphrodite

heterosexuality

heterosexism

homophobia

homosexuality

incest taboo

pornography

primary sex characteristics

prostitution

queer theory

secondary sex characteristics

sex

sexual orientation

transsexuals

PART IV: IMPORTANT RESEARCHERS

Alfred Kinsey   Helen Colton

Simon LeVay   Kingsley Davis

PART V: STUDY QUESTIONS

True-False

1. T F Social scientists long considered sex *off limits* for research. It was not until the middle of the twentieth century that researchers turned attention to this pervasive dimension of social life.
2. T F In *fertilization*, the male contributes either an X or Y chromosome.
3. T F *Primary sex characteristics* are those that develop during puberty.
4. T F *Hermaphrodites* are people who feel they are one sex even though biologically they are of the other.
5. T F Sexuality has a *biological* foundation.
6. T F Almost any *sexual practice* shows considerable variation from one society to another.
7. T F Every known culture has some form of *incest taboo*--it is a cultural universal.
8. T F The *sexual revolution* identified by Alfred Kinsey's research occurred prior to World War II.
9. T F According to the author, the *sexual counterrevolution* occurred in our society during the 1960s.
10. T F During this century, *premarital sexual behavior* among females has changed more dramatically than it has for males.
11. T F According to research data cited in the text, sexual *behavior* in the U.S. appears to be more permissive *than sexual* attitudes.
12. T F Research data suggests that married people have *sexual intercourse* more frequently than single people.
13. T F *Sexual orientation* refers to the biological distinction of being female or male.
14. T F Most research indicates that among *homosexuals*, lesbians outnumber gays by a ratio of about two-to-one.
15. T F *Pornography* refers to sexually explicit material that causes sexual arousal.
16. T F Around the world, *prostitution* is greatest in poor countries where patriarchy is strong and traditional cultural norms limit women's ability to make a living.
17. T F Among the types of *prostitutes*, call girls have the lowest status.
18. T F A common myth is that most victims of *rapes* are raped by strangers.
19. T F Most people born in the U.S. between the years 1963 and 1974 married as *virgins*.
20. T F According to national survey research, over forty percent of adults in the U.S. think that a woman should be able to obtain a legal *abortion* for any reason if she wants to.

Multiple-Choice

1. _____ refers to the biological distinction between females and males.

    (a) Gender
    (b) Sex
    (c) Sexual orientation
    (d) Human sexuality

2.	In reproduction, a female ovum and a male sperm, each containing_____ chromosomes, combine to form a fertilized embryo. One of these chromosome pairs determines the child's sex.

	(a)	12
	(b)	7
	(c)	23
	(d)	31
	(e)	48

3.	_____ are people who feel they are one sex even though biologically they are of the other sex.

	(a)	Hermaphrodites
	(b)	Transvestites
	(c)	Homophobics
	(d)	Transsexuals

4.	If an Islamic woman is disturbed by another person while she is bathing, what body part is she most likely to cover?

	(a)	her feet
	(b)	her breasts
	(c)	her navel
	(d)	her genitals
	(e)	her face

5.	During the last century, people witnessed profound changes in sexual attitudes and practices. The first indications of this change occurred in the

	(a)	1920s.
	(b)	1940s.
	(c)	1960s.
	(d)	1970s.

6.	Sixty-two percent of males born in the U.S. between 1953 and 1962 claim to have had two or more sex partners before age twenty. What is the corresponding figure for females born during that same time period?

	(a)	20
	(b)	28
	(c)	36
	(d)	48
	(e)	57

7. According to the _____, society allows (and even encourages) men to be sexually active, while expecting women to remain chaste before marriage and faithful to their husbands afterwards.

   (a)   sexual counterrevolution
   (b)   sexual revolution
   (c)   double-standard
   (d)   permissiveness index

8. Approximately _____ *percent* of U.S. adults say that premarital sexual intercourse is "always wrong."

   (a)   20
   (b)   35
   (c)   15
   (d)   60
   (e)   8

9. _____ refers to a person's preference in terms of sexual partner: same sex, other sex, either sex, neither sex.

   (a)   Sexual orientation
   (b)   Sex
   (c)   Gender
   (d)   Sexual response

10. Which of the following is a conclusion of the *Kinsey studies*?

   (a)   The sexual response cycle for women includes eight stages, while for men there is a four stage sexual response cycle.
   (b)   Homosexuality and heterosexuality are not mutually exclusive categories, but rather exist on a continuum.
   (c)   Sexual orientation changes two or three times for the average person over his or her lifetime.
   (d)   none of the above

11. Approximately _____ percent of men and _____ percent of women in the U.S. define themselves as partly or entirely *homosexual*.

   (a)   10.4/12.4
   (b)   12.1/ 8.7
   (c)   6.5/ 7.0
   (d)   11.3/ 2.6
   (e)   2.8/ 1.4

12.   What percentage of *men* in the U.S. claim to have experienced "any homosexual activity" during his lifetime?

(a)   12.7
(b)   20.1
(c)   5.7
(d)   9.1

13.   In recent decades, the public attitude toward *homosexuality* has been moving toward greater acceptance. Today, what percentage of people in the U.S. think that sexual relations between two adults of the same sex is always wrong?

(a)   25
(b)   15
(c)   40
(d)   55
(e)   85

14.   Which of the following are accurate concerning *teen pregnancy* in the United States?

(a)   Approximately one million teens become pregnant each year.
(b)   Most teens who get pregnant did not intend to.
(c)   Teens who become pregnant are at great risk of poverty.
(d)   The U.S. has a higher rate of teen pregnancy than that found in other industrial societies.
(e)   All of the above are accurate.

15.   Which of the following is *inaccurate* about *prostitution*?

(a)   Most prostitutes are women.
(b)   Most prostitutes offer heterosexual services.
(c)   Call girls are the lowest prestige type of prostitution.
(d)   Prostitution is greatest in poor countries where patriarchy is strong and traditional cultural norms limit women's ability to earn a living.

16.   *Prostitution* is classified as being what type of crime?

(a)   property
(b)   victimless
(c)   white-collar
(d)   violent

17.   Official *rape* statistics indicate that approximately _____ percent of rape victims are *male*.

(a)   10
(b)   16
(c)   less than 2
(d)   21

18.   Which of the following is/are evidence of a societal need to *regulate* sex?

(a)   Most societies condemn married people for having sex with someone other than their spouse.
(b)   Every society has some form of incest taboo.
(c)   Historically, the social control of sexuality was strong, mostly because sex commonly led to childbirth.
(d)   all of the above

19.   Which of the following is *inaccurate* concerning the perspective offered by the *structural-functionalist paradigm*?

(a)   It helps us to appreciate how sexuality plays an important part in how society is organized.
(b)   It focuses attention on how societies, through the incest taboo and other cultural norms have always paid attention to who has sex with who, especially who reproduces with whom.
(c)   This approach pays considerable attention to the great diversity of sexual ideas and practices found around the world.
(d)   All of the above a re accurate.

20.   Which of the following is a criticism of the *symbolic-interactionist paradigm*?

(a)   It fails to take into account how social patterns regarding sexuality are socially constructed.
(b)   It fails to help us appreciate the variety of sexual practices found over the course of history and around the world.
(c)   It fails to identify the broader social structures that establish certain patterns of sexual behaviors cross-culturally.
(d)   None of the above are criticisms of symbolic-interactionism.

21.   _____ refers to a view stigmatizing anyone who is not heterosexual as "queer."

(a)   Asexuality
(b)   Heteterosexism
(c)   Bisexuality
(d)   Homophobia

22.   Overall, there are approximately _____ *abortions* performed each year in the United States.

(a)   2.5 million
(b)   900,000
(c)   500,000
(d)   1.3 million

Matching

1. ___ The biological distinction between females and males.
2. ___ The genitals, organs used for reproduction.
3. ___ A human being with some combination of female and male genitalia.
4. ___ People who feel they are one sex even though biologically they are of the other.
5. ___ Refers to a person's preference in terms of sexual partners.
6. ___ Sexual attraction to someone of the same sex.
7. ___ No sexual attraction to people of either sex.
8. ___ Sexual attraction to people of both sexes.
9. ___ Refers to sexually explicit material that causes sexual arousal.
10. ___ The selling of sexual services.
11. ___ A view stigmatizing anyone who is not heterosexual as "queer."
12. ___ Refers to a growing body of knowledge that challenges an allegedly heterosexual bias in sociology.

a. transsexuals
b. queer theory
c. asexuality
d. primary sex characteristics
e. heterosexism
f. sexual orientation

g. prostitution
h. bisexuality
i. sex
j. pornography
k. homosexuality
l. hermaphrodite

Fill-In

1. _____ refers to the biological distinction between females and males.
2. One of the twenty-three chromosome pairs found in humans determines one's sex. If the father contributes an (X) chromosome, the offspring will be a _____.
3. _____ *sex characteristics* refer to bodily differences, apart from the genitals, that distinguish biologically mature females and males.
4. Human beings with some combination of female and male genitalia are referred to as _____.
5. One cultural universal--an element found in every society the world over--is the _____ _____, a norm forbidding sexual relations or marriage between certain relatives.
6. The most recent studies, targeting men and women born in the 1970s, show that _____ percent of *men* and _____ percent of *women* had premarital sexual intercourse by their senior year in high school.
7. Some research suggests that *sexual orientation* is rooted in biology. Simon LeVay links sexual orientation to the structure of the _____ _____.
8. Given current scientific research evidence, the best guess at present is that *sexual orientation* is derived from both _____ and _____.
9. Recent research suggests that about _____ percent of U.S. *males* and _____ percent of U.S. *females* aged between eighteen and fifty-nine reported *homosexual activity* at some time in their lives.
10. _____ describes the dread of close personal interaction with people thought to be gay, lesbian, or bisexual.
11. Traditionally, people have criticized *pornography* on _____ grounds. Today, however, pornography is seen as a _____ issue because it depicts women as the sexual playthings of men.

12. At the bottom of the *sex-worker hierarchy* are _____ _____.
13. *Prostitution* is against the law almost everywhere in the United States, but many people consider it a _____ *crime*.
14. In the United States, among those born between 1963 and 1974, just _____ percent of men and _____ percent of women report being *virgins* at first marriage.

Definition and Short-Answer

1. What are the important anatomical differences between *males* and *females*? In what ways are these differences important in term of the relatives statuses and roles of women and men in social institutions such as the family and the economy?
2. What evidence was used by Alfred Kinsey to suggest considerable *cultural variation* exists in terms of sexual practices?
3. What are the functions served by the *incest taboo* for both individuals and society as a whole?
4. What does the author mean by saying that sexual attitudes in the United States are both *restrictive* and *permissive*?
5. When was the *sexual revolution*? What social and cultural factors influenced this revolution? What was the *sexual counterrevolution*? What social and cultural factors helped bring it about?
6. How would you summarize our society's attitudes concerning *premarital sex*?
7. What does Alfred Kinsey mean by the *sexual orientation continuum*? What is the data he uses to argue for its existence?
8. What is the evidence that sexual orientation is a *product of society*? What is the evidence that it is a *product of biology*?
9. Why do you think *teen pregnancy* rates are higher in the United States than in other modern industrial societies?
10. To what extent would you agree that *pornography* today is less a moral issue than it is an issue concerning power? Why?
11. Is *prostitution* really a victimless crime? Why?
12. What are the *functions* of prostitution for society?
13. Why is it important for society to *regulate* sexuality?
14. What evidence do symbolic-interactionists use to suggest sexuality is *socially constructed*?
15. Social-conflict theorists argue that sexuality is at the root of *inequality* between women and men. How is this so?

PART VI: ANSWERS TO STUDY QUESTIONS

True-False

1.	T	(p. 221)	11.	T	(p. 227)
2.	T	(p. 222)	12.	T	(p. 228)
3.	F	(p. 222)	13.	F	(p. 228)
4.	F	(p. 222)	14.	F	(p. 230)
5.	T	(p. 222)	15.	T	(p. 232)
6.	T	(p. 224)	16.	T	(p. 233)
7.	T	(p. 224)	17.	F	(p. 233)
8.	F	(p. 226)	18.	T	(p. 235)
9.	F	(p. 226)	19.	F	(p. 238)
10.	T	(p. 227)	20.	T	(pp. 240-241)

Multiple-Choice

1.	b	(p. 221)	12.	d	(p. 230)
2.	c	(p. 221)	13.	d	(pp. 230-231)
3.	d	(p. 223)	14.	e	(pp. 231-232)
4.	e	(p. 224)	15.	c	(p. 233)
5.	a	(p. 225)	16.	b	(p. 234)
6.	d	(p. 226)	17.	a	(p. 235)
7.	c	(p. 226)	18.	d	(pp. 236-237)
8.	b	(p. 227)	19.	c	(pp. 236-237)
9.	a	(p. 228)	20.	c	(p. 238)
10.	b	(p. 228)	21.	b	(p. 239)
11.	e	(p. 230)	22.	d	(p. 240)

Matching

1.	i	(p. 221)	7.	c	(p. 228)
2.	d	(p. 222)	8.	h	(p. 228)
3.	l	(p. 223)	9.	j	(p. 232)
4.	a	(p. 223)	10.	c	(p. 233)
5.	f	(p. 228)	11.	e	(p. 239)
6.	k	(p. 228)	12.	b	(p. 239)

Fill-In

1. Sex (p. 221)
2. female (p. 222)
3. Secondary (p. 222)
4. Hermaphrodite (p. 223)
5. incest taboo (p. 224)
6. 76, 66 (p. 227)
7. human brain (p. 229)
8. society, biology (p. 229)
9. 9, 4 (p. 230)
10. Homophobia (p. 231)
11. moral, power (p. 232)
12. street walker (p. 233)
13. victimless (p. 234)
14. 16.3, 20.1 (p. 238)

PART VII: IN FOCUS--IMPORTANT ISSUES

- Understanding Sexuality

  Differentiate between sex as a *biological issues* and as a *cultural issue*:

  What evidence exists to support the theory that there is considerable variation in *sexual practices* around the world?

- Sexual Attitudes In the United States

  What does the author mean by saying that our cultural orientation toward sexuality has always been *inconsistent*?

  How strong do you believe the *sexual double standard* is in our society today?

What does the research suggest about behavioral patterns for each of the following?

premarital sex

sex among adults

extramarital sex

- Sexual Orientation

What is the evidence concerning each of the following in terms of giving us our *sexual orientation?*

biology

society

How have attitudes toward *homosexuality* changed in our society over the last fifty years? What factors have influenced our society's altitudes toward homosexuality?

- Sexual Controversies

  Identify two major points made in the text concerning each of the following four controversial issues:

  teen pregnancy

  pornography

  prostitution

  sexual violence

- Theoretical Analysis of Sexuality

  According to *structural-functionalists,* why is it important for society to regulate sexuality?

  What are three *latent functions* of prostitution?

  Can you think of two latent functions of *pornography*? What are they?

Provide an illustration of how global comparisons can be used to illustrate the symbolic-interactionists view that sexuality is *socially constructed*.

According to social-conflict theorists, how is sexuality involved in the creation and maintenance of *social inequality*?

PART VIII: ANALYSIS AND COMMENT

Critical Thinking

"Sex Education: Problem or Solution?"

Key Points: Questions:

"Date Rape: Exposing Dangerous Myths"

Key Points: Questions:

Global Sociology

"Sexual Slavery: A Report from Thailand"

Key Points: Questions:

Controversy and Debate

"The Abortion Controversy"

Key Points: Questions:

Window on the World--Global Map 9-1

"Prostitution in Global Perspective"

Key Points: Questions:

Seeing Ourselves--National Map 9-1

"Teenage Pregnancy Rates across the United States"

Key Points: Questions:

10 Social Stratification

PART I: CHAPTER OUTLINE

I. What is Social Stratification?
II. Caste and Class Systems
   A. The Caste System
      1. Two Illustrations: India and South Africa
      2. Caste and Agrarian Life
   B. The Class System
      1. Meritocracy
      2. Status Consistency
   C. Birth and Achievement: The United Kingdom
      1. The Estate System
      2. The United Kingdom Today
   D. Another Example: Japan
      1. Feudal Japan
      2. Japan Today
   E. The Former Soviet Union
      1. A Classless Society?
      2. The Second Russian Revolution
   F. Ideology: The Power Behind Stratification
      1. Plato and Marx on Ideology
      2. Historical Patterns of Ideology
III. The Functions of Social Stratification
   A. The Davis-Moore Thesis
IV. Stratification and Conflict
   A. Karl Marx: Class and Conflict
   B. Why No Marxist Revolution?
      1. A Counterpoint
   C. Max Weber: Class, Status, and Power
      1. The Socioeconomic Status Hierarchy
      2. Inequality in History
V. Stratification and Technology in Global Perspective
   A. Hunting and Gathering Societies
   B. Horticultural, Pastoral, and Agrarian Societies
   C. Industrial Societies
   D. The Kuznets Curve

PART II: LEARNING OBJECTIVES

1. To understand the four basic principles of social stratification.
2. To be able to differentiate between the caste and class system of stratification.
3. To begin to understand the relationship between ideology and stratification.
4. To be able to differentiate between the structural-functional and social-conflict perspectives of stratification.
5. To be able to describe the views of Max Weber concerning the dimensions of social class.
6. To be able to describe the approach to understanding social stratification as presented by the Lenskis.

PART III: KEY CONCEPTS

blue-collar occupation

burakumin

capitalists

caste system

class system

Davis-Moore thesis

endogamous

ideology

Kuznets curve

meritocracy

perestroika

primogeniture

proletariat

samurai

179

shoguns

social mobility

social stratification

socioeconomic status

status consistency

structural social mobility

white-collar occupation

PART IV: IMPORTANT RESEARCHERS

Karl Marx   Max Weber

Gerhard and Jean Lenski   Herbert Spencer

Kurt Vonnegut   Plato

Ralph Dahrendorf   Melvin Turin

PART V: STUDY QUESTIONS

True-False

1. T   F   Social stratification is *universal*--found in all societies.
2. T   F   *Ascription* is fundamental to social-stratification systems based on *castes*.
3. T   F   Social stratification is a characteristic of society, not simply a reflection of individual differences.
4. T   F   *Social mobility* is defined as the system by which a society ranks categories of people in a hierarchy.
5. T   F   *Caste* systems tend to be characterized by *endogamous marriages*.
6. T   F   Caste systems tend to be more common among hunting and gathering than *agrarian* societies.
7. T   F   A *meritocracy* is a social stratification system based on birth and other ascribed statuses.
8. T   F   Caste systems are characterized by greater *status consistency* than class systems.
9. T   F   The *working class* is the largest segment of the population in *Great Britain*.
10. T   F   The nobility of *feudal Japan* were known as the *burakumin*.
11. T   F   Greater *income inequality* exists in the U.S. than in any other society in the world.
12. T   F   *Ideology* refers to cultural beliefs that serve to justify social stratification.
13. T   F   The ancient Greek philosopher *Plato* defined *justice* as agreement about who should have what.
14. T   F   The *Davis-Moore thesis* is a component of the social-conflict perspective of social stratification.
15. T   F   *Structural-functionalists* argue that social stratification encourages a matching of talents and abilities to appropriate positions in society.
16. T   F   *Karl Marx's* social conflict theory of social stratification identified two basic relationships to the means of production--those who own productive property, and those labor for others.
17. T   F   *Max Weber* developed a unidimensional model of social stratification which was dominant earlier this century.
18. T   F   Unlike Karl Marx, *Max Weber* believed that socialism would increase inequality by expanding government and concentrating power in the hands of political elite.
19. T   F   *Gerhard* and *Jean Lenski* argued that hunting and gathering societies have greater social inequality than agrarian or horticultural societies.
20. T   F   The *Kuznets curve* projects greater social inequality as industrial societies advance technologically.

1.   A system by which a society ranks categories of people in a hierarchy is called

      (a)   social inequality.
      (b)   meritocracy.
      (c)   social stratification.
      (d)   social mobility.

2.   Which of the following principles is *not* a basic factor in explaining the existence of social stratification?

      (a)   Although universal, social stratification also varies in form.
      (b)   Social stratification persists over generations.
      (c)   Social stratification rests on widely held beliefs.
      (d)   Social stratification is a characteristic of society, not simply a function of individual differences.
      (e)   All are factors in explaining social stratification.

3.   A change in one's position in a social hierarchy refers to

      (a)   ideology.
      (b)   social mobility.
      (c)   meritocracy.
      (d)   social inequality.
      (e)   endogamy.

4.   What is a *caste system*?

      (a)   social stratification based on ascription
      (b)   social stratification based on meritocracy
      (c)   social stratification based on achievement
      (d)   any system in which there is social inequality

5.   Which of the following is *not* one of the four *castes* in India's traditional caste system?

      (a)   Vaishya
      (b)   Jaishra
      (c)   Shudra
      (d)   Brahmin
      (e)   Kshatriya

6. In a *caste system*, birth shapes people's lives in all but which of the following ways?

    (a) Traditional caste groups have specific occupations.
    (b) Castes require the norm of exogamous marriages.
    (c) Caste norms guide people to stay in the company of "their own kind."
    (d) Caste systems rest on powerful cultural beliefs.

7. *Apartheid* became law in South Africa in

    (a) 1916.
    (b) 1971.
    (c) 1948.
    (d) 1876.

8. What is the term for a system of social stratification based entirely on *personal merit*?

    (a) classlessness
    (b) meritocracy
    (c) primogeniture
    (d) egalitarianism

9. Which of the characteristics that follow are most accurate in terms of *class systems*?

    (a) They are more clearly defined than castes.
    (b) They have variable status consistency.
    (c) They have occupations based on ascription.
    (d) all of the above
    (e) none of the above

10. What is the term for the degree of consistency in a person's social standing across various dimensions of social inequality?

    (a) status consonance
    (b) status congruity
    (c) status balance
    (d) status consistency
    (e) socioeconomic status

11. In the Middle Ages, social stratification in England was a system of three

    (a) open classes.
    (b) absolute castes.
    (c) meritocracies.
    (d) closed classes.
    (e) caste-like estates.

12. The social stratification system in the United Kingdom today still has vestiges of its feudal system of the past. Which of the following was characteristic of their feudal system?

   (a)   It was a caste-like estate system.
   (b)   It was based on the law of primogeniture.
   (c)   It consisted of the nobility, the clergy, and the commoners.
   (d)   all of the above

13. The *United Kingdom* today is identified as a(n)

   (a)   neomonarchy.
   (b)   caste system.
   (c)   estate system.
   (d)   open estate system.
   (e)   class society.

14. Which of the following comprises one-half of all persons in the United Kingdom's class system?

   (a)   working class
   (b)   upper class
   (c)   lower class
   (d)   middle class

15. In *feudal Japan*, the warrior caste was known as the

   (a)   samurai.
   (b)   shoguns.
   (c)   burakumin.
   (d)   gurukula.

16. The former Soviet Union had four levels in their social stratification system. The highest level was known as

   (a)   intelligentsia.
   (b)   perestroika.
   (c)   apparatchiks.
   (d)   primogeniture.
   (e)   nogoodniks.

17. What do sociologists call a shift in the social position of large numbers of people due more to changes in society itself than to individual efforts?

   (a)   perestroika
   (b)   bureaucratization
   (c)   linear social stratification
   (d)   structural social mobility

18.   What is *ideology*?

   (a)   a system in which entire categories of people are ranked in a hierarchy
   (b)   ideas that are generated through scientific investigation
   (c)   views and opinions that are based on the principle of cultural relativism
   (d)   ideas that limit the amount of inequality of a society
   (e)   cultural beliefs that serve to justify social stratification

19.   The *Davis-Moore thesis* asserts that

   (a)   social stratification has beneficial consequences for the operation of society.
   (b)   industrialization produces greater, and more harmful social stratification than previous forms of subsistence.
   (c)   social stratification based on meritocracy has dysfunctional consequences for society and its individual members.
   (d)   ideology undermines social stratification.
   (e)   industrial capitalism is moving toward a classless social order.

20.   Which perspective of social stratification views social inequality as the domination of some categories of people by others?

   (a)   symbolic-interactionism
   (b)   sociocultural evolution
   (c)   social-conflict
   (d)   structural-functionalism

21.   In Karl Marx's analysis of social stratification, another name for the working class is the

   (a)   primogeniture.
   (b)   perestroika.
   (c)   apparatchiks.
   (d)   proletariat.
   (e)   bourgeoisie.

22.   Which of the following is/are reasons given as to why there has been *no Marxist revolution*?

   (a)   the fragmentation of the capitalist class
   (b)   a higher standard of living
   (c)   more extensive worker organization
   (d)   more extensive legal protections
   (e)   all of the above

23. Which of the following is *not* one of the dimensions of social stratification according to Max Weber?

   (a) class
   (b) education
   (c) power
   (d) status

24. According to the model of *sociocultural evolution* developed by *Gerhard* and *Jean Lenski*, social stratification is at its peak in

   (a) hunting and gathering societies.
   (b) postindustrial societies.
   (c) large-scale agrarian societies.
   (d) industrial societies.

25. The *Kuznets curve* suggests

   (a) industrialization and social stratification are unrelated.
   (b) industrial societies are represented by greater social inequality than agrarian societies.
   (c) the emergence of postindustrial society may signal greater social inequality.
   (d) greater technological sophistication is generally accompanied by greater social equality.

26. Which of the following is/are accurate statements?

   (a) Generally speaking, countries that have had centralized, socialist economies display the least income inequality.
   (b) The standard of living in countries that have had centralized, socialist economies tend to have a relatively low standard of living.
   (c) Industrial societies with capitalist economies have higher overall living standards compared to other countries.
   (d) Severe income disparity characterizes industrial societies with capitalist economies.
   (e) all of the above

27. The novel by Kurt Vonnegut, Jr., about an imaginary account of a future United States concerned

   (a) a society in which social inequality was abolished and was not as appealing as one might expect.
   (b) a caste-like society in which extreme inequality has emerged from capitalist roots.
   (c) a technocratic society in which human productive labor is no longer required.
   (d) a return to an agrarian way of life in which social stratification was based on family lineage and land ownership.

28. Which of the following is/are arguments being made in the book *The Bell Curve* by Charles Murray and Richard Herrnstein?

    (a) Something called "general intelligence" exists.
    (b) At least one-half the variation in human intelligence is genetic.
    (c) Higher education and the work place is being dominated by a cognitive elite.
    (d) Increasingly, poor people are individuals with lower intelligence.
    (e) All of the above are arguments being made in this book.

Matching

1. ___ Social stratification based on *ascription*.
2. ___ The degree of consistency in a person's social standing across various dimensions of social inequality.
3. ___ Social stratification based on personal merit.
4. ___ An economic program, meaning *restructuring*, developed by Mikhail Gorbachev.
5. ___ Cultural beliefs that justify social stratification.
6. ___ The assertion that social stratification is universal because it has beneficial consequences for the operation of society.
7. ___ According to Karl Marx, the people who own and operate factories and other productive businesses in pursuit of profit.
8. ___ According to Karl Marx, the people who sell their productive labor for wages.
9. ___ Developed a multidimensional model of social class which included the variables of *class, status,* and *power*.
10. ___ Reveals that greater *technological* sophistication is generally accompanied by more pronounced *social-stratification*, to a point.

a.	proletariat	f.	the Davis-Moore thesis
b.	perestroika	g.	Max Weber
c.	Kuznets curve	h.	meritorcracy
d.	capitalists	i.	status consistency
e.	caste	j.	ideology

Fill-In

1. *Social* _____ refers to a system by which a society ranks categories of people in a hierarchy.
2. Social stratification is a matter of four *basic principles*: it is a characteristic of _____, not simply a reflection of individual differences; it _____ over generations; it is _____ but variable; and, it involves not just inequality but _____.
3. A _____ _____ is a system of social stratification based *ascription*.
4. Caste systems mandate that people marry others of the same ranking. Sociologists call this pattern _____ *marriage*.
5. Social stratification based on *personal merit* is called a _____.
6. In feudal past of the United Kingdom, the *law of* _____ mandated that only the eldest son inherited property of parents.

7. In feudal Japan, the *warrior caste* was known as _____.

8. The four levels of jobs in the former Soviet Union included the top government officials, or the _____, the _____, and the rural _____.

9. _____ *social mobility* refers to a shift in the social position of large numbers of people due more to changes in society itself than to individual efforts.

10. _____ refers to cultural beliefs that justify social stratification.

11. From Karl Marx's point of view, capitalist society _____ *the class structure in each new generation.*

12. Four reasons are given as to why there has been *no Marxist revolution*, including: the _____ of the capitalist class, a _____ standard of living, more extensive worker _____, and more extensive legal _____.

13. Advocates of *social-conflict analysis* believe that Karl Marx's analysis of capitalism is still largely valid. They offer the following reasons: wealth remains largely _____, _____ work offers little to workers, progress requires _____. And the _____ still favors the rich.

14. The three components of *Max Weber's* model of social class are _____, _____, and _____.

15. _____ *status* refers to a composite ranking based on various dimensions of social inequality.

16. Gerhard and Jean Lenski argue that the level of _____ representative of a society is a very significant factor in determining the nature of social stratification in that society.

17. The *Kuznets curve* shows that greater _____ sophistication is generally accompanied by more pronounced social stratification.

18. The authors of the _____ *Curve* argue that there is something called "general intelligence," that much of it is related to genetics, that it is important for the type of work required in the period of the Information Revolution, and that it is related to social class.

Definition and Short-Answer

1. What are the four *fundamental principles* of social stratification?
2. Briefly describe the social-stratification system of the *United Kingdom*.
3. What are the four reasons given in the text for why the *Marxist Revolution* has not occurred?
4. What are the basic qualities of a *caste system*?
5. What are the components of *Max Weber's* multidimensional model of social stratification? Define each.
6. What are three criteria of the *Davis-Moore thesis*? What is your opinion of this thesis and its relevance for helping us understand our social stratification? What evidence exists in support of this thesis? What evidence exists that contradicts it?
7. Define *Karl Marx's* concepts of *proletariat* and *capitalists*. What value does Marx's perspective offer to the understanding of modern social stratification?
8. Review the basic points being made by *Gerhard* and *Jean Lenski* concerning global inequality in historical perspective.
9. Describe the *second Russian Revolution*.
10. Provide an illustration of *structural social mobility* in our society.

PART VI: ANSWERS TO STUDY QUESTIONS

True-False

1.	T	(p. 248)
2.	T	(p. 248)
3.	T	(p. 248)
4.	F	(p. 248)
5.	T	(p. 249)
6.	F	(p. 249)
7.	F	(p. 250)
8.	T	(p. 251)
9.	T	(p. 252)
10.	F	(p. 253)

11.	F	(p. 255)
12.	T	(p. 256)
13.	T	(p. 257)
14.	F	(p. 257)
15.	T	(pp. 257-258)
16.	T	(pp. 258-259)
17.	F	(p. 261)
18.	T	(p. 261)
19.	F	(p. 263)
20.	F	(p. 263)

Multiple Choice

1.	c	(p. 248)
2.	e	(p. 248)
3.	b	(p. 248)
4.	a	(p. 248)
5.	b	(p. 249)
6.	b	(p. 249)
7.	c	(p. 250)
8.	b	(p. 250)
9.	b	(p. 251)
10.	a	(p. 251)
11.	e	(p. 251)
12.	d	(p. 252)
13.	e	(p. 252)
14.	a	(p. 252)

15.	a	(p. 253)
16.	c	(p. 255)
17.	d	(p. 255)
18.	e	(p. 256)
19.	a	(p. 257)
20.	c	(p. 258)
21.	d	(p. 259)
22.	e	(pp. 260-261)
23.	b	(p. 261)
24.	c	(p. 263)
25.	c	(p. 263)
26.	e	(p. 264)
27.	a	(p. 265)
28.	e	(p. 266-267)

Matching

1.	e	(p. 248)
2.	i	(p. 251)
3.	h	(pp. 250-251)
4.	b	(p. 255)
5.	j	(p. 256)

6.	f	(p. 257)
7.	d	(p. 259)
8.	a	(p. 259)
9.	g	(p. 261)
10.	c	(p. 263)

Fill-In

1. stratification (p. 248)
2. society, persists, universal, beliefs (p. 248)
3. caste (p. 248)

4. endogamous (p. 249)
5. meritocracy (p. 250)
6. primogeniture (p. 252)
7. samurai (p. 253)
8. appararchiks, intelligentsia, manual workers, rural peasantry (p. 254)
9. Structural (p. 255)
10. Ideology (p. 256)
11. reproduces (p. 259)
12. fragmentation, higher, organization, protection (pp. 260-261)
13. concentrated, white-collar, struggle, law (p. 261)
14. class, status, power (p. 261)
15. Socioeconomic (p. 262)
16. technology (p. 263)
17. technological (p. 263)
18. Bell (p. 266)

PART VII: IN FOCUS--IMPORTANT ISSUES

- What is Social Stratification?

  What are the four basic *principles of social stratification*?

  1.

  2.

  3.

  4.

- Caste and Class Systems

  Identify three major characteristics of a *caste system*:

  Identify three major characteristics of a *class system*:

190

What are the Functions of Social Stratification?

What is the *Davis-Moore thesis*?

What is the evidence that this thesis is valid?

What are three major criticisms of this thesis?

- Stratification and Conflict

What was Karl Marx's argument about *class and conflict*?

What is the evidence that Marx's view is still relevant today?

What are four reasons why a *Marxist Revolution* has not occurred in capitalist societies?

Define each of the three *dimensions of social stratification* as identified by Max Weber:

class

status

power

- Stratification and Technology: A Global Perspective

According to the *Kuznets curve*, describe the relationship between technology and social stratification throughout history:

hunting and gathering societies

horticultural, pastoral, and agrarian

industrial societies

postindustrial societies

- Social Stratification: Facts and Values

  What are the major questions being raised by the novel by Kurt Vonnegut, Jr. cited in the text concerning social stratification?

PART VIII: ANALYSIS AND COMMENT

Global Sociology

"Race as Caste: A Report From South Africa"

Key Points: Questions:

Critical Thinking

"Is Getting Rich "The Survival of the Fittest"?"

Key Points: Questions:

"Big Bucks: Are the Rich Worth What They Earn?"

Key Points: Questions:

Controversy and Debate

"The Bell Curve Debate: Are Rich People Really Smarter?"

Key Points: Questions:

Window on the World--Global Map 9-1

"Income Disparity in Global Perspective"

Key Points: Questions:

11 Social Class in the United States

PART II: LEARNING OBJECTIVES

1.   To develop a sense of the extent of social inequality in the United States.
2.   To consider the meaning of the concept of socioeconomic status and to be aware of its dimensions.
3.   To be able to review the role of economic resources, power and occupational prestige, and schooling in the U.S. class system.
4.   To be able to identify and trace the significance of various ascribed statuses for the construction and maintenance of social stratification in the United States.
5.   To begin to see the significance of the global economy and its impact on our economic system.
6.   To be able to generally describe the various social classes in our social stratification system.
7.   To become aware of how health, values, family life, and gender are related to the social-class system in our society.
8.   To begin to develop a sociological understanding about the nature of social mobility in the United States.
9.   To develop a general understanding of the demographics of poverty in the United States.
10.   To become aware and critical of different explanations of poverty.
11.   To develop an awareness of the problem of homelessness in the United States.
12.   To consider some of the dilemmas involved in public assistance and welfare reform.

PART III: KEY CONCEPTS

absolute poverty

culture of poverty

197

femininization of poverty

horizontal social mobility

income

intergenerational social mobility

intragenerational social mobility

lower-class

marginal poor

middle-class

pink-collar occupations

prestige

proletariat

relative poverty

social inequality

social mobility

social stratification

socioeconomic status

status consistency

structural social mobility

upper-class

wealth

white-collar occupation

PART IV: IMPORTANT RESEARCHERS

William Julius Wilson   Edward Banfield

Oscar Lewis   Max Weber

Elizabeth Bott

PART V: STUDY QUESTIONS

True-False

1.	T	F	*Wealth* in the United States is distributed more equally than income.
2.	T	F	*Wealth* is defined as the total value of money and other assets, minus outstanding debts.
3.	T	F	Recent government calculations place the wealth of the average U.S. household at about $50 000.
4.	T	F	When financial assets are balanced against debits, the lowest--ranking 40 percent of families in the U.S. have virtually no wealth at all.
5.	T	F	The United States has far less *income inequality* than is found in many other industrial societies.
6.	T	F	Eighty-two percent of adults in the U.S. have a high school diploma.
7.	T	F	African American families earn about eighty percent of what white families earn.
8.	T	F	Over one-third of U.S. adults have a college degree.
9.	T	F	Average *wealth* for whites families in the U.S. is over ten times that for black families.
10.	T	F	The *working class* is the largest social class in the United States.
11.	T	F	About 40 percent of *lower-class* families own their own homes, though typically in the least desirable neighborhoods.
12.	T	F	Cultural values vary by social class. *Affluent* people with greater education and financial security are more tolerant of controversial behavior such as homosexuality.
13.	T	F	Parents in *working-class* families are characterized by an emphasis on *conformity* to conventional beliefs and practices, more so than are middle- class families.
14.	T	F	*Intragenerational social mobility* refers to a change in social position occurring during a person's lifetime.
15.	T	F	The *earnings gap* between men and women has been increasing in the U.S. over the past thirty years.
16.	T	F	The *middle-class slide* is an example of downward structural mobility.

17.	T	F	Compared to the period of 1950-1973, the period of 1974-1997 provided greater growth in *median family income*, particularly with more dual earner families in existence.
18.	T	F	The official *poverty rate* in the United States in 1997 was approximately 13.3 percent.
19.	T	F	The *poverty threshold* is three times what the government estimates people must spend to eat.
20.	T	F	Two-thirds of all poor people in the U.S. are African American.
21.	T	F	The poverty rate among the elderly in the U.S. is higher than the rate for children.
22.	T	F	The *culture of poverty* is a concept relating poverty to a lower-class subculture that inhibits personal achievement and foster resignation.
23.	T	F	William Julius Wilson believes that the solution to the problems of inner cities is the *creation of jobs*.
24.	T	F	Among the poor in the U.S., over sixty percent of the heads of households are employed *full-time*.
25.	T	F	Estimates are that one-quarter of *homeless* people in the U.S. are mentally ill.
26.	T	F	People in the U.S. are more likely to blame individuals rather than society for poverty compared to people in other industrialized societies.

Multiple Choice

1. We in the United States tend to *underestimate* the amount of inequality in our society. Which of the following is *not* a reason for this phenomenon?

   (a) because we embrace the legal principle of equality
   (b) because we are an affluent society
   (c) because we emphasize statuses conferred at birth
   (d) because our culture celebrates individual autonomy and achievement
   (e) because in principle, the law gives equal standing to all

2. Census Bureau data show that *income* and *wealth* are unequally distributed in the United States. Which of the following statements is most accurate?

   (a) The median household income in the U.S. in 1997 was $63,036.
   (b) The top five percent of households (by income) receive sixty-five percent of the income earned in the U.S.
   (c) The poorest twenty percent of households only receive ten percent of the income earned in the U.S.
   (d) Wealth is distributed more unequally in the U.S. than is income.

3. Recent government calculations put the *wealth* of the average U.S. household at about

   (a) $10,000.
   (b) $25,000.
   (c) $38,000.
   (d) $50,000.
   (e) $67,000.

4. *Education* is distributed unequally in the U.S. as evidenced by the fact that

    (a)   only a little more than twenty percent of the adult population has a college education.
    (b)   only about fifty-five percent of the adult population has a high school education.
    (c)   thirty percent of adults have not completed high school.
    (d)   all of the above

5. In 1997, African American families earned _____ percent of that earned by white families.

    (a)   90
    (b)   84
    (c)   73
    (d)   67
    (e)   61

6. African American households have an average *wealth* that is _____ of white households.

    (a)   one-half
    (b)   one-third
    (c)   one-tenth
    (d)   one-fifth

7. The *middle class* includes approximately what percentage of the U.S. population?

    (a)   20-25
    (b)   40-45
    (c)   30-35
    (d)   55-60

8. Which of the following is inaccurate about the *Social Register*?

    (a)   It lists families, not individuals.
    (b)   It lists addresses and phone numbers.
    (c)   It lists occupations.
    (d)   It lists schools attended by a family's children.

9. The *lower-class* comprises about ____ percent of our society's population.

    (a)   5
    (b)   10
    (c)   15
    (d)   20
    (e)   25

10. In 1997, the federal government officially classified _____ percent of the U.S. population as being *poor*.

   (a) 8.2
   (b) 13.3
   (c) 18.5
   (d) 22.7

11. The term *conspicuous consumption* refers to

   (a) the practice of buying things to get noticed.
   (b) purchasing food and other necessities.
   (c) items purchased by the poor using public assistance funds.
   (d) buying items on credit.

12. Which of the following statements is/are accurate regarding general patterns in our society?

   (a) Working-class parents tend to encourage children to conform to conventional norms and obey and respect authority.
   (b) Middle-class parents tend to teach children to express their individuality.
   (c) Most working-class couples divide their responsibilities according to gender.
   (d) Middle-class couples tend to be more egalitarian than working-class couples.
   (e) all of the above

13. Regarding *politics*, which of the following is most accurate?

   (a) Wealthier people tend to support the Democratic Party.
   (b) Higher income people are less likely to vote than poorer people.
   (c) On social issues, wealthier and more highly educated people tend to be more liberal than people of lower social standing.
   (d) People of lower social standing are more conservative on economic issues than wealthier people.

14. What does research reveal about *social mobility* in the United States?

   (a) Social mobility, at least among men, has been relatively low.
   (b) The long-term trend in social mobility has been downward.
   (c) Within a single generation, social mobility is usually dramatic, not incremental.
   (d) The short-term trend has been stagnation, with some income polarization.

15. A change in social position of children relative to that of their parents is called

   (a) horizontal social mobility.
   (b) structural social mobility.
   (c) intergenerational social mobility.
   (d) intragenerational social mobility.

16. Which of the following is accurate concerning how U.S. families in different income levels fared between *1980 and 1997*?

    (a)   Well-to-do families (the highest 20 percent) saw a moderate decline in their incomes.
    (b)   Middle-income families saw their incomes increase by over forty percent.
    (c)   The lowest-income category suffered a over a three percent decline in earnings.
    (d)   All income categories experienced a decline in earnings.

17. What evidence exists to suggest that there is *income stagnation* in our society in recent years?

    (a)   For many workers, earnings have stalled.
    (b)   Multiple-job holding is up.
    (c)   More jobs offer little income.
    (d)   More young people are remaining at home.
    (e)   all of the above

18. Which of the following statements is/are accurate?

    (a)   Most young people aged eighteen to twenty-four are now living with their parents.
    (b)   Over the last twenty years the earnings gap between women and men has been narrowing.
    (c)   In 1997, women in the U.S. earned approximately seventy-four percent of what men earned.
    (d)   The percentage of workers who the government classifies as "low-income workers" has increased since 1979.
    (e)   All of the above are accurate statements.

19. High-paying jobs in *manufacturing* accounted for twenty-six percent of jobs in 1960; today, such jobs support _____ percent of our workforce.

    (a)   30
    (b)   15
    (c)   25
    (d)   4
    (e)   10

20. Approximately what percentage of the U.S. population is officially classified as being poor?

    (a)   5
    (b)   13
    (c)   19
    (d)   26

21. Poverty statistics in the United States reveal that

    (a)   the elderly are more likely than any other age group to be poor.
    (b)   almost 70 percent of all African Americans are poor.
    (c)   urban and suburban poverty rates are considerably higher than rural poverty rates.
    (d)   about 63 percent of the poor are female.

22.   The *culture of poverty* view concerning the causes of poverty

      (a)   holds that the poor are primarily responsible for their own poverty.
      (b)   blames poverty on economic stagnation relating to the globalization of the U.S. economy.
      (c)   sees lack of ambition on the part of the poor as a consequence, not a cause for poverty.
      (d)   views the conservative economic policies of the last two decades in the U.S. as the primary reason for relatively high poverty rates.

23.   According to evidence cited in the text

      (a)   nineteen percent of poor families have at least one person who is employed full-time.
      (b)   thirty-nine percent of poor have at least one member who is employed part-time.
      (c)   twenty-five of homeless people in the U.S. are mentally ill.
      (d)   one-third of the homeless in the U.S. are entire families.
      (e)   all of the above

24.   What does sociologist William Julius Wilson see as a solution to the problem of *inner-city poverty*?

      (a)   busing children to better schools
      (b)   improving welfare programs
      (c)   creating jobs
      (d)   enforcing the law

Matching

1. ____ The total value of money and other assets, minus outstanding debts.
2. ____ Encompasses 40 to 45 percent of the U.S. population and exerts a tremendous influence on U.S. culture.
3. ____ Accounts for about one-third of the U.S. population.
4. ____ A change in social position occurring within a person's lifetime.
5. ____ Upward or downward social mobility of children in relation to their parents.
6. ____ A form of downward structural social mobility.
7. ____ The deprivation of some people in relation to those who have more.
8. ____ Describes the trend by which women represent an increasing proportion of the poor.
9. ____ Developed the concept of the *culture of poverty*, or a lower-class subculture that inhibits personal achievement and fosters resignation to one's plight.
10. ____ Argued that *society* is primarily responsible for poverty and that any lack of ambition on the part of the poor is a *consequence* of insufficient opportunity.

a.	William Julius Wilson	f.	the working-class
b.	intergenerational social mobility	g.	Oscar Lewis
c.	femininization of poverty	h.	the middle-class
d.	wealth	i.	the middle-class slide
e.	intragenerational social mobility	j.	relative poverty

1. We underestimate the extent of stratification in the United States for several reasons, including: In principle, the law gives _____ standing to all, our culture celebrates individual _____ and _____, we tend to _____ with people like ourselves, and the United States is an _____ society.

2. In 1997, the richest twenty percent of families in the U.S. controlled _____ percent of all *income*.

3. _____ is the total value of money and other assets, minus outstanding debts.

4. When financial assets are balanced against debits, the lowest-ranking _____ percent of U.S. families have virtually no *wealth* at all.

5. Much of the disparity in income between whites and African Americans is due to the larger share of single-parent families among African Americans. Comparing only families headed by *married couples*, African-Americans earn _____ percent as much as whites.

6. The *median family income* for African Americans in 1997 was _____.

7. The *working-class* comprises about _____ percent of the U.S. population.

8. In 1997, the federal government classified _____ of our population as *poor*.

9. _____ *consumption* refers to the practice of buying expensive things to "make a statement."

10. While the relationship between social class and politics is complex, generally, members of high social standing tend to have _____ *views on economic issues* and _____ *views on social issues*.

11. _____ *social mobility* refers to a change in social position occurring within a person's lifetime.

12. Evidence of "income stagnation" in our society today includes: for many workers, earnings have _____, _____ job-holding is up, more jobs offer little _____, and young people are remaining _____.

13. _____ *poverty* refers to deprivation of some people in relation to those who have more.

14. For an urban family of four, in 1997, the poverty threshold was _____.

15. In 1997, _____ of people under the age of eighteen were poor. During that same year _____ percent of the poor were over the age of sixty-five.

16. The trend by which females represent an increasing proportion of the poor is called the _____ *of poverty*.

17. In the United States in 1997, _____ the poverty rate in *urban* areas (inner-cites and suburbs) was _____ percent and in *rural* areas was _____ percent.

18. _____ percent of poor families *own their homes*.

19. According to William Julius Wilson sees any apparent lack of ambition on the part of the poor as a _____ of insufficient opportunity rather than a _____ of poverty.

20. In 1997, _____ percent of the heads of poor families labored at least fifty weeks a year and yet could not escape poverty.

21. Virtually all *homeless people* have one status in common: _____.

22. *Conservatives* believe government assistance undermines _____ among the poor, and erodes the traditional _____.

23.   More of the U.S. population attributes poverty to personal _____ than _____ _____.

24.   Welfare reform has included replacing the federal AFDC program with TANF or _____ _____ _____, a program with funding for new state-run programs.

Definition and Short-Answer

1.   What are the four *fundamental principles* of social stratification?
2.   Briefly describe the social-stratification system of *Great Britain*.
3.   What are the four reasons given in the text for why the *Marxist Revolution* has not occurred?
4.   What are the basic qualities of a *caste system*?
5.   What is meant by the concept *structural social mobility*? Provide two illustrations.
6.   What are the components of *Max Weber's* multidimensional model of social stratification? Define each.
7.   What are three criteria of the *Davis-Moore thesis*? What is your opinion of this thesis and its relevance for helping us understand our social stratification? What evidence exists in support of this thesis? What evidence contradicts it?
8.   What are some of the reasons why people in the United States might tend to underestimate the extent of social inequality in our society?
9.   How are *wealth* and *income* distributed throughout the population in the United States?
10.   What are the basic components of *socioeconomic status*? How are they measured? How do these components differ from Max Weber's components of social class?
11.   To what extent do *ascribed statuses* affect a person's place in our social-stratification system? Provide examples using the variables of race, ethnicity, and gender.
12.   Using the factors of health, values, and politics, discuss the difference social class makes in the lives of people within our society.
13.   Identify six significant *demographic characteristics* of the poor in our society today.
14.   What is meant by the term *culture of poverty*? What policies and programs do you think could be instituted to counteract this phenomenon?
15.   What is meant by the term *femininization of poverty*? What can be done to reverse this trend in our society?
16.   Review the basic points being made by *Gerhard* and *Jean Lenski* concerning global inequality in historical perspective.
17.   What are the four general conclusions being made about *social mobility* in the United States today?
18.   What is the evidence that the *American Dream* is waning in our society?

PART VI: ANSWERS TO STUDY QUESTIONS

True-False

1.	F	(p. 272)	14.	T	(p. 283)
2.	T	(p. 273)	15.	F	(p. 284)
3.	T	(p. 273)	16.	T	(p. 285)
4.	T	(pp. 273-274)	17.	F	(p. 285)
5.	F	(p. 273)	18.	T	(p. 286)
6.	T	(p. 275)	19.	T	(p. 286)
7.	F	(p. 275)	20.	F	(p. 289)
8.	F	(p. 276)	21.	F	(p. 288)
9.	T	(p. 276)	22.	T	(p. 290)
10.	F	(pp. 279-280)	23.	T	(p. 290)
11.	T	(p. 280)	24.	F	(p. 292)
12.	T	(p. 281)	25.	T	(p. 293)
13.	T	(p. 282)	26.	T	(p. 295)

Multiple Choice

1.	c	(p. 272)	13.	c	(p. 282)
2.	d	(p. 273)	14.	d	(p. 283)
3.	d	(p. 273)	15.	c	(p. 283)
4.	a	(p. 275)	16.	c	(p. 283)
5.	e	(p. 275)	17.	e	(p. 285)
6.	c	(p. 276)	18.	e	(p. 285)
7.	b	(p. 279)	19.	b	(p. 286)
8.	c	(p. 278)	20.	b	(p. 286)
9.	d	(p. 280)	21.	d	(pp. 287-289)
10.	b	(p. 280)	22.	a	(p. 290)
11.	a	(p. 281)	23.	e	(p. 290)
12.	e	(p. 282)	24.	c	(p. 291)

Matching

1.	d	(p. 272)	6.	i	(p. 285)
2.	h	(p. 279)	7.	j	(p. 286)
3.	f	(p. 280)	8.	c	(p. 289)
4.	e	(p. 283)	9.	g	(p. 290)
5.	b	(p. 283)	10.	a	(p. 291)

Fill-In

1. equal, autonomy, achievement, interact, affluent (p. 272)
2. 47.2 (p. 272)
3. wealth (p. 273)
4. 40 (p. 272)

5.   87 (p. 275)
6. $28,602 (p. 275)
7.   33 (p. 280)
8.   13.3 (p. 280)
9.   conspicuous (p. 281)
10.   conservative, liberal (p. 282)
11.   intergenerational (p. 283)
12.   stalled, multiple, income, home (p. 283)
13.   relative (p. 286)
14. $16,400 (p. 287)
15.   19.9, 10.5 (p. 287)
16.   femininization (p. 289)
17.   9.0, 12.6 (p. 289)
18.   41 (p. 290)
19.   result, cause (p. 291)
20.   19.2 (p. 292)
21.   poverty (p. 293)
22.   self-reliance, family (pp. 294-295)
23.   laziness, societal injustice (pp. 294-295)
24.   temporary assistance for needy families (pp. 294-295)

PART VII: IN FOCUS--IMPORTANT ISSUES

- Dimensions of Social Inequality

    Our author suggests that U.S. society is *highly stratified*. What are two pieces of evidence that support this view?

    Identify the five variables discussed in the text which are used to determine the *socioeconomic status* of a household.

    Briefly describe how each of these are distributed in the United States today.

- Social Stratification and Birth

  In what five ways does the ascribed status of *birth* affect a person's status in our social class system? Provide evidence for two of these as influencing one's social class status.

- Social Classes In the United States

  Briefly describe each of the following *social classes* in the United States:

  the upper class

       upper-uppers

       lower-uppers

  the middle class

       upper-middles

       middle-middles

  the working class

  the lower class

- The Difference Class Makes

  Social stratification affects many dimensions of our lives. How are each of the following connected to social class?

  health

  values

  politics

  family and gender

- Social Mobility

  What are the four *general conclusions* being made in the text concerning social mobility in the United States?

  1.

  2.

  3.

  4.

What are the four pieces of evidence identified in the text suggesting that upward social mobility in the U.S. is becoming harder to achieve, particularly for middle-class families?

1.

2.

3.

4.

- Poverty in the United States

Describe the *demographics of poverty* using the following variables:

age

race and ethnicity

gender and family patterns

urban and rural poverty

Briefly summarize the following two *explanations of poverty*:

blame the poor

blame society

Research suggest that there are more *homeless* people in our society than ever before. Identify two examples for each of the following explanations for this increase.

personal traits

societal factors

PART VIII: ANALYSIS AND COMMENT

Social Diversity

"The Color of Money: Being Rich in Black and White"

Key Points: Questions:

Critical Thinking

"Caste and Class: The Social Register and Who's Who"

Key Points: Questions:

"When Work Disappears: The Result Is Poverty"

Key Points: Questions:

Applying Sociology

"U.S. Children: Bearing the Burden of Poverty"

Key Points: Questions:

Controversy and Debate

"The Welfare Dilemma"

Key Points: Questions:

Seeing Ourselves--National Maps 11-1, 11-2, 11-3

""Fear of Falling" across the United States"

Key Points: Questions:

"Child Poverty across the United States"

Key Points: Questions:

"Median Household Income across the United States"

Key Points: Questions:

Global Stratification

PART I: CHAPTER OUTLINE

PART II: LEARNING OBJECTIVES

1.	To be able to define and describe the demographics of the three "economic development" categories used to classify nations of the world.
2.	To begin to understand both the severity and extensiveness of poverty in the low-income nations of the world.
3.	To recognize the extent to which women are overrepresented among the poor of the world and the factors leading to this condition.
4.	To be able to identify and define the different types of human slavery that still exists around the globe.
5.	To be able to identify and discuss the correlates of global poverty.
6.	To be able to identify and discuss the two major theories used to explain global inequality.
7.	To be able to identify and describe the stages of modernization.
8.	To be able to recognize the problems facing women as a result of modernization in the low-income nations of the world.
9.	To be able to identify the keys to combating global inequality over the next century.

PART III: KEY CONCEPTS

absolute poverty

colonialism

dependency theory

high-income countries

low-income countries

middle-income countries

modernization theory

multinational corporation

neocolonialism

relative poverty

traditionalism

PART IV: IMPORTANT RESEARCHERS

Immanuel Wallerstein   W. W. Rostow

PART V: STUDY QUESTIONS

<u>True-False</u>

1.   T   F   Because global income is so concentrated, even people in the United States with income *below the government's poverty line* live far better than the majority of the earth's people.

2.   T   F   The wealth of the world's three *richest people* equals the annual economic output of the world's forty-eight poorest countries.

3.   T   F   The richest twenty percent of the global population receive about fifty percent of all the *income*.

4.   T   F   The *high-income countries*, representing 15 percent of humanity, control over one-half of the world's income.

5.   T   F   Approximately 50 percent of the world's population live in *low-income countries*.

6.   T   F   Approximately one-fourth of the population of *low-income countries* live in urban areas.

7.   T   F   *Low-income countries* are plagued by constant hunger, unsafe housing, and high rates of disease.

8.   T   F   Only about 20 percent of the people living in *low-income societies* farm the land.

9.   T   F   *Australia* has the highest *quality of life score* in the world.

10. T   F   A key reason why the *quality of life* differs so much around the world is that economic productivity is lowest in precisely the regions of the globe where population growth is highest.

11. T   F   *Relative poverty* refers to a lack of resources that is life threatening.

12. T   F   There is a greater disparity of wealth along lines of *gender* in low-icome countries than in high-income, industrial societies.

13. T   F   *Modernization theory* suggests the greatest barrier to economic development is *traditionalism*.

14. T   F   *Immanuel Wallerstein's* capitalist world economy model is used to illustrate and support *dependency theory*.

15.	T	F	*Modernization theory* draws criticism for suggesting that the causes of global poverty lie almost entirely in poor societies themselves.
16.	T	F	*Dependency theory* claims that the increasing prosperity of high-income countries has largely come at the expense of low-income countries.
17.	T	F	According to *dependency theory*, global inequality must be seen in terms of the distribution of wealth, as opposed to highlighting the productivity of wealth.
18.	T	F	Empirical evidence indicates that most people in the countries of the world are living better than they have in the past.
19.	T	F	Ten million of the world's children die each year as a result of *hunger*.
20.	T	F	With such high mortality rates, particularly among children, poor countries are showing a net decline in population by about 10 million people *annually*.
21.	T	F	The keys to combating global inequality during the next century lie in seeing it as partly a *problem of technology* and also a *political problem*.
22.	T	F	As low-income countries increase their standard of living, *less stress* is expected to be placed on the *physical environment*.

Multiple Choice

1. The poorest twenty percent of the world's nations controls _____ percent of the *global income*.

    (a)   12
    (b)   10
    (c)   15
    (d)   1
    (e)   5

2. The *high-income countries*, representing 15 percent of the world's population, control over _____ percent of the world's income.

    (a)   25
    (b)   35
    (c)   50
    (d)   80

3. Which of the following statements concerning the *high-income countries* is/are accurate?

    (a)   Taken together, countries with the most developed economies cover roughly twenty-five percent of the earth's land area.
    (b)   About three-fourths of the people in high-income countries live in or near cities.
    (c)   Significant cultural differences exist among high-income countries.
    (d)   Production in rich nations is capital-intensive.
    (e)   All of the above are accurate statements.

4. Which of the following is an *inaccurate* statement concerning *middle-income countries*?

    (a)   In middle-income countries, per capita income ranges between $2,500 and $10,000.
    (b)   About half the people in middle-income countries still live in rural areas and work in agriculture.
    (c)   One cluster of middle-income countries includes the former Soviet Union and the nations of Eastern Europe.
    (d)   Taken together, middle-income countries span roughly sixty-five percent of the earth's land area.

5. *Middle-income countries* cover _____ percent of the earth's land area and contains one-third of humanity.

    (a)   40
    (b)   30
    (c)   25
    (d)   10
    (e)   65

6. What percentage of the world's population live in the *low-income countries* of the world?

    (a)   25
    (b)   50
    (c)   77
    (d)   85
    (e)   95

7. The nickname of the *Manila dump* is

    (a)   Rohooven Heights.
    (b)   Svendoven Mire.
    (c)   Swollen Hollow.
    (d)   Smokey Mountain.

8. The *per-capita GDP* in the United States in 1997 was

    (a) $10,033.
    (b) $51,300.
    (c) $15,400.
    (d) $29,010.
    (e) $37,028.

9.   Which country has the highest score on the *Quality of Life Index*?

    (a)   Canada
    (b)   the United States
    (c)   Brazil
    (d)   Germany

10.   Half of all deaths in *low-income countries* occur among

    (a)   the elderly beyond the age of 65.
    (b)   children under the age of 10.
    (c)   adults between the age of 40 and 59.
    (d)   young adults aged 18-35.

11.   Which of the following is *inaccurate*?

    (a)   Families in poor societies do not depend on women's incomes.
    (b)   In high-income countries, the median age at death is over 65 years of age.
    (c)   The United Nations estimates that in poor countries men own 90 percent of the land.
    (d)   About 70 percent of the world's 1 billion people living near absolute poverty are women.

12.   Which of the following is *not* a type of *slavery* identified in the text?

    (a)   chattel
    (b)   child
    (c)   colonial
    (d)   servile forms of marriage
    (e)   debt bondage

13.   Which of the following is *not* discussed as a correlate of *global poverty*?

    (a)   cultural patterns
    (b)   population growth
    (c)   technology
    (d)   social stratification
    (e)   all are discussed

14.   *Neocolonialism* is

    (a)   primarily an overt political force.
    (b)   a form of economic exploitation that does not involve formal political control.
    (c)   the economic power of the low-income countries being used to control the consumption
            patterns in the high-income countries.
    (d)   the exploitation of the high-income countries by the low-income countries.
    (e)   none of the above

220

15. A model of economic and social development that explains global inequality in terms of technological and cultural differences among societies is _____ theory.

   (a) colonial
   (b) dependency
   (c) modernization
   (d) ecological

16. *Modernization theory* identifies _____ as the greatest barrier to economic development.

   (a) technology
   (b) social equality
   (c) social power
   (d) tradition

17. Which of the following is *not* a stage in *Rostow's model of modernization*?

   (a) colonialism
   (b) traditional
   (c) take-off
   (d) drive to technological maturity
   (e) high mass consumption

18. According to *W. W. Rostow's* modernization model, which stage is Thailand currently in?

   (a) traditional
   (b) take-off
   (c) drive to technological maturity
   (d) residual-dependency

19. Which of the following is *not* a criticism of modernization theory?

   (a) It tends to minimize the connection between rich and poor societies.
   (b) It tends to blame the low-income countries for their own poverty.
   (c) It ignores historical facts that thwart development in poor countries.
   (d) It has fallen short of its own standards of success.
   (e) All are criticisms of this theory.

20. _____ *theory* is a model of economic and social development that explains global inequality in terms of the historical exploitation of poor societies by rich ones.

   (a) Modernization
   (b) Colonial
   (c) Dependency
   (d) Evolutionary
   (e) Ecological

21. Which of the following is *not* mentioned in *Immanuel Wallerstein's* capitalist world-economy model as a reason for the perpetuation of the dependency of the low-income countries?

   (a) narrow, export-oriented economies
   (b) lack of industrial capacity
   (c) foreign debt
   (d) All are mentioned.
   (e) None are mentioned.

22. Which of the following is *not* a criticism of *dependency theory*?

   (a) It assumes that the wealth of the high-income countries is based solely on appropriating resources from low-income societies.
   (b) It tends to blame the low-income countries for their own poverty.
   (c) It does not lend itself to clear policy making.
   (d) It assumes that world capitalism alone has produced global inequality.
   (e) all of these are criticisms of this theory

23. In approximately _____ of the world's countries, living standards are lower than they were in 1980.

   (a) one-third
   (b) one-half
   (c) three-fourths
   (d) eighty-eight percent

24. Which of the following is an *inaccurate* statement regarding *global stratification*?

   (a) According to the United Nations, one-third of the world's countries are living better than they were in the past.
   (b) One insight, offered by modernization theory, is that poverty is partly a problem of technology.
   (c) One insight, derived from dependency theory, is that global inequality is also a political issue.
   (d) While economic development increases living standards, it also establishes a context for less strain being placed on the environment.

Matching

1. ____ Percentage of the world's income controlled by the poorest fifth of the world's population.
2. ____ Two middle-income countries.
3. ____ Two high-income countries.
4. ____ The percentage of people in low-income countries who live in cities.
5. ____ The percentage of the world's population living in low-income countries.
6. ____ The percentage of births attended by trained health personnel in Mexico.
7. ____ The process by which some nations enrich themselves through political and economic control of other nations.
8. ____ Huge businesses that operate in many countries.
9. ____ A model of economic and social development that explains global inequality in terms of technological and cultural differences among societies.
10. ____ A model of economic and social development that explains global inequality in terms of the historical exploitation of poor societies by rich ones.

a.	Venezuela and Malaysia	f.	52
b.	modernization theory	g.	Canada and Singapore
c.	multinational corporations	h.	75
d.	colonialism	i.	dependency theory
e.	8	j.	25

Fill-In

1. Compared to the older "three worlds" model, the new classification system used in the text has two main advantages, including a focus on the single most important dimension that underlies social life-- _____.
2. The richest twenty percent of the U.S. population earns about forty-seven percent of the national income. The richest twenty percent of the *global population* receives about _____ percent of the world income.
3. The *middle-income countries* of the world represent about _____ nations and _____ of the world's population.
4. According to our author, poverty in *low-income countries* is more _____ and more _____ than it is in the United States.
5. The United States had a GDP in 1997 of over _____ dollars.
6. Every day, about _____ pople die around the world of *starvation*.
7. The four types of slavery identified in the text include: _____, _____, _____, and _____ forms of marriage.
8. The *correlates of global poverty* include _____, population _____, _____ patterns, social _____, _____ inequality, and global _____ relationships.
9. _____ is a new form of economic exploitation that does not involve formal political control.
10. _____ *theorists* suggest global inequality reflects differing levels of technological development and cultural differences among societies.

223

11. *W. W. Rostow's* stages of modernization include: the _____,
_____, drive to _____ maturity, and high
mass _____.

12. _____ *theory* maintains that global poverty historically stems from the exploitation of poor societies by rich societies.

13. Immanuel Wallerstein calls the *rich nations* the _____ of the world economy, while he says the *low-income countries* represent the _____ of the world economy.

14. *Modernization theory* maintains that rich societies _____ _____ through capital investment and technological innovation.

15. *Dependency theory* claims that the world economy makes poor nations dependent on rich ones. This dependency involves three factors: narrow, _____ *economies*, lack of _____ *capacity*, and _____ *debt*.

16. Two key to combating global inequality during the next century will be seeing it partly as a problem of _____ and that it is also a _____ problem.

Definition and Short-Answer

1. Define the terms *high-income, middle-income,* and *low-income countries*. Identify the key characteristics of each category. Does this resolve the "terminology" problem?

2. How do the economies in each of the three *levels* or *categories* of countries differ from one another? Make specific reference to *Figures 11-1* and *11-2* in your answer.

3. What factors create the condition of *women* being overrepresented in poverty around the world?

4. What are the *correlates* of global poverty? Describe each.

5. What is *neocolonialism*? Provide an illustration.

6. What are the four stages of *modernization* in Rostow's model of societal change and development?

7. What are the *problems* faced by women in poor countries as a result of modernization?

8. According to *modernization* theorists, in what respects are rich nations part of the solution to global poverty?

9. Differentiate between how *modernization theory* and *dependency theory* view the primary causes of global inequality. Critique each of these theories, identifying the strengths and weaknesses of each in terms of explaining global poverty. How do each differ in terms of recommendations to improve the conditions in low-income countries?

10. Write an essay about *poverty in low-income countries*. What are the statistics of *global poverty*?

PART VI: ANSWERS TO STUDY QUESTIONS

True-False

1.	T	(p. 300)	12.	T	(p. 308)
2.	T	(p. 300)	13.	T	(p. 311)
3.	F	(p. 301)	14.	F	(pp. 314-315)
4.	T	(p. 303)	15.	T	(p. 314)
5.	T	(p. 303)	16.	T	(p. 314)
6.	T	(p. 303)	17.	F	(p. 316)
7.	T	(p. 303)	18.	F	(p. 319)
8.	F	(p. 303)	19.	T	(p. 320)
9.	F	(p. 304)	20.	F	(p. 320)
10.	T	(p. 305)	21.	T	(p. 320)
11.	F	(p. 305)	22.	F	(p. 320)

Multiple Choice

1.	d	(p. 308)	13.	e	(pp. 308-309)
2.	c	(p. 301)	14.	b	(p. 310)
3.	e	(p. 301)	15.	c	(p. 311)
4.	d	(pp. 301-302)	16.	d	(p. 311)
5.	a	(p. 302)	17.	a	(p. 312)
6.	b	(p. 303)	18.	b	(p. 312)
7.	d	(p. 303)	19.	e	(p. 314)
8.	d	(p. 304)	20.	c	(p. 314)
9.	a	(p. 304)	21.	d	(p. 316)
10.	b	(pp. 306-307)	22.	b	(pp. 317-318)
11.	a	(pp. 306-307)	23.	a	(p. 319)
12.	c	(p. 308)	24.	d	(pp. 319-320)

Matching

1.	e	(p. 300)	6.	h	(p. 308)
2.	a	(p. 301)	7.	d	(p. 309)
3.	g	(p. 301)	8.	c	(p. 310)
4.	j	(p. 303)	9.	b	(p. 311)
5.	f	(p. 305)	10.	i	(p. 314)

Fill-In

1. economic development (p. 300)
2. 80 (p. 300)
3. 90, one-third (pp. 301-302)
4. severe, extensive (pp. 304-305)

5. 7.8 trillion (p. 304)
6. 40,000 (p. 307)
7. chattel, child, debt bondage, servile (p. 308)
8. technology, growth, cultural, stratification, gender, power (pp. 309)
9. neocolonialism (p. 310)
10. modernization (p. 311)
11. traditional, take-off, technological, consumption (p. 312)
12. dependency (p. 314)
13. core, periphery (315)
14. produce wealth (p. 316)
15. export-oriented, industrial, foreign (p. 316)
16. technology, political (p. 320)

PART VII: IN FOCUS—IMPORTANT ISSUES

- Global Stratification

  Describe the general characteristics for each of the following categories of countries:

  high-income countries

  middle-income countries

  low-income-countries

- Global Wealth and Poverty

What is the evidence that poverty in poor countries is *more severe* and *more extensive* than in the rich nations?

Identify and illustrate the four types of *slavery* found around the world.

Describe how each of the following are *correlates of poverty*:

   technology

   population growth

   cultural patterns

   social stratification

   gender inequality

   global power relationships

- Global Stratification: Theoretical Analysis

What are the major tenets of *modernization theory*?

Outline and describe *Rostow's stages of modernization*:

According to modernization theory, what is the *role of rich nations* in terms of global stratification?

What are the five basic *criticisms* of modernization theory?

What are the basic tenets of *dependency theory*?

According to Immanuel Wallerstein, what are the three factors involved in the dependency of poor nations on rich nations?

What are the five basic *criticisms* of dependency theory?

- Global Stratification: Looking Ahead

What is the evidence that global stratification is both an issue of *technology* and *politics*?

What do you suggest can be done to reduce the polarization of high-income and low-income countries?

PART VIII: ANALYSIS AND COMMENT

Global Sociology

"God Made Me to Be a Slave"

Key Points: Questions:

"A Different Kind of Poverty: A Report from India"

Key Points: Questions:

"Modernization and Women: A Report From Rural Bangladesh"

Key Points: Questions:

Controversy and Debate

"Will the World Starve?"

Key Points: Questions:

Window on the World--Global Maps 12-1 and 12-2

"Median Age at Death in Global Perspective"

Key Points: Questions:

"Prosperity and Stagnation in Global Perspective"

Key Points: Questions:

13   Gender Stratification

PART I: CHAPTER OUTLINE

I.   Gender and Inequality
- A.   Male-Female Differences
- B.   Gender In Global Perspective
  1. The Israeli Kibbutzim
  2. Margaret Mead's Research
  3. George Murdock's Research
  4. In Sum: Gender and Culture
- C.   Patriarchy and Sexism
  1. The Cost of Sexism
  2. Is Patriarchy Inevitable?

III.   Gender and Socialization
- A.   Gender and the Family
- B.   Gender and the Peer Group
- C.   Gender and Schooling
- D.   Gender and the Mass Media

IV.   Gender and Social Stratification
- A.   Working Women and Men
  1. Gender and Occupations
- B.   Housework
- C.   Gender, Income, and Wealth
- D.   Gender and Education
- E.   Gender and Politics
- F.   Gender and the Military
- G.   Are Women A Minority?
- H.   Minority Women
- I.   Violence Against Women
  1. Sexual Harassment
  2. Pornography

PART II: LEARNING OBJECTIVES

1. To know the distinction between male-female differences and gender stratification.

2. To become aware of the various types of social organizations found globally based upon the relationship between females and males.

3. To be able to describe the link between patriarchy and sexism, and to see how the nature of each is changing in modern society.

4. To be able to describe the role that gender plays in socialization in the family, the peer group, schooling, the mass media, and adult interaction.

5. To see how gender stratification occurs in the work world, education, and politics.

6. To consider key arguments in the debate over whether women constitute a minority.

7. To consider how the structural-functional and social-conflict paradigms help explain the origins and persistence of gender inequality.

8. To begin to recognize the extent to which women are victims of violence, and to begin to understand what we can do to change this problem.

9. To consider the central ideas of feminism, the variations of feminism, and resistance to feminism.

PART III: KEY CONCEPTS

expressive qualities

femininity

feminism

gender

gender identity

gender roles

gender stratification

instrumental qualities

kibbutzim

liberal feminism

masculinity

matriarchy

minority

patriarchy

pornography

radical feminism

sexism

sexual harassment

socialist feminism

PART IV: IMPORTANT RESEARCHERS

Margaret Mead   George Murdock

Talcott Parsons   Janet Lever

Jesse Bernard   Carol Gilligan

Friedrich Engels   Felice Schwartz

PART V: STUDY QUESTIONS

<u>True-False</u>

1.   T   F   *Gender* refers to the biological distinction between females and males.
2.   T   F   *Gender stratification* is perhaps most clearly illustrated by the fact that men's life
               expectancy is greater than the life expectancy for women.
3.   T   F   The experience of the *Israeli Kibbutzim* suggests that cultures have considerable
               latitude in defining what is masculine and feminine.
4.   T   F   The conclusions made by *Margaret Mead* in her research on three New Guinea
               societies is consistent with the sociobiological argument that "persistent biological
               distinctions may undermine gender equality."
5.   T   F   *George Murdock's* cross-cultural research has shown some general patterns in terms
               of which type of activities are classified as *masculine* or *feminine;* however, beyond
               this general pattern, significant variation exists.
6.   T   F   Globally, *hunting* and *warfare* generally fall to men, while home-centered tasks such
               as cooking and child care generally fall to women.
7.   T   F   In global perspective, societies consistently define only a few specific activities as
               feminine or *masculine.*

234

8.	T	F	*Patriarchy* is a form of social organization in which males dominate females.
9.	T	F	Research suggests that the vast majority of young people in the United States develop consistently "masculine" or "feminine" personalities.
10.	T	F	Janet Lever's research on *play* suggests that boys favor team sports with complex rules and clear objectives.
11.	T	F	Carol Gilligan's research on patterns of moral reasoning suggests that boys learn to reason according to "rules and principles" more so than girls.
12.	T	F	In 1997, almost 70 percent of people in the U.S. ages sixteen and over were working for income: 75 percent of men and 59.8 percent of women.
13.	T	F	Women with children under the age of six years have a much smaller proportion of their number working in the labor force than married women with no children.
14.	T	F	According to Naomi Wolf, the *beauty myth* arises, first, because society teaches women to measure themselves in terms of physical appearance, with standards that are unattainable.
15.	T	F	In 1998, women made up about thirty-five percent of the *paid labor force*.
16.	T	F	With women's entry into the labor force, the amount of *housework* performed by women has declined, but the share women do has stayed about the same.
17.	T	F	Approximately two-thirds of the *pay gap* between men and women is the result of two factors--types of work and family responsibilities.
18.	T	F	The *mommy track* is a concept developed by Felice Schwartz that is applied to educated women who marry, have children, and choose to stay home as full-time homemakers.
19.	T	F	Today, over one-half of all Bachelor's degrees are earned by *women*.
20.	T	F	*Minority females* earn more on average than minority males.
21.	T	F	According to the definition given in the text, *sexual harassment* always involves physical contact.
22.	T	F	According to structural-functionalist Talcott Parsons, gender, at least in the traditional sense, forms a *complementary* set of roles that links men and women together.
23.	T	F	The *ERA* was first proposed to Congress in 1972.
24.	T	F	*Liberal feminists* feel that individuals should be free to develop their own abilities and talents.

Multiple Choice

1. The personal traits and social positions that members of a society attach to being female and male refers to

   (a)   gender.
   (b)   sex.
   (c)   sexual orientation.
   (d)   gender stratification.

2.   The unequal distribution of wealth, power, and privilege between men and women refers to

(a)   secondary sex characteristics.
(b)   gender division.
(c)   gender stratification.
(d)   gender discrimination.
(e)   sexual orientation.

3.   Which of the following has been found to be *true* about men and women?

(a)   Global data show their average weights to be about the same.
(b)   There are no overall differences in intelligence between males and females.
(c)   Men consistently outperform women in tests of long-term endurance.
(d)   Global data show their average longevity is about the same.

4.   Investigations of the *Israeli Kibbutzim* have indicated

(a)   they are collective settlements.
(b)   their members historically have embraced social equality.
(c)   they support evidence of wide cultural latitude in defining what is feminine and masculine.
(d)   men and women living there share both work and decision making.
(e)   all of the above

5.   The social inequality of men and women has been shown to be culturally based rather than exclusively biological by which of the following studies?

(a)   Murdock's study of preindustrial societies
(b)   Israeli kibbutzim studies
(c)   New Guinea studies by Margaret Mead
(d)   all of the above

6.   Margaret Mead's research on gender in three societies in New Guinea illustrates that

(a)   diffusion tends to standardize gender role assignments for women and men.
(b)   gender is primarily biologically determined.
(c)   gender is treated virtually the same across societies.
(d)   gender is a variable creation of culture.
(e)   while gender roles vary cross-culturally for men, they are very consistent for women.

7.   Among the *Mundugumor*, Margaret Mead found

(a)   both females and males to be very passive.
(b)   females to be very aggressive and males to be passive.
(c)   both males and females to be aggressive and hostile.
(d)   sex roles to be very similar to what they are in the U.S.

8. A form of social organization in which females are dominated by males is termed

   (a) matriarchal.
   (b) oligarchal.
   (c) patriarchy.
   (d) egalitarian.

9. The belief that one sex is innately superior to the other refers to

   (a) homophobia.
   (b) heterosexism.
   (c) sexism.
   (d) sexual individualism.

10. _____ are attitudes and activities that a society links to each sex.

   (a) Gender roles
   (b) Sexual orientation
   (c) Gender stratification
   (d) Gender identity

11. Which sociologist suggests that, soon after birth, family members introduce infants to either a *pink* or a *blue* world, depending on whether the infant is a she or a he?

   (a) Karl Marx
   (b) Jessie Bernard
   (c) George Peter Murdock
   (d) Talcott Parsons

12. Research by Carol Gilligan and Janet Lever demonstrates the influence of _____ on gender roles.

   (a) the peer group
   (b) biology
   (c) religion
   (d) personality

13. Which of the following statements about women in the labor force is *inaccurate*?

   (a) Most married women are in the paid labor force.
   (b) Most married women without children are in the paid labor force.
   (c) Most married women with children under the age of six are in the paid labor force.
   (d) About 46 percent of all women in the paid labor force work in either clerical or service type jobs.
   (e) Less than one-half of all divorced women with children work in the paid labor force.

14. What percentage of *married couples* in the U.S. today count on two incomes?

    (a) 25
    (b) 60
    (c) 87
    (d) 36

15. On average, what percentage of a male's income does a female earn?

    (a) 39
    (b) 48
    (c) 57
    (d) 74
    (e) 89

16. Two-thirds of the *earnings disparity* between men and women is explained by two variables

    (a) age and geography.
    (b) marital status and education.
    (c) type of work and family responsibilities.
    (d) father's occupation and health.

17. After the 1998 national elections, how many of the 100 U.S. Senators were women?

    (a) 0
    (b) 2
    (c) 9
    (d) 20
    (e) 31

18. As a woman, where are you most likely to suffer *physical violence*?

    (a) at work
    (b) at home
    (c) among friends
    (d) on the streets

19. Many feminists want our society to use a(n) _____ standard when measuring for *sexual harassment*.

    (a) effect
    (b) intention
    (c) quid pro quo
    (d) quid pro quid

238

20. *Talcott Parsons* argued that there exist two *complementary role sets* which exist to link males and females together with social institutions. He called these

   (a) rational and irrational.
   (b) effective and affective.
   (c) fundamental and secondary.
   (d) residual and basic.
   (e) instrumental and expressive.

21. Which theorist suggested that the male dominance over women was linked to technological advances which led to surpluses of valued resources?

   (a) Talcott Parsons
   (b) Erving Goffman
   (c) Friedrich Engels
   (d) Janet Lever

22. Which of the following nations has the highest rate of *contraception use* by women of childbearing age?

   (a) Norway
   (b) the United Kingdom
   (c) the United States
   (d) Ireland

23. Which of the following is *not* a variation with *feminism*?

   (a) liberal
   (b) socialist
   (c) radical
   (d) expressive

24. What variant of feminism links the social disadvantage of women primarily to the *capitalist economic system*?

   (a) socialist
   (b) expressive
   (c) communal
   (d) liberal

1. ____ The personal traits and social positions that members of a society attach to being female and male.
2. ____ The unequal distribution of wealth, power, and privilege between men and women.
3. ____ Did groundbreaking research on gender in New Guinea.
4. ____ A form of social organization in which females dominate males.
5. ____ The belief that one sex is innately superior to the other.
6. ____ Attitudes and activities that a society links to each sex.
7. ____ After spending a year watching children at play, concluded that boys favor team sports with complex rules and clear objectives.
8. ____ Any category of people, distinguished by physical or cultural difference, that is socially disadvantaged.
9. ____ Comments, gestures, or physical contact of a sexual nature that are deliberate, repeated, and unwelcome.
10. ____ A structural-functionalist, differentiated between instrumental and expressive roles.
11. ____ Argued that capitalism intensifies male dominance.
12. ____ The advocacy of social equality for the men and women in opposition to patriarchy and sexism.

a.	matriarchy	g.	gender
b.	feminism	h.	sexual harassment
c.	Friedrich Engels	i.	a minority
d.	Janet Lever	j.	gender roles
e.	gender stratification	k.	Talcott Parsons
f.	sexism	l.	Margaret Mead

Fill-In

1. According to research cited in the text, adolescent males exhibit greater _____ ability, while adolescent females excel in _____ skills.
2. _____ are collective Jewish settlements in Israel in which remarkable strides have been made in social equality between women and men.
3. In her research on gender roles, Margaret Mead focused on three New Guinea societies, the _____, _____, and the _____.
4. _____ is the belief that one sex is innately superior to the other.
5. _____ _____ are attitudes and activities that a society links to each sex.
6. Today in the United States, _____ percent of *married women with children under the age of six* are in the labor force.
7. In the United States, _____ percent of women over the age of 16 were working for income in 1998. The comparable figure for men was _____.
8. In 1998, women were _____ percent of the *labor force* in the United States.
9. With women's entry into the labor force, the amount of *housework* performed by women has declined, but the _____ women do has stayed about the same.

10. Two factors--type of _____ and _____ responsibilities--account for about two-thirds of the earnings disparities between women and men.

11. A _____ is any category of people, distinguished by physical or cultural difference, that is socially disadvantaged.

12. The two types of *violence* against women focused on in the text include _____ and _____ .

13. _____ _____ refers to comments, gestures, or physical contact of a sexual nature that are deliberate, repeated, and unwelcome.

14. Talcott Parsons identified two *complementary roles* that link men and women. These include the _____ and _____ .

15. _____ refers to the advocacy of social equality for men and women, in opposition to patriarchy and sexism.

16. Basic *feminist ideas* include the importance of _____ , the expanding human _____ , eliminating gender _____ , ending sexual _____ , and promoting sexual _____ .

17. The three types of *feminism* are _____ , _____ , and _____ .

Definition and Short-Answer

1. Briefly review the significant events in the history of the *Women's Movement* during the nineteenth century.

2. Compare the research by *Margaret Mead* in New Guinea with the research done at the Israeli *Kibbutzim* in terms of the cultural variability of gender roles.

3. What generalizations about the linkage between *sex* and *gender* can be made based on the cross-cultural research of *George Murdock*?

4. According to the author, is *patriarchy* inevitable? Why? What roles have technological advances and industrialization played in the changes in the relative statuses of women and men in society?

5. *Table 13-1* presents lists of traits linked to the traditional gender identities of *femininity* and *masculinity*. Develop a questionnaire using the traits identified in this table to survey females and males to determine to what extent these traits differentiate between the sexes.

6. Identify five important points about *gender stratification* within the occupational domain of our society.

7. What are the explanations as to why males dominate *politics*? To what extent are the roles of women changing in this sphere of social life? What factors are influencing these changes?

8. Review the issue of *violence against women* in our society. What are the types of violence discussed? What are the demographics of violence?

9. Are women a *minority group*? What are the arguments for and against this idea? What is the evidence being presented in the Controversy and Debate box at the end of the chapter to suggest men may be a minority group?

10. Compare the analyses of gender stratification as provided through the *structural-functional* and *social-conflict* paradigms.

11. What are the five *basic principles* of *feminism*? Discuss the specific examples for each.

12. What are the three types of *feminism*? Briefly differentiate between them in terms of the basic arguments being made about gender roles in society.

13.   What are the three general criticisms of the conclusions being made by *social-conflict* theorists concerning gender stratification?
14.   What evidence can you provide from your own experience and observations concerning the argument being made by *Jessie Bernard* about the *pink* and *blue* worlds?

PART VI: ANSWERS TO STUDY QUESTIONS

True-False

1.	F	(p. 325)	13.	F	(p. 333)
2.	F	(p. 326)	14.	T	(pp. 334-335)
3.	T	(pp. 326-327)	15.	F	(p. 334)
4.	F	(p. 327)	16.	T	(pp. 336-337)
5.	T	(p. 327)	17.	T	(p. 337)
6.	T	(p. 327)	18.	F	(p. 337)
7.	F	(p. 328)	19.	T	(p. 338)
8.	T	(p. 328)	18.	F	(pp. 337-338)
9.	F	(p. 330)	19.	T	(p. 338)
10.	T	(p. 331)	20.	F	(p. 340)
11.	T	(p. 331)	21.	F	(p. 341)
12.	T	(pp. 331-332)	22.	T	(p. 343)

Multiple-Choice

1.	a	(p. 325)	13.	d	(pp. 333-335)
2.	c	(p. 326)	14.	b	(p. 335)
3.	b	(p. 326)	15.	d	(p. 337)
4.	e	(pp. 326-327)	16.	c	(p. 338)
5.	d	(pp. 326-327)	17.	c	(p. 339)
6.	d	(p. 327)	18.	b	(p. 341)
7.	b	(p. 327)	19.	a	(p. 343)
8.	c	(p. 328)	20.	e	(pp. 343-344)
9.	c	(p. 328)	21.	c	(p. 344)
10.	a	(p. 330)	22.	b	(p. 346)
11.	b	(p. 231)	23.	d	(p. 346)
12.	a	(p. 331)	24.	a	(p. 346)

Matching

1.	g	(p. 325)	7.	d	(p. 331)
2.	e	(p. 326)	8.	i	(p. 340)
3.	l	(p. 327)	9.	h	(p. 341)
4.	a	(p. 328)	10.	k	(p. 343)
5.	f	(p. 328)	11.	c	(p. 344)
6.	j	(p. 330)	12.	b	(p. 345)

1.   mathematical, verbal (p. 326)
2.   Kibbutzim (p. 326)
3.   Arapesh, Mundugumor, Tchambuli (p. 327)
4.   Sexism (p. 328)
5.   Gender roles (p. 330)
6.   64 (p. 335)
7.   59.8, 74.9 (p. 333)
8.   46 (p. 334)
9.   share (p. 338)
10.   work, family (p. 338)
11.   minority (p. 340)
12.   sexual harassment, pornography (p. 341)
13.   Sexual harassment (p. 341)
14.   instrumental, expressive (p. 344)
15.   Feminism (p. 345)
16.   change, choice, stratification, violence, autonomy (pp. 345-346)
17.   liberal, socialist, radical (p. 346)

PART VII: IN FOCUS--IMPORTANT ISSUES

• Gender and Inequality

What does *Figure 13-1* indicate about the biological differences between females and males?

What are the significant biological differences between females and males?

What conclusions do you make when weighing the evidence presented by Margaret Mead and George Murdock concerning cross-cultural patterns of *gender roles*?

What are three *costs of sexism*?

- Gender and Socialization

  Provide one illustration from the text concerning each of the following influences on *gender role socialization*.

  the family

  the peer group

  schooling

  the mass media

- Gender and Social Stratification

  Identify the percentages of employed people for each of the following categories:

  males (sixteen and older): _____
  females (sixteen and older): _____
  married women with children under the age of six: _____
  married women with children between the ages of six and seventeen: _____
  divorced women with children: _____

What does *Figure 13-2* tell us? Why do you think these changes in labor force participation rates have occurred?

How does employment status affect women's *housework* labor? How about marital status? Presence of children? What about for men?

What are the two factors that most influence the differences in pay for women and men?

How has women's participation in the *military* changed since the Revolutionary War?

Are women a *minority group*? Why?

How is *sexual harassment* defined?

How is *pornography* defined?

In what ways do sexual harassment and pornography represent *violence against women*?

- Theoretical Analysis of Gender

  Briefly discuss how each of the following theoretical paradigms views the issue of gender in society:

     structural-functionalism

     social-conflict

- Feminism

  What are the four basic *feminist ideas* identified in the text?

  Describe each of the following *types of feminism*:

     liberal

     socialist

     radical

  Why is there *opposition to feminism*?

246

- Looking Ahead: Gender In the Twenty-First Century

What is the vision offered by the author concerning the role of gender in society over the next century?

PART VIII: ANALYSIS AND COMMENT

Applying Sociology

"Masculinity as Contest"

Key Points: Questions:

Critical Thinking

"Pretty Is as Pretty Does: The Beauty Myth"

Key Points: Questions:

Global Sociology

"Female Genital Mutilation: Violence in the Name of Morality"

Key Points: Questions:

Controversy and Debate

"Men's Rights! Are Men Really So Privileged?"

Key Points: Questions:

Window on the World--Global Maps 13-1, 13-2, 13-3

"Women's Power in Global Perspective"

Key Points: Questions:

"Women's Paid Employment in Global Perspective"

Key Points: Questions:

"Housework in Global Perspective"

Key Points: Questions:

Seeing Ourselves--National Map 13-1

"Women in State Government across the U.S."

Key Points: Questions:

14 Race and Ethnicity

PART I: CHAPTER OUTLINE

I. The Social Meaning of Race and Ethnicity
    A. Race
        1. Racial Typology
        2. A Trend toward Mixture
    B. Ethnicity
    C. Minorities

II. Prejudice
    A. Stereotypes
    B. Racism
    C. Theories of Prejudice
        1. Scapegoat Theory
        2. Authoritarian Personality Theory
        3. Cultural Theory
        4. Conflict Theory

III. Discrimination
    A. Institutional Prejudice and Discrimination
    B. Prejudice and Discrimination: The Vicious Cycle

IV. Majority and Minority: Patterns of Interaction
    A. Pluralism
    B. Assimilation
    C. Segregation
    D. Genocide

V. Race and Ethnicity in the United States
    A. Native Americans
    B. White Anglo-Saxon Protestants
    C. African Americans
    D. Asian Americans
        1. Chinese Americans
        2. Japanese Americans
        3. Recent Asian Immigrants

PART II: LEARNING OBJECTIVES

1.   To develop an understanding about the biological basis for definitions of race.
2.   To be able to distinguish between the biological concept of race and the cultural concept of ethnicity.
3.   To be able to identify the characteristics of a minority group.
4.   To be able to identify and describe the two forms of prejudice.
5.   To be able to identify and describe the four theories of prejudice.
6.   Be able to distinguish between prejudice and discrimination.
7.   To be able to provide examples of institutional prejudice and discrimination.
8.   To be able to see how prejudice and discrimination combine to create a vicious cycle.
9.   To be abe to describe the patterns of interaction between minorities and the majority.
10.   To be able to describe the histories and relative statuses of each of the racial and ethnic groups identified in the text.

PART III: KEY CONCEPTS

affirmative action

American dilemma

assimilation

authoritarian personality

Brown vs. the Board of Education of Topeka

de facto segregation

de jure segregation

discrimination

ethnicity

genocide

hypersegregation

internal colonialism

institutional discrimination

institutional prejudice

minority

miscegenation

pluralism

prejudice

race

racism

scapegoat theory

segregation

stereotype

WASP

white ethnics

PART IV: IMPORTANT RESEARCHERS

Robert Merton   Emory Bogardus

T. W. Adorno   Thomas Sowell

PART V: STUDY QUESTIONS

True-False

1.   T   F   Physical diversity appeared among our human ancestors as the result of living in different *geographic regions* of the word.

2.   T   F   Although *racial categories* point to some biological elements, *race* is a socially constructed concept.

3.   T   F   According to the author of our text, for sociological purposes the concepts of *race* and *ethnicity* can be used interchangeably.

4.   T   F   A racial or ethnic *minority* is a category of people, distinguished by physical or cultural traits, who are socially disadvantaged.

5.   T   F   Ethnicity involves *even more variability* than race.

6.   T   F   The *scapegoat theory* links prejudice to frustration and suggests that prejudice is likely to be pronounced among people who themselves are disadvantaged.

7.   T   F   Emory Bogardus' concept of *social distance* is used in the *cultural theory* of prejudice, which suggests that some prejudice is found in everyone because it is embedded in culture.

8.   T   F   Thomas Sowell has argued that *IQ* is directly related to biological forces, citing the great stability in average IQ scores for different categories of racial and ethnic groups.

9.   T   F   In *Robert Merton's* typology of patterns of prejudice and discrimination, an unprejudiced-nondiscriminator is labeled an "all-weather liberal."

10.   T   F   According to the author, as a cultural process, *assimilation* involves changes in ethnicity but not in race.

11.   T   F   The United States Supreme Court decisions such as the *1954 Brown case* have reduced the presence of *de jure segregation* in the United States.

12.   T   F   *Genocide* is the systematic annihilation of one category of people by another.

13.   T   F   *Native Americans* were not granted citizenship in the United States until 1924.

14.   T   F   *White Anglo-Saxon Protestants* (WASPS) represent less than ten percent of the population of the United States.

15.   T   F   The *Dred Scott* Supreme Court decision declared that blacks were to have full rights and privileges as citizens of the United States.

16.   T   F   *Jim Crow Laws* illustrate institutional discrimination.

17.   T   F   The largest category of *Asian Americans* is people of Chinese ancestry.

18.   T   F   Though a "silent minority," *Chinese Americans* have higher poverty rates and lower average family incomes than African Americans and Hispanics.

19.   T   F   *Issei* is a term referring to foreign-born Japanese.

20.   T   F   More than one-half of *Hispanics* in the United States are *Mexican Americans*.

21.   T   F   *Cuban Americans* have the lowest average family income and highest poverty rates of all Hispanic Americans.

22.   T   F   The highest rates of *immigration* to the United States occurred during the 1920s and 1930s.

1.   Linda Brown was not permitted to enroll in the second grade at an elementary school near her home in Topeka, Kansas because she was

    (a)   Jewish.
    (b)   African American.
    (c)   blind.
    (d)   HIV positive.
    (e)   Iranian.

2.   A socially constructed category composed of people who share biologically transmitted traits that members of a society deem socially significant is the definition for

    (a)   race.
    (b)   minority group.
    (c)   ethnicity.
    (d)   assimilation.

3.   Today in the United States, *interracial births* account for _____ percent of all births.

    (a)   less than 1
    (b)   2
    (c)   4
    (d)   6
    (e)   9

4.   A shared cultural heritage is the definition for

    (a)   a minority group.
    (b)   race.
    (c)   assimilation.
    (d)   pluralism.
    (e)   ethnicity.

5.   Members of an *ethnic category* share

    (a)   common ancestors, language, and religion.
    (b)   only biological distinctions.
    (c)   residential location.
    (d)   social class ranking.
    (e)   none of the above.

6. Among people of *European descent,* the largest number of people in the U.S. trace their ancestry back to

   (a) Italy.
   (b) Ireland.
   (c) England.
   (d) Germany.
   (e) Russia.

7. *Minority groups* have two major characteristics:

   (a) race and ethnicity.
   (b) religion and ethnicity   .
   (c) physical traits and political orientation.
   (d) sexual orientation and race.
   (e) distinctive identity and subordination.

8. What is the term for a category of people, set apart by physical or cultural traits, that is socially disadvantaged?

   (a) minority group
   (b) stereotype
   (c) ethnicity
   (d) race

9. What is the term for a rigid and irrational generalization about an entire category of people?

   (a) racism
   (b) discrimination
   (c) stereotype
   (d) prejudice

10. What is the term for an exaggerated description applied to every person in some category?

   (a) racism
   (b) stereotype
   (c) discrimination
   (d) prejudice

11. A *form of prejudice* referring to the belief that one racial category is innately superior or inferior to another is called

    (a) stereotyping.
    (b) discrimination.
    (c) racism.
    (d) scapegoating.

12. One explanation of the origin of prejudice is found in the concept of the *authoritarian personality*. Such a personality exhibits

    (a) an attitude of authority over others believed to be inferior.
    (b) frustration over personal troubles directed toward someone less powerful.
    (c) rigid conformity to conventional cultural norms and values.
    (d) social distance from others deemed inferior.

13. Treating various categories of people unequally refers to

    (a) prejudice.
    (b) stereotyping.
    (c) miscegenation.
    (d) discrimination.

14. *Robert Merton's* study of the relationship between prejudice and discrimination revealed one behavioral type that discriminates against persons even though he or she is not prejudiced. This person would be called a(n)

    (a) active bigot.
    (b) all-weather liberal.
    (c) timid bigot.
    (d) fair-weather liberal.

15. According to the work of W. I. Thomas, a *vicious cycle* is formed by which variables?

    (a) miscegenation and authoritarianism
    (b) race and ethnicity
    (c) pluralism and assimilation
    (d) segregation and integration
    (e) prejudice and discrimination

16. A state in which racial and ethnic minorities are distinct but have social parity is termed

    (a) segregation.
    (b) pluralism.
    (c) integration.
    (d) assimilation.

17. *Pluralism* has only limited application in U.S. society because

    (a)   most Americans only want to maintain their distinctive identities to a point.
    (b)   our society's tolerance for diversity is limited.
    (c)   people of different colors and cultures don't have equal standing.
    (d)   all of the above

18. The process by which minorities gradually adopt patterns of the dominant culture is known as

    (a)   pluralism.
    (b)   amalgamation.
    (c)   assimilation.
    (d)   miscegnation.

19. *Miscegenation* is

    (a)   the biological reproduction by partners of different racial categories.
    (b)   the process by which minorities gradually adopt patterns of the dominant culture.
    (c)   a state in which all categories of people are distinct but have social parity.
    (d)   a condition of prejudice leading to discrimination.

20. In _____ the U.S. government made Native Americans wards of the state and set out to resolve the "Indian problem."

    (a)   1770
    (b)   1807
    (c)   1871
    (d)   1911
    (e)   1946

21. Which of the following statements is/are accurate concerning *white Anglo Saxon Protestants (WASPs)?*

    (a)   They represent about twenty percent of our nation's population.
    (b)   Historically, WASP immigrants were highly skilled and motivated to achieve by what we now call the Protestant work ethic.
    (c)   WASPs were never one single social group.
    (d)   The majority of people in the upper-class in the United States are still WASPs.
    (e)   All of the above are accurate statements about WASPs.

22. In 1865, the _____ to the Constitution *outlawed slavery.*

    (a)   Thirteenth Amendment
    (b)   Civil Rights Act
    (c)   Equal Rights Amendment
    (d)   Twenty-sixth Amendment

23.   *Jim Crow Law:*

   (a)   protected freed slaves prior to the Civil War.
   (b)   gave Native Americans residency rights west of the Mississippi.
   (c)   integrated schools.
   (d)   are examples of institutional discrimination.
   (e)   emerged during the post-World War II economic boom period.

24.   Approximately what percentage of African Americans are living in poverty today?

   (a)   10
   (b)   41
   (c)   19
   (d)   62
   (e)   24

25.   Which of the following statements concerning *Chinese Americans* is/are accurate?

   (a)   In 1882, the U.S. government passed the first of several laws restricting Chinese immigration.
   (b)   Census data puts the median Chinese American family income above the national average.
   (c)   Chinese Americans have a higher poverty rate than the national average.
   (d)   The percentage of Chinese Americans who have graduated college is twice the national average.
   (e)   All of the above are accurate statements.

26.   Which category of *Asian Americans* has the highest median family income?

   (a)   Chinese
   (b)   Filipino
   (c)   Japanese
   (d)   Korean

27.   *Mexican Americans* account for _____ of all Hispanics living in the United States.

   (a)   one-third
   (b)   two-thirds
   (c)   one-fifth
   (d)   one-half

28.   In 1997, the *median family income* for whites was about $46,800. For African Americans the median family income was $28,600. What was the figure for Hispanics?

(a) $22,700
(b) $28,200
(c) $31,600
(d) $37,900

Matching

1. ___   A socially constructed category composed of people who share biologically transmitted traits that members of a society consider important.
2. ___   A shared cultural heritage.
3. ___   A category of people, distinguished by physical or cultural traits, that is socially disadvantaged.
4. ___   An approach contending that while extreme prejudice may characterize some people, some prejudice is found in everyone.
5. ___   A person or category of people, typically with little power, whom people unfairly blame for their troubles.
6. ___   A theory holding that prejudice springs from frustration among people who are themselves disadvantaged.
7. ___   A state in which racial and ethnic minorities are distinct but have social parity.
8. ___   The process by which minorities gradually adopt patterns of the dominant culture.
9. ___   Non-WASPs whose ancestors lived in Ireland, Poland, Germany, Italy, or other European countries.
10. ___   Hostility toward foreigners.

a.	xenophobia	f.	white ethnic Americans
b.	assimilation	g.	cultural theory
c.	minority	h.	pluralism
d.	scapegoat	i.	race
e.	ethnicity	j.	scapegoat theory

Fill-In

1.   The term _____ refers to a socially constructed category composed of men and women who share biologically transmitted traits that members of society consider important.
2.   The three part scheme of racial classification developed by biologists during the nineteenth century included _____, _____, and

       _____.
3.   While *race* is a _____ concept, *ethnicity* is a _____ concept.
4.   Two major characteristics of *minorities* are that they have a _____ identity and are _____ by the social-stratification system.

5.	A _____ refers to prejudicial views or descriptions of some category of people.

6.	_____ *theory* holds that prejudice springs from frustration.

7.	Thomas Sowell has demonstrated that most of the documented racial difference in intelligence are not due to _____ but to people's _____.

8.	_____ prejudice or discrimination refers to bias in attitudes or actions inherent in the operation of any of society's institutions.

9.	_____ is the process by which minorities gradually adopt patterns of the dominant culture.

10.	_____ is the systematic annihilation of one category of people by another.

11.	In _____, the United States declared Native Americans wards of the government and set out to resolve "the Indian problem" through forced assimilation. Not until _____ were Native Americans entitled to U.S. citizenship.

12.	In the _____ _____ *case* of 1857, the U.S. Supreme Court addressed the question, "Are blacks citizens?" by writing "We think they are not...."

13.	In 1865, the _____ _____ to the Constitution outlawed slavery.

14.	*Gunnar Myrdal* argued that the denial of basic rights and freedoms to entire categories of Americans was the _____.

15.	In 1997 the *median family income* for the entire population of the U.S. was $44,568. For *African Americans* this figure was _____.

16.	Approximately _____ percent of *Asian Americans* live in California.

17.	In 1999, *Hispanics* represented _____ percent of the U.S. population.

18.	More than _____ *immigrants* have come to the U.S. each year during the 1990s.

Short-Answer and Definition

1.	Identify and describe the four *explanations* of why prejudice exists.

2.	Differentiate between the concepts *prejudice* and *discrimination*.

3.	What are the four types of people identified by *Robert Merton's* typology of patterns of prejudice and discrimination? Provide an illustration for each.

4.	What is *institutional prejudice and discrimination*? Provide two illustrations.

5.	What are three criticisms of *affirmative action*? What are three reasons given by proponents of affirmative action to continue this social policy.

6.	What are the four models representing the *patterns of interaction* between minority groups and the majority group? Define and discuss an illustration for each of these.

7.	In what three important ways did Japanese immigration and assimilation into U.S. society differ from the Chinese?

8.	How do Native Americans, African Americans, Hispanic Americans, and Asian Americans compare to whites in terms of relative social standing using the variables of *educational achievement, family income,* and *poverty rates?*

9.	What was the *Dred Scott* ruling by the Supreme Court?

10.	What was the Court's ruling in *Brown vs. the Board of Education of Topeka case?*

11.	What is the *American Dilemma?*

12.	Referring to *Figure 14-3,* discuss the changing patterns in immigration to the United States. What factors do you think have most influenced these patterns?

14. What are the two major characteristics of a *minority group*?
15. Differentiate between the concepts of *race* and *ethnicity*.
16. How are the changing patterns in *immigration* likely to influence the future of the United States?

PART VI: ANSWERS TO STUDY QUESTIONS

True-False

1.	T	(p. 354)	12.	T	(p. 365)
2.	T	(p. 354)	13.	T	(p. 367)
3.	F	(p. 355)	14.	F	(p. 367)
4.	T	(p. 356)	15.	F	(p. 369)
5.	T	(p. 356)	16.	T	(p. 369)
6.	T	(p. 359)	17.	T	(p. 370)
7.	T	(p. 360)	18.	F	(p. 371)
8.	F	(p. 361)	19.	T	(p. 372)
9.	T	(p. 362)	20.	T	(p. 375)
10.	T	(p. 364)	21.	F	(p. 376)
11.	T	(pp. 364-365)	22.	F	(p. 377)

Multiple Choice

1.	b	(p. 353)	15.	e	(p. 362)
2.	a	(p. 354)	16.	b·	(p. 363)
3.	c	(p. 355)	17.	d	(p. 363)
4.	e	(p. 355)	18.	c	(p. 363)
5.	a	(p. 356)	19.	a	(p. 364)
6.	d	(p. 356)	20.	c	(p. 365)
7.	e	(p. 356)	21.	a	(p. 367)
8.	a	(p. 356)	22.	d	(p. 369)
9.	d	(p. 357)	23.	e	(p. 367)
10.	b	(p. 359)	24.	e	(p. 371)
11.	c	(p. 359)	25.	e	(p. 371)
12.	c	(p. 359)	26.	c	(p. 371)
13.	d	(p. 361)	27.	d	(p. 375)
14.	d	(p. 362)	28.	b	(p. 375)

Matching

1.	i	(p. 354)	6.	j	(p. 359)
2.	e	(p. 355)	7.	h	(p. 363)
3.	c	(p. 356)	8.	b	(p. 363)
4.	g	(p. 360)	9.	f	(p. 376)
5.	d	(p. 359)	10.	a	(p. 378)

1. race (p. 3654
2. Caucasian, Negroid, Mongoloid (p. 355)
3. biological, cultural (p. 356)
4. distinctive, subordination (p. 356)
5. stereotype (p. 357)
6. Scapegoat (p. 359)
7. biology, environments (p. 359)
8. institutional (p. 362)
9. assimilation (p. 363)
10. Genocide (p. 365)
11. 1871, 1924 (p. 367)
12. Dred Scott (p. 369)
13. Thirteenth Amendment (p. 369)
14. American dilemma (p. 369)
15. $28,602 (p. 369)
16. 40 (p. 370)
17. 11 (p. 375)
18. 1 million (p. 378)

PART VII: IN FOCUS--IMPORTANT ISSUES

- The Social Meaning of Race and Ethnicity

  Differentiate between the concepts of *race* and *ethnicity*.

  What does the author mean by saying that ethnicity involves more *variability* than race?

  What are the basic characteristics of a *minority group*?

262

Briefly describe each of the following *theories of prejudice*:

scapegoat theory

authoritarian personality theory

cultural theory

conflict theory

- Discrimination

How does discrimination differ from prejudice?

Provide two illustrations of *institutional discrimination*.

263

- Majority and Minority: Patterns of Interaction

  Define and illustrate each of the following *patterns of interaction* between racial and ethnic groups:

  pluralism

  assimilation

  segregation

  genocide

- Race and Ethnicity in the United States

  Identify three important characteristics for the following racial and ethnic groups that differentially characterize them in our society's social stratification system.

  Native Americans

  White Anglo-Saxon Protestants

African Americans

Asian Americans

Chinese Americans

Japanese Americans

recent Asian Immigrants

Hispanic Americans

Mexican Americans

Puerto Ricans

Cuban Americans

- Race and Ethnicity: Looking Ahead

  What are the issues today that are different from the past concerning *immigration* to the United States? What issues have not changed?

PART VIII: ANALYSIS AND COMMENT

Social Diversity

"The Immigrant Life in the United States"

Key Points: Questions:

Critical Thinking

"Does Race Affect Intelligence?"

Key Points: Questions:

Controversy and Debate

"Affirmative Action: Problem or Solution?"

Key Points: Questions:

Seeing Ourselves--National Maps 14-1, 14-2, 14-3, 14-4

"Where the Minority-Majority Already Exists"

Key Points: Questions:

"Land Controlled by American Indians, 1790-1998"

Key Points: Questions:

"The Concentration of People of WASP Ancestry across the United States"

Key Points: Questions:

"The Concentration of Asian Americans, African Americans, and Hispanics/Latinos, by County, Projections for 2001"

Key Points: Questions:

15

Aging and the Elderly

PART I: CHAPTER OUTLINE

I.   The Graying of the United States
    A.   The Birth Rate: Going Down
    B.   Life Expectancy: Going Up
    C.   An Aging Society: Cultural Change
    D.   The "Young Old" and the "Old Old"

II.   Growing Old: Biology and Culture
    A.   Biological Changes
    B.   Psychological Changes
    C.   Aging and Culture
    D.   Age Stratification: A Global Assessment
        1.   Hunting and Gathering Societies
        2.   Pastoral, Horticultural, and Agrarian Societies
        3.   Industrial Societies
        4.   Japan: An Exceptional Case

III.   Transitions and Challenges of Aging
    A.   Finding Meaning
    B.   Social Isolation
    C.   Retirement
    D.   Aging and Poverty
    E.   Caregiving
        1.   Who are the Caregivers?
        2.   Elder Abuse
    F.   Ageism
    G.   The Elderly: A Minority?

IV.   Theoretical Analysis of Aging
    A.   Structural-Functional Analysis: Aging and Disengagement
    B.   Symbolic-Interaction Analysis: Aging and Activity
    C.   Social-Conflict Analysis: Aging and Inequality

V.   Death and Dying
    A.   Historical Patterns of Death
    B.   The Modern Separation of Life and Death
    C.   Ethical Issues: Confronting Death
        1.   When Does Death Occur?
        2.   The "Right to Die" Debate
    D.   Bereavement

VI.   Looking Ahead: Aging In the Twenty-First Century

LEARNING OBJECTIVES

1.   To define and review the development of the graying of the United States.
2.   To be able to describe the interrelationship and respective roles of biology and culture in growing old.
3.   To be able to describe the role of the elderly in global and historical perspectives.
4.   To be able to describe the relationship between adjusting to old age and personality type.
5.   To be able to describe the problems and transitions involved in growing old.
6.   To become aware of the viewpoints on old age being offered by three different sociological perspectives--structural-functional, symbolic-interactionism, and social-conflict.
7.   To consider the effects of ageism on society.
8.   To be able to identify the key arguments in the debate over whether the elderly constitute a minority group.
9.   To be able to describe the changing character of death throughout history and into modern times.
10.   To be able to describe the process of bereavement in the United States.

PART III: KEY CONCEPTS

activity theory

ageism

age stratification

caregiving

death

defended personality

disengagement theory

disintegrated and disorganized personality

euthanasia

integrated personality

geronticide

gerontocracy

270

gerontology

hospice movement

old-age dependency theory

open status

passive-dependent personality

PART IV: IMPORTANT RESEARCHERS

Bernice Neugarten   Betty Friedan

Gordon Streib   Elaine Cumming and William Henry

Steven Spitzer   Elisabeth Kubler-Ross

PART V: STUDY QUESTIONS

<u>True-False</u>

1.   T   F   Today in the United States, people over the age of sixty-five account for twenty percent of the population.

2.   T   F   The elderly population in the U.S. is growing *twice as fast* as the general population.

3.   T   F   The *old-age dependency ratio* refers to the number of ill or disabled elderly people for every one hundred healthy elderly people in a society.

4.   T   F   *Gerontology* refers to a form of social organization in which the elderly have the most wealth, power, and prestige.

5.   T   F   Overall, about seventy percent of the aged consider their overall health condition "good" or "excellent."

6.   T   F   The *sensory abilities* of people tend to diminish in old age.

7.   T   F   Psychological research shows that *personalities* change little as people grow old.

8.   T   F   The average *life span* in the world's poorest countries is less than thirty years.

9.   T   F   A *gerontrocracy* is more likely to exist in hunting and gathering society than in a horticultural or agrarian society.

10.   T   F   Industrialization tends to *erode* the power and prestige of the elderly.

11.   T   F   A *gerontocracy* is a form of social organization in which elderly people have the most wealth, power, and prestige.

12.   T   F   Most elderly people in the U.S. *live alone*.

13.   T   F   Bernice Neugarten found that the most common personality type found among the aged is referred to as *passive-dependent personalities*.

14.   T   F   Most U.S. workers *retire* at age sixty-five or earlier.

15.   T   F   Children are more likely to be *poor* in the U.S. than are the aged.

16.   T   F   Females working full-time past the age of sixty-five *earn more* than their male counterparts.

17.   T   F   About seventy-five percent of all *caregivers* for the elderly are women.

18.   T   F   *Ageism* refers to prejudice and discrimination against the elderly.

19.   T   F   *Symbolic-interactionists* readily accept *disengagement theory*, arguing that the elderly need to remove themselves from positions of responsibility in order to achieve a healthy lifestyle.

20.   T   F   From a *structural-functionalist* point of view, a limitation of *activity theory* is the tendency to exaggerate the well-being and competence of the elderly.

21.   T   F   In 1900, about one-third of all deaths in the United States occurred before the age of five, while today, eighty-five percent of deaths involve people over the age of fifty-five.

22.   T   F   *Euthanasia* refers to the unequal distribution of wealth, power, and privilege among people at different stages of the life course.

1.   In 1900, the United States was a young nation with half the population under the age of twenty-three; just _____ percent had reached the age of sixty-five.

      (a)   one
      (b)   four
      (c)   ten
      (d)   twenty

2.   Currently, the aged represent about _____ *percent* of our population.

      (a)   6
      (b)   13
      (c)   18
      (d)   21

3.   Between now and 2050 the *median age* in the U.S. will rise to _____ and the *percent* of our population over the age of 65 will be

      (a)   40/20.
      (b)   30/15.
      (c)   50/50.
      (d)   25/40.
      (e)   36/14.

4.   The ratio of elderly people to working-age adults, termed the *old-age dependency ratio*, will rise dramatically by 2050--rising from twenty to _____ elderly people per one hundred people aged eighteen to sixty-four.

      (a)   twenty-five
      (b)   thirty
      (c)   thirty-seven
      (d)   forty-six

5.   _____ refers to the study of aging and the elderly.

      (a)   Gerontocracy
      (b)   Ageism
      (c)   Elderology
      (d)   Gerontology
      (e)   Oldograpphy

273

6. Most counties in the U.S. with a high percentage of older people are found in

   (a) the Sunbelt.
   (b) the Northeast.
   (c) the Midwest.
   (d) the West.

7. *Gerontocracy* is most likely to be a characteristic of what type of society?

   (a) hunting and gathering
   (b) pastoral, horticultural, and agrarian
   (c) industrial
   (d) postindustrial
   (e) nomadic

8. The Abkhasian society exhibits exceptional *longevity* due to

   (a) a healthy diet.
   (b) regular exercise.
   (c) positive self-image of the elderly in society.
   (d) all of the above

9. Which of the following is *not* a personality type identified by Bernice Neugarten in her study of adjustment to old age?

   (a) disintegrated and disorganized
   (b) residual-active
   (c) passive-dependent
   (d) integrated
   (e) defended

10. Most elderly men

    (a) live alone.
    (b) live in nursing homes.
    (c) live with extended family members.
    (d) live with their spouse.

11. Approximately ___ percent of elderly women *live alone*.

    (a) 41
    (b) 23
    (c) 68
    (d) 16

274

12. Approximately what percentage of the aged population in the U.S. live in *poverty*?

    (a)   less than 5
    (b)   18
    (c)   25
    (d)   33
    (e)   11

13. Which of the following statements concerning the elderly is *inaccurate*?

    (a)   The poverty rate among elderly African Americans is over twice the rate for their white, non-Hispanic counterparts.
    (b)   Women over the age of sixty-five who are working full-time earn about 63 percent of their male counterparts.
    (c)   The poverty rate among the elderly is higher today than it was forty years ago.
    (d)   The majority of elderly people have retired from the labor force.

14. Some sociologists argue that the elderly constitute a *minority group*, while others disagree. Which of the following reasons is an argument *against* the elderly being a minority group?

    (a)   The status of being elderly is an open status.
    (b)   The elderly think of themselves in terms of sex, race, and ethnicity.
    (c)   The social disadvantages of the elderly are not as great as for other categories of people.
    (d)   all of the above

15. According to _____ analysis, *disengagement* is a strategy to ensure the orderly operation of society by removing aging people from productive roles while they are still able to perform them.

    (a)   symbolic-interaction
    (b)   structural-functional
    (c)   social-conflict
    (d)   social-exchange

16. *Activity theory* is a sociological theory of aging based upon

    (a)   structural-functional analysis.
    (b)   social-conflict analysis.
    (c)   symbolic-interaction analysis.
    (d)   social-exchange analysis.

17. In modern U.S. society *death* has become

   (a) more common to everyday experience.
   (b) less of an ethical issue.
   (c) easier to accept.
   (d) an event that occurs often in the home of the dying person.
   (e) defined as an unnatural event.

18. Which of the following statements is *inaccurate*?

   (a) Less than two-thirds of deaths in the U.S. involve people over the age of fifty-five.
   (b) In 1900, one-third of all deaths in the U.S. involved children under the age of five.
   (c) Living wills are documents stating which medical procedures an individual wants and does not want under specific conditions.
   (d) Euthanasia refers to assisting in the death of a person suffering from an incurable disease.

19. Which of the following is *not* a stage of *bereavement* according to the Elisabeth Kubler-Ross' stage model?

   (a) integration
   (b) anger
   (c) acceptance
   (d) resignation
   (e) denial

20. The major purpose of the *hospice movement* is

   (a) to lobby the federal government and state governments for support of "right-to-die" legislation.
   (b) to help terminally ill patients find cures for their illnesses.
   (c) to provide care and support for dying people.
   (d) assist people who wish to end their own lives.

Matching

1. ___ The projected percentage of the U.S. population who will be over the age of sixty-five in the year 2050.
2. ___ The study of aging and the elderly.
3. ___ A form of social organization in which the elderly have the most wealth, power, and prestige.
4. ___ The percentage of aged women living with a spouse.
5. ___ Prejudice and discrimination against the elderly.
6. ___ A theory associated with symbolic-interaction analysis.
7. ___ A theory associated with the structural-functional paradigm.
8. ___ Assisting in the death of a person suffering from an incurable disease.
9. ___ A country with extremely liberal euthanasia laws.
10. ___ Found that people usually confront their own death in stages.

a.	Elizabeth Kubler-Ross	h.	gerontology
b.	the Netherlands	i.	ageism
c.	gerontocracy	j.	Talcott Parsons
d.	activity	k.	euthanasia
e.	40	l.	20
f.	disengagement	m.	the United States
g.	15		

Fill-In

1. The *birth rate* in the United States has been _____ for over a century.
2. Typically, two factors combine to *drive up* the elderly population in a society. These include a low _____ _____ and increasing _____.
3. The ratio of elderly people to working-age adults is termed the *old age* _____ _____.
4. _____ is the study of aging and the elderly.
5. Today in the United States, _____ percent of people over the age of sixty-five characterize their overall health as "good" or "excellent."
6. _____ is a form of social organization in which the elderly have the most wealth, power, and prestige.
7. In her study of the transitions of aging, Bernice Neugarten found that most common type of *personality* among people seventy years of age or older was what she labeled _____.
8. Approximately _____ percent of elderly women in the U.S. live with a spouse.
9. By age sixty-five, ____ percent of *men* and ____ percent of *women* are not in the paid labor force.
10. Among full-time workers in 1996, *women* over the age of sixty-five had median earnings of $27,070, compared to $ _____ for *men*.
11. _____ refers to prejudice and discrimination against the elderly.
12. _____ refers to informal and unpaid care provided to a dependent person by family member, other relatives, or friends.
13. Our author believes the aged should not be identified as a minority group, but rather be considered a _____ *segment* of the U.S. population.
14. One criticism of *social-conflict theory* is that rather than blaming capitalism for the lower standard of living of the elderly, the real culprit is _____.

15. _____ is the killing of infants and _____ is the killing of the elderly.

16. _____ refers to assisting in the death of a person suffering from an incurable disease.

17. Medical and legal experts in the United States now define *death* as an _____ state involving no response to stimulation, no movement or breathing, no reflexes, and no indication of brain activity.

18. According to Elisabeth Kubler-Ross, like *death*, _____ involves four stages, including denial, anger, negotiation, and acceptance.

Definition and Short-Answer

1. What is the *AARP*? What are your thoughts and feelings about this organization and its role in our society today?

2. Define *gerontology*. Further, many different demographic facts concerning the aged in our society are presented on pages 388-390. Select the two which most interest you and discuss their significance for our society using your own opinions and experiences.

3. Define and illustrate the concept of *age stratification*. How does it vary by a society's level of technological development?

4. What are the four types of *personalities* identified by Bernice Neugarten? In what ways are they different in helping people adjust to old age? Are there people in your life whom you can identify with having any of these personality types?

5. Differentiate between *activity theory* and *disengagement theory* in terms of how each helps us understand the changing status of the aged in society.

6. Why is *elder abuse* so common in our society? What are some of the demographic facts concerning this critical social problem in our society?

7. Discuss the relative economies of the aged in our society today.

8. According to *social-conflict* theorists, why is the status of the aged diminished in capitalist societies? What do critics of this theory suggest?

9. What are the arguments in the debate concerning whether the aged are a *minority group*?

10. What are Daniel Callahan's points concerning how much old age the U.S. can afford?

11. Review the points being made by Betty Friedan concerning the aged in our society. Do you agree with her viewpoint?

12. How is the relative status of the aged related to the level of *technological development* of a society?

PART VI: ANSWERS TO STUDY QUESTIONS

True-False

1.	F	(p. 384)		12.	T	(p. 387)
2.	T	(p. 384)		13.	T	(p. 391)
3.	F	(p. 386)		14.	F	(p. 394)
4.	F	(p. 386)		15.	F	(p. 394)
5.	T	(p. 387)		16.	F	(p. 394)
6.	T	(pp. 386-387)		17.	T	(p. 395)
7.	T	(p. 387)		18.	T	(p. 395)
8.	F	(p. 389)		19.	F	(p. 398)
9.	F	(p. 390)		20.	T	(p. 398)
10.	T	(p. 390)		21.	T	(p. 399)
11.	T	(p. 390)		22.	F	(p. 400)

Multiple-Choice

1.	b	(p. 384)		11.	d	(p. 392)
2.	b	(p. 384)		12.	e	(p. 394)
3.	a	(p. 384)		13.	c	(p. 394)
4.	c	(p. 386)		14.	a	(p. 396)
5.	d	(p. 386)		15.	b	(p. 396)
6.	c	(p. 387)		16.	c	(p. 397)
7.	b	(p. 390)		17.	e	(p. 398)
8.	d	(p. 391)		18.	a	(pp. 398-399)
9.	b	(p. 392)		19.	a	(pp. 401-402)
10.	d	(p. 392)		20.	c	(p. 403)

Matching

1.	l	(p. 384)		6.	d	(p. 397)
2.	h	(p. 386)		7.	f	(p. 397)
3.	c	(p. 390)		8.	k	(p. 400)
4.	e	(p. 394)		9.	b	(p. 400)
5.	i	(p. 395)		10.	a	(p. 401)

Fill-In

1. falling (p. 384)
2. birth rate, longevity (p. 384)
3. dependency ratio (p. 386)
4. gerontology (p. 386)
5. 70 (p. 387)
6. gerontocracy (p. 390)
7. integrated (p. 392)
8. 40 (p. 393)
9. 83, 91 (p. 393)

10. 42,836 (p. 394)
11. ageism (p. 395)
12. Caregiving (p. 394)
13. distinctive (p. 396)
14. industrialization (p. 398)
15. Infanticide, gentrocide (p. 399)
16. euthanasia (p. 400)
17. irreversible (p. 400)
18. bereavement (pp. 401-402)

PART VII: IN FOCUS--IMPORTANT ISSUES

- The Graying of the United States

  What are the two major factors identified in the text that are contributing to the *graying* of the United States population? What evidence is being presented concerning each of these?

  What is meant by the *old-age dependency ratio*? How is it changing? Why should we be concerned about this change?

- Growing Old: Biology and Culture

Review the major changes for the aged in each of the following domains:

    biological

    psychological

Provide three examples of how aging is related to *culture*:

What is *age stratification*?

How is age stratification related to a society's level of *technological development*?

- Transitions and Challenges of Aging

  Summarize the key points being made in the text concerning each of the following transitions and challenges of aging:

  finding meaning

  social isolation

  retirement

  aging and poverty

  caregiving

  Are the elderly a *minority group*? Provide one point to argue for this idea and one to argue against it.

- Theoretical Analysis of Aging

Review the major arguments concerning the aged in society according to structural-functionalists who use *disengagement theory*.

What is one major criticism of this perspective?

Review the major arguments concerning the aged in society according to symbolic-interactionists who use *activity theory*.

What is one major criticism of this perspective?

How do *conflict theorists* understand the relationship between industrial society and the social stratification of the aged?

283

- Death and Dying

How has the place of death in society changed since Medieval times?

What are two arguments being made on each side of the *"right-to-die"* debate?

- Looking Ahead: Aging In the Twenty-First Century

  What are three major issues that will be confronting our society over the next fifty to sixty years given the growing number of aged people in the United States?

PART VIII: ANALYSIS AND COMMENT

Global Sociology

"Growing (Very) Old: A Report From Abkhasia"

Key Points: Questions:

"Death on Demand: A Report From the Netherlands"

Key Points: Questions:

Controversy and Debate

"Setting Limits: Must We "Pull the Plug" on Old Age?"

Key Points: Questions:

Window on the World--Global Map 15-1

"The Elderly in Global Perspective: 2020"

Key Points: Questions:

Window on the World--Global Map 15-2

"Life Expectancy in Global Perspective"

Key Points: Questions:

Seeing Ourselves

"National Map 15-1: The Elderly Population of the United States"

Key Points: Questions:

16 The Economy and Work

PART I: CHAPTER OUTLINE

I.   The Economy: Historical Overview
   A.   The Agricultural Revolution
   B.   The Industrial Revolution
   C.   The Information Revolution and the Postindustrial Society
   D.   Sectors of the Economy
   E.   The Global Economy
II.   Economic Systems: Paths to Justice
   A.   Capitalism
   B.   Socialism
      1.   Social and Communism
   C.   Welfare Capitalism and State Capitalism
   D.   Relative Advantages of Capitalism and Socialism
      1.   Economic Productivity
      2.   Economic Equality
      3.   Personal Freedom
   E.   Changes in Socialist Countries
III.   Work in the Postindustrial Economy
   A.   The Decline of Agricultural Work
   B.   From Factory Work to Service Work
   C.   The Dual Labor Market
   D.   Labor Unions
   E.   Professions
   F.   Self-Employment
   G.   Unemployment and Underemployment
   H.   The Underground Economy
   I.   Social Diversity in the Workplace
   J.   New Information Technology and Work
IV.   Corporations
   A.   Economic Concentration
   B.   Conglomerates and Corporate Linkages
   C.   Corporations: Are They Competitive?
   D.   Corporations and the Global Economy

PART II: LEARNING OBJECTIVES

1.   To be able to identify the elements of the economy.
2.   To be able to review the history and development of economic activity from the Agricultural Revolution through to the Postindustrial Revolution.
3.   To be able to identify and describe the three sectors of the economy.
4.   To be able to compare the economic systems of capitalism, state capitalism, socialism, and democratic socialism.
5.   To be able to explain the difference between socialism and communism.
6.   To be able to describe the general characteristics and trends of work in the U.S. postindustrial society.
7.   To begin to see the impact of multinational corporations on the world economy.

PART III: KEY CONCEPTS

capitalism

communism

conglomerates

corporation

economy

global economy

interlocking directorate

labor unions

monopoly

oligopoly

postindustrial economy

primary sector

profession

secondary sector

socialism

state capitalism

tertiary sector

welfare capitalism

PART IV: IMPORTANT RESEARCHERS

Karl Marx

PART V: STUDY QUESTIONS

True-False

1.	T	F	The *economy* includes the production, distribution, and consumption of both goods and services.
2.	T	F	*Agriculture*, as a subsistence strategy, first emerged some five thousand years ago.
3.	T	F	In Medieval Europe, people living in cities often worked at home, a pattern called *cottage industry*.
4.	T	F	Most workers in the New England textile factories in the early nineteenth century were *women*.
5.	T	F	The *primary sector* of the economy is the part of the economy that generates raw material directly from the natural environment.
6.	T	F	The terms *primary, secondary,* and *tertiary* referring to sectors in the economy, imply a ranking in importance for our society.
7.	T	F	Agriculture occupies more than seventy percent of the labor force in *low-income countries* .
8.	T	F	The largest economic sector of *middle-income countries* is the secondary sector.
9.	T	F	*Socialism* is being defined as both a political and economic system.
10.	T	F	Per capita GDP tended to be significantly higher in capitalist as compared to socialist economies during the 1970s and 1980s.
11.	T	F	The *income ratio*, as a measure of the distribution of income in a society, tended to be higher in socialist systems as compared to capitalist systems during the 1970s and 1980s.
12.	T	F	More than two-thirds of employed men and women in the U.S. hold *white-collar jobs*.
13.	T	F	The *primary labor market* includes jobs providing minimal benefits to workers.
14.	T	F	The pattern of *union decline* holds in other high-income countries besides just the United States.
15.	T	F	A larger percentage of workers today are *self-employed* as compared to any other period in the history of the United States.

289

16.	T	F	Most *self-employed* people in the U.S. are in white-collar jobs.
17.	T	F	According to the text, the Information Revolution is changing the kind of work people do and where they do it. Part of the consequence of this process is that computers are *deskilling labor*.
18.	T	F	There are approximately five million *incorporated* companies in the United States. The top five-hundred of these represent over three-fourths of total corporate assets.
19.	T	F	The largest corporation in the U.S. is IBM.
20.	T	F	An *oligopoly* refers to domination of a market by a few producers.

Multiple Choice

1. A productive system based on service work and extensive use of information technology refers to

    (a)   the postindustrial economy.
    (b)   the primary sector.
    (c)   the secondary sector.
    (d)   a cottage industry.

2. Which of the following was not a way in which *industrialization* changed the economy?

    (a)   new forms of energy
    (b)   centralization of work into factories
    (c)   manufacturing and mass production
    (d)   generalization
    (e)   wage labor

3. The *sector* of the economy that transforms raw materials into manufactured goods is termed the

    (a)   primary sector.
    (b)   competitive sector.
    (c)   secondary sector.
    (d)   basic sector.
    (e)   manifest sector.

4. Which of the following is *not a sector* of the modern economy?

    (a)   primary
    (b)   manifest
    (c)   secondary
    (d)   tertiary

5.	Your occupation is teaching. In what production *sector* of the economy?

	(a)	primary
	(b)	secondary
	(c)	tertiary
	(d)	manifest

6.	You mine gold for a living. In what production *sector* of the economy do you work?

	(a)	tertiary
	(b)	manifest
	(c)	secondary
	(d)	auxiliary
	(e)	primary

7.	Today, about _____ percent of the U.S. labor force is in *service work*, including secretarial and clerical work and positions in food service, sales, law, advertising, and teaching.

	(a)	98
	(b)	88
	(c)	70
	(d)	60
	(e)	52

8.	What is the *economic system* in which natural resources and the means of producing goods and services are privately owned?

	(a)	capitalism
	(b)	socialism
	(c)	communism
	(d)	state capitalism

9.	Which of the following is/are accurate statements concerning *capitalism*?

	(a)	Justice, in a capitalist context, amounts to freedom of the marketplace where one can produce, invest, and buy according to individual self-interest.
	(b)	A purely capitalist economy is a free-market system with no government interference, sometimes called a laissez-faire economy.
	(c)	Consumers regulate a free-market economy.
	(d)	All are accurate statements concerning capitalism.

10. Which of the following is/are accurate concerning *socialism*?

    (a) Socialism is characterized by collective ownership of property.
    (b) Socialism rejects the laissez-faire approach.
    (c) Justice, in a socialist context, is not freedom to compete and accumulate wealth but, rather, meeting everyone's basic needs in a more or less equal manner.
    (a) All of the above are accurate statements concerning socialism.

11. _____ is a hypothetical economic and political system in which all members of a society are socially equal.

    (a) Socialism
    (b) Communism
    (c) Welfare capitalism
    (d) State capitalism

12. Sweden and Italy represent what type of economic and political system?

    (a) capitalism
    (b) socialism
    (c) communism
    (d) welfare capitalism

13. An economic and political system that combines a mostly market-based economy with government programs to provide for people's basic needs is termed

    (a) socialism.
    (b) market socialism.
    (c) market communism.
    (d) an oligarchy.
    (e) welfare capitalism.

14. An economic and political system in which companies are privately owned although they cooperate closely with the government is known as

    (a) state socialism.
    (b) state capitalism.
    (c) welfare capitalism.
    (d) communism.

15.   *Capitalist* economies had about _____ times the per capita GDP during the 1980s as *socialist* economies.

    (a)   2.7
    (b)   12.9
    (c)   8.2
    (d)   .75
    (e)   1.3

16.   During the 1970s and 1980s, *socialist economies* had about _____ as much *income inequality* as was found in capitalist economies during the same time period.

    (a)   one-tenth
    (b)   twice
    (c)   three times
    (d)   one-half
    (e)   four times

17.   What percentage of women in the U.S. had *income-producing jobs* in 1998?

    (a)   31.7
    (b)   67.5
    (c)   44.6
    (d)   81.5
    (e)   57.1

18.   By 2000, _____ percent of *new jobs* were in the *service sector*.

    (a)   50
    (b)   60
    (c)   70
    (d)   80
    (e)   90

19.   Today in the United States, two percent of the labor force is engaged in farming. In 1900 the figure was

    (a)   10 percent.
    (b)   25 percent.
    (c)   40 percent.
    (d)   55 percent.

20. In 1997, _____ percent of the U.S. labor force was *unionized*.

    (a) less than 5
    (b) 16
    (c) 25
    (d) 36
    (e) over 50

21. A _____ is a prestigious, white-collar occupation that requires extensive formal education.

    (a) profession
    (b) career
    (c) technical occupation
    (d) primary sector work

22. Currently, what percentage of the U.S. labor force is *self-employed*?

    (a) less than 1
    (b) 3.8
    (c) 6.5
    (d) 15.3
    (e) 21.7

23. Which of the following statements is *most accurate*?

    (a) White males have a much higher rate of unemployment than white females.
    (b) A much higher proportion of African American females are unemployed than African American men.
    (c) College graduates actually have a higher unemployment rate than the general population.
    (d) The overall unemployment rate today in the U.S. is about ten percent.
    (e) Teens have a higher rate of unemployment than people over the age of twenty.

24. Economic activity involving income unreported to the government as required by law refers to the _____ *economy*

    (a) tertiary.
    (b) residual.
    (c) secondary.
    (d) underground.

294

25. What is the term for an organization with legal existence, including rights and liabilities, apart from those of its members?

    (a)   corporation
    (b)   bureaucracy
    (c)   business
    (d)   conglomerate

26. What is the term for giant corporations composed of many smaller corporations?

    (a)   megacorporations
    (b)   monopolies
    (c)   multinational corporations
    (d)   conglomerates
    (e)   oligarchies

27. Which U.S. corporation leads the nation in sales and assets?

    (a)   IBM
    (b)   General Motors
    (c)   Exxon
    (d)   Ford Motor Company
    (e)   Proctor and Gamble

28. What is the term for a social network made up of people who simultaneously serve on the board of directors of many corporations?

    (a)   conglomerate
    (b)   interlocking directorate
    (c)   oligopoly
    (d)   monopoly

29. The domination of a market by a single producer is called a(n)

    (a)   conglomerate.
    (b)   interlocking directorate.
    (c)   monopoly.
    (d)   oligopoly.

30. In 1996, the average *hourly wage* for a U.S. worker in manufacturing was $12.78. At $23.00 per hour, which country had the highest average wage for working in the manufacturing sector?

    (a)   France
    (b)   Russia
    (c)   Canada
    (d)   Germany
    (e)   South Korea

Matching

1. ___ The social institution that organizes a society's production, distribution, and consumption of goods and services.
2. ___ A production system based on service work and extensive use of information.
3. ___ The part of the economy that transforms raw materials into manufactured goods.
4. ___ The part of the economy involving services rather than goods.
5. ___ Economic activity spanning many nations of the world with little regard for national borders.
6. ___ An economic system in which natural resources and the means of producing goods and services are collectively owned.
7. ___ An economic and political system in which companies are privately owned although they cooperate closely with the government.
8. ___ Jobs that provide minimal benefits to workers.
9. ___ An organization with a legal existence, including rights and liabilities, apart from those of its members.
10. ___ Giant corporations composed of many smaller corporations.

a.	socialism	f.	state capitalism
b.	conglomerates	g.	economy
c.	secondary sector	h.	postindustrial economy
d.	tertiary sector	i.	global economy
e.	secondary labor market	j	corporation

Fill-In

1. _____ range from necessities like food to luxuries like swimming pools, while _____ include various activities that benefit others.
2. *Industrialization* introduced five fundamental changes in the economies of Western societies, including: new forms of _____, the centralization of work in _____, manufacturing and _____ _____, _____, and _____ _____.
3. A _____ *economy* is a productive system based on service work and high technology.
4. The Information Revolution unleashed three key changes, including: From tangible products to _____, from mechanical skills to _____ skills, and the movement of work from factories to _____.

296

5. The _____ _____ is the part of the economy generating raw materials directly from the natural environment.

6. The _____ _____ is the part of the economy generating services rather than goods.

7. Four major consequences of a *global economy* include: a global _____ ___ _____, an increasing number of products passing through the _____ of more than one nation, _____ _____ no longer control the economic activity that takes place within their boundaries, and a _____ number of businesses, operating internationally, control a vast share of the world's economic activity.

8. A *capitalist system* has three distinctive features, including: _____ ownership of property, pursuit of personal _____, and free _____ and consumer sovereignty.

9. A *socialist system* has three distinctive features, including: _____ ownership of property, pursuit of _____ goals, an _____ control of the economy.

10. _____ is a hypothetical economic and political system in which all members of a society are socially equal.

11. _____ _____ is an economic and political system in which companies are privately owned although they cooperate closely with the government.

12. A comparison of economic performance between *capitalist* and *socialist* economies supports the conclusion that capital economies produce a _____ overall standard of living but with _____ income disparity.

13. *Socialist* systems in Eastern Europe prior to the great transformations of 1989 and 1990 did away with _____ *elites*, but expanded the clout of _____ *elites*.

14. While _____ percent of males over the age of 16 in the U.S. have income-producing jobs, _____ of the females do.

15. By 2000, _____ percent of new jobs of new jobs were in the service sector, and _____ percent of the entire labor force performed *service work*.

16. Sociologists divide the jobs in today's economy into two categories: the _____ *labor market* that includes occupations that provide extensive benefits to workers, and the _____ *labor market*, that includes jobs that provide minimal benefits to workers.

17. People describe their occupations as *professions* to the extent that they demonstrate the following four characteristics: _____ knowledge, _____ practice, _____ over clients, and _____ to community rather than to self-interest.

18. The *Information Revolution* is changing the kind of work people do as well as where they do it. Computers are altering the character of work in four additional ways: they are _____ labor, making work more _____, _____ workplace interaction, and enhancing employer's _____ of workers.

19. _____ are giant corporations comprised of many smaller corporations.

20. _____ refers to domination of a market by a few producers.

Definition and Short-Answer

1. What were the five revolutionary changes brought about by the *Industrial Revolution*?
2. Define the concept *postindustrial society*, and identify three key changes unleashed by the *Information Revolution*.

3. What are the three basic characteristics of *capitalism*? What are the three basic characteristics of *socialism*? What is *democratic socialism*?

4. Comparing productivity and economic equality measures for *capitalist* and *socialist* economic systems, what are the relative advantages and disadvantages of each? Make comparisons in terms of *productivity, economic inequality,* and *civil liberties.*

5. What are the three main consequences of the development of a *global economy*?

6. What are the three major *sectors* of the economy? Define and illustrate each of these.

7. What are the basic characteristics of a *profession*?

8. What are your interpretations of the data being presented in *Figure 16-2*?

PART VI: ANSWERS TO STUDY QUESTIONS

True-False

1.	T	(p. 410)	11.	F	(p. 418)
2.	T	(p. 410)	12.	T	(p. 420)
3.	T	(p. 410)	13.	F	(p. 420)
4.	T	(p. 411)	14.	T	(p. 421)
5.	T	(p. 412)	15.	F	(p. 422)
6.	F	(p. 412)	16.	F	(p. 422)
7.	T	(p. 413)	17.	T	(p. 425)
8.	F	(p. 413)	18.	T	(p. 425)
9.	F	(p. 416)	19.	F	(p. 426)
10.	T	(p. 418)	20.	T	(p. 427)

Multiple Choice

1.	a	(p. 410)	16.	d	(p. 418)
2.	d	(p. 410)	17.	e	(p. 419)
3.	c	(p. 412)	18.	e	(p. 420)
4.	b	(p. 412)	19.	c	(p. 420)
5.	c	(p. 412)	20.	b	(p. 421)
6.	e	(p. 412)	21.	a	(p. 421)
7.	c	(p. 412)	22.	c	(p. 422)
8.	a	(p. 415)	23.	e	(pp. 422-423)
9.	d	(p. 415)	24.	d	(p. 423)
10.	d	(pp. 416-417)	25.	a	(p. 425)
11.	b	(p. 417)	26.	d	(p. 426)
12.	d	(p. 417)	27.	a	(p. 426)
13.	e	(p. 417)	28.	b	(p. 427)
14.	b	(p. 418)	29.	d	(p. 427)
15.	a	(p. 418)	30.	d	(p. 427)

1.	h	(p. 410)	6.	i.	(p. 416)
2.	e	(p. 410)	7.	c	(p. 418)
3.	a	(p. 412)	8.	j	(p. 420)
4.	g	(p. 412)	9.	b	(p. 425)
5.	d	(pp. 412-413)	10.	f	(p. 426)

Fill-In

1.   goods, services (p. 410)
2.   energy, factories, mass production, specialization, wage labor (p. 410)
3.   postindustrial (p. 410)
4.   ideas, literacy, almost anywhere (pp. 411-412)
5.   primary sector (p. 412)
6.   tertiary sector (p. 412)
7.   division of labor, economies, national governments, small (p. 413)
8.   private, profit, competition (p. 415)
9.   collective, collective, government (p. 416)
10.   Communism (p. 417)
11.   State capitalism (p. 418)
12.   higher, greater (p. 418)
13.   economic, political (p. 419)
14.   71.6, 57.1 (p. 424)
15.   90, 70 (p. 419)
16.   primary, secondary (p. 420)
17.   theoretical, self-regulating, authority, orientation (pp. 421-422)
18.   deskilling, abstract, limiting, control (p. 425)
19.   Conglomerates (p. 426)
20.   Oligopoly (p. 427)

PART VII: IN FOCUS--IMORTANT ISSUES

- The Economy: Historical Overview

   Identify and describe the five fundamental ways in with *industrialization* changed the economy.

   In what ways is *postindustiral society* different from industrial society?

What are the four major consequences of the *global economy*?

- Economic Systems: Paths to Justice

What are the three distinctive features of *capitalism?*

1.

2.

3.

How is *justice* understood in a capitalist context?

What are the three distinctive features of *socialism*?

1.

2.

3.

How is *justice* understood in a socialist context?

What are the relative advantages of capitalism and socialism in each of the following domains?

economic productivity

economic equality

personal freedom

- Work In the Postindustrial Economy

Differentiate between the major qualities of *industrial society* and *postindustrial society*.

What are the four characteristics of a *profession*?

1.

2.

3.

4.

The *unemployment rate* in the U.S. today is about four percent. What is *underemployment*? Why is it perhaps a bigger problem in our society than unemployment today?

What are the four ways in which *computers* are changing the character of work in the United States? Provide an illustration for each of these.

                change   illustration

1.

2.

3.

4.

- Corporations

What is the evidence that there is *economic concentration* in the United States?

What are three important consequences of a *global economy*?

- Looking Ahead: The Economy of the Twenty-First Century

What are three major patterns that are expected to continue to occur in terms of the our economy?

1.

2.

3.

PART VIII: ANALYSIS AND COMMENT

Social Diversity

"Women in the Mills of Lowell, Massachusetts"

Key Points: Questions:

"Diversity in the New Century: Changes in the Workplace"

Key Points: Questions:

Applying Sociology

"Them That's Got, Gets: The Case of Corporate Welfare"

Key Points: Questions:

Controversy and Debate

"The Market: Does the "Invisible Hand" Look Out for Us or Pick Our Pockets"

Key Points: Questions:

Window on the World--Global Map 16-1, 16-2

"Agricultural Employment in Global Perspective"

Key Points: Questions:

"Industrial Employment in Global Perspective"

Key Points: Questions:

Seeing Ourselves--National Maps 16-1, 16-2

"Labor Force Participation across the United States"

Key Points: Questions:

"Where the Jobs Will Be: Projections to 2010"

Key Points: Questions:

17 Politics And Government

PART I: CHAPTER OUTLINE

I. Power and Authority
    A.   Traditional Authority
    B.   Rational-Legal Authority
    C.   Charismatic Authority
II. Politics in Global Perspective
    A.   Monarchy
    B.   Democracy
        1.   Democracy and Freedom: Capitalist and Socialist Approaches
    C.   Authoritarianism
    D.   Totalitarianism
    E.   A Global Political System?
III. Politics in the United States
    A.   U.S. Culture and the Rise of the Welfare State
    B.   The Political Spectrum
        1.   Economic Issues
        2.   Social Issues
        3.   Mixed Positions
        4.   Party Identification
    C.   Special-Interest Groups
    D.   Voter Apathy
IV. Theoretical Analysis of Power in Society
    A.   The Pluralist Model: The People Rule
    B.   The Power-Elite Model: A Few People Rule
    C.   The Marxist Model: Bias in the System Itself
        1.   Critical Evaluation
V. Power Beyond the Rules
    A.   Revolution
    B.   Terrorism

VI.   War and Peace
A.   The Causes of War
B.   The Costs and Causes of Militarism
C.   Nuclear Weapons
D.   Pursuing of Peace
VII.   Looking Ahead: Politics in the Twenty-First Century
VIII. Summary
IX.   Key Concepts
X.   Critical-Thinking Questions
XI.   Applications and Exercises
XII.   Sites to See

PART II: LEARNING OBJECTIVES

1.   To recognize the difference between power and authority.
2.   To be able to identify, define, and illustrate the different types of authority.
3.   To be able to compare the four principal kinds of political systems.
4.   To be able to describe the nature of the American political system of government, and discuss the principal characteristics of the political spectrum of the U.S.
5.   To be able to compare the pluralist and power-elite models of political power.
6.   To be able to describe the types of political power that exceed, or seek to eradicate, established politics.
7.   To be able to identify the factors which increase the likelihood of war.
8.   To recognize the historical pattern of militarism in the United States and around the world, and to consider factors which can be used in the pursuit of peace.

PART III: KEY CONCEPTS

arms race

authoritarianism

authority

charismatic authority

democracy

government

Marxist political-economy model

military-industrial complex

monarchy

nuclear proliferation

pluralist model

political action committees

political revolution

politics

power

power-elite model

rational-legal authority

revolution

routinization of charisma

special-interest group

state terrorism

terrorism

totalitarianism

traditional authority

voter apathy

war

welfare state

PART IV: IMPORTANT RESEARCHERS

Max Weber   C. Wright Mills

Robert and Helen Lynd   Quincy Wright

Floyd Hunter   Robert Dahl

Nelson Polsby

PART V: STUDY QUESTIONS

<u>True-False</u>

1. T   F   *Authority* is power people perceive as legitimate rather than coercive.
2. T   F   *Charismatic authority* is limited to the preindustrialized world.
3. T   F   *Traditional authority* is sometimes referred to as bureaucratic authority.
4. T   F   Currently, the world has 422 *nation-states*.
5. T   F   *Socialist* societies claim they are democratic because their economies meet everyone's basic needs.
6. T   F   In 1999, eighty-eight of the world's nations, containing forty percent of all people, were *politically free*--that is, they offered their citizens extensive political rights and civil liberties.
7. T   F   *Authoritarianism* refers to a political system that denies popular participation in government.
8. T   F   Singapore is characterized by limited government intervention and extreme personal liberty and freedom.
9. T   F   In the United States today, tax revenue, as a share of gross domestic product, is higher than in any other industrialized society.
10. T   F   For every thirteen U.S. citizens, there is one government employee.
11. T   F   Generally, the *Democratic Party* supports the role of government in U.S. society, including government regulation of the economy.
12. T   F   Most U.S. adults claim identification with the *Republican Party*.
13. T   F   *Political Action Committees* are organizations formed by special-interest groups, independent of political parties, to pursue political aims by raising and spending money.
14. T   F   *Voter apathy* is a problem, as evidenced by the fact that citizens in the U.S. are less likely to vote today than they were a century ago.
15. T   F   Most high-income people *do vote* and most low-income people *do not* vote.
16. T   F   According to the *pluralist model* of U.S. politics, we are a democracy in which power is widely dispersed and in which apathy amounts to indifference.

308

17.	T	F	Research by *Robert* and *Helen Lynd* in Muncie, Indiana (the Middletown study) supported the *pluralist model* concerning how power is distributed in the United States.
18.	T	F	One of the four insights offered concerning *terrorism* is that democracies are especially vulnerable to it because these governments afford extensive civil liberties to their people and have limited police networks.
19.	T	F	More U.S. soldiers were killed during *World War II* than in all other wars in which the U.S. has ever participated.
20.	T	F	In recent years, defense has been the largest single expenditure by the U.S. government, accounting for nineteen percent of federal spending.
21.	T	F	*War* is rooted in social dynamics on both national and international levels.
22.	T	F	It is estimated that by 2010 about five nations will have the ability to fight a *nuclear war*.

Multiple Choice

1. Who defined *power* as the ability to achieve desired ends despite resistance?

   (a)   C. Wright Mills
   (b)   Max Weber
   (c)   Alexis de Tocqueville
   (d)   Robert Lynd

2. Power that people perceive as being *legitimate* rather than coercive is the definition for

   (a)   a monarchy.
   (b)   totalitarianism.
   (c)   government.
   (d)   politics.
   (e)   authority.

3. Which of the following is *not* one of the general contexts in which power is commonly defined as authority?

   (a)   traditional
   (b)   charismatic
   (c)   rational-legal
   (d)   democratic

4. Power that is legitimated by respect for long-established cultural patterns is called

   (a)   traditional.
   (b)   sacred.
   (c)   political.
   (d)   charismatic.
   (e)   power-elite.

5.   According to *Max Weber*, the survival of a charismatic movement depends upon

        (a)   pluralism.
        (b)   political action.
        (c)   routinization.
        (d)   assimilation.

6.   Norway, Spain, Belgium, Great Britain, the Netherlands, and Denmark are all contemporary exampl
        of what form of government?

        (a)   totalitarian democracies
        (b)   authoritarian
        (c)   constitutional monarchies
        (d)   absolute monarchies
        (e)   communist democracies

7.   What percentage of humanity live in nations that are classified as being *not free*?

        (a)   14
        (b)   21
        (c)   34
        (d)   43
        (e)   50

8.   _____ refers to a political system that extensively regulates people's lives.

        (a)   Authoritarianism
        (b)   Totalitarianism
        (c)   Absolute monarchy
        (d)   State capitalism

9.   Relatively speaking, which of the following nations has the largest government, based in tax reven
        as a share of gross national product?

        (a)   Japan
        (b)   France
        (c)   the United States
        (d)   Canada
        (e)   Sweden

10. A _____ refers to a range of government agencies and programs that provides benefits to the population.

    (a)   socialist system
    (b)   democracy
    (c)   authoritarian government
    (d)   welfare state
    (e)   political spectrum

11. In 1997, the federal budget amounted to a *per capita* dollar amount of

    (a)   5,600.
    (b)   1,100.
    (c)   9,050.
    (d)   780.

12. In making sense of people's *political attitudes*, analysts distinguish between two kinds of issue, including

    (a)   institutional and personal.
    (b)   economic and social.
    (c)   structural and moral.
    (d)   national and international.

13. Approximately 46.5 percent of adults in the United States identify with the *Democratic Party*. What percentage identify with the Republican Party?

    (a)   25.3
    (b)   51.9
    (c)   48.2
    (d)   34.1

14. Which of the following statements is/are accurate concerning *voting* in the United States?

    (a)   The long-term trend has been for greater eligibility to vote.
    (b)   A smaller and smaller share of eligible citizens actually do vote.
    (c)   Women and men are equally likely to cast a ballot.
    (d)   People over the age of sixty-five are three times as likely to vote as young adults aged eighteen to twenty-four.
    (a)   All of the above are accurate statements.

15. Which idea below represents the *pluralist model* of power?

(a) Power is highly concentrated.
(b) Voting cannot create significant political changes.
(c) The U.S. power system is an oligarchy.
(d) Power is widely dispersed throughout society.

16. With which general sociological paradigm is the *power-elite model* associated?

(a) social-conflict
(b) symbolic-interaction
(c) structural-functional
(d) social-exchange

17. An analysis that explains politics in terms of the operation of society's *economic system* is referred to as

(a) pluralist theory.
(b) Marxist political-economy model.
(c) power-elite model.
(d) welfare state model.

18. Researchers using the _____ view voter apathy as *indifference*.

(a) power-elite model
(b) liberal-democratic model
(c) pluralist model
(d) Marxist model

19. In which stage of *revolution* does the danger of counterrevolution occur?

(a) rising expectations
(b) unresponsive government
(c) establishing a new legitimacy
(d) radical leadership by intellectuals

20. According to Paul Johnson, which of the following is/are distinguishing characteristics of *terrorism*?

(a) Terrorists try to paint violence as a legitimate political tactic.
(b) Terrorism is employed not just by groups, but by governments against their own people.
(c) Democratic societies reject terrorism in principle, but they are especially vulnerable to terrorists because they afford extensive civil liberties.
(d) Terrorism is always a matter of definition.
(e) all of the above

21. *Quincy Wright* has identified several circumstances as conditions which lead humans to go to war? Which of the following is not one of these?

    (a)   perceived threat
    (b)   political objectives
    (c)   social problems
    (d)   moral objectives
    (e)   wide-ranging alternatives

22. Together, the world's nations spend some _____ *trillion* annually for military purposes.

    (a)   5
    (b)   4
    (c)   1
    (d)   8
    (e)   2

23. *Military spending* accounts for _____ percent of the federal budget of the United States.

    (a)   less than 5
    (b)   10
    (c)   19
    (d)   35
    (e)   50

24. Over one-half of all Americans *killed* in war were killed during

    (a)   World War I.
    (b)   the Vietnam War.
    (c)   the Revolutionary War.
    (d)   the Civil War.
    (e)   World War II.

25. Which of the following was *not* listed as a means of reducing the danger of nuclear war?

    (a)   deterrence
    (b)   high-technology defense
    (c)   diplomacy and disarmament
    (d)   resolving underlying conflict
    (e)   multi-national corporate investment

Matching

1. ____ The ability to achieve desired ends despite resistance.
2. ____ Power people perceive as legitimate rather than coercive.
3. ____ A political system that extensively regulates people's lives.
4. ____ A political system that denies popular participation in government.
5. ____ Tax revenues as a share of the gross domestic product for Sweden in 1996.
6. ____ The percentage adults in the U.S. who identify with the Republican party.
7. ____ An analysis of politics that views power as dispersed among many competing interest groups.
8. ____ An analysis of politics that views power as concentrated among the rich.
9. ____ Random acts of violence or the threat of such violence by an individual or group as a political strategy.
10. ____ Organized, armed conflict among the people of various societies, directed by their government.

a.	power-elite model	f.	34.1
b.	war	g.	pluralist model
c.	authoritarianism	h.	power
d.	authority	i.	55.6
e.	terrorism	j.	totalitarianism

Fill-In

1. _____ is the social institution that distributes power, sets a social agenda, and makes decisions.
2. _____ is a formal organization that directs the political life of a society.
3. *Power* people perceive as legitimate rather than coercive is referred to as _____.
4. Max Weber differentiated between three types of *authority*, including _____, _____, and _____.
5. _____ *authority* is power legitimated through extraordinary personal abilities that inspire devotion and obedience.
6. Currently there are _____ independent *nation-states* in the world.
7. A _____ is a political system in which a single family rules from generation to generation.
8. According to the author, countries like the United States are not truly *democratic* for two reasons. One, is the problem of _____. The vast majority of political officials are not elected. Two, there is the problem of economic _____.
9. _____ is a political system that denies popular participation in government.
10. _____ refers to a political system that extensively regulates people's lives.
11. Singapore is a tiny nation on the tip of the Malay peninsula with a population of four million. It gained its independence from _____ in *1965*.

12. A _____ _____ refers to a range of government agencies and programs that provides benefits to the population.

13. The political culture of the United States can be summed up in a word: _____. As the great nineteenth century poet and essayist Ralph Waldo Emerson said, "The government that governs best is the government that governs least."

14. Today's *welfare state* in the U.S. is the result of a gradual increase in the size of government. However, as much as government has expanded in this country, the U.S. welfare state is still smaller than that in other industrial nations. As measured by *tax revenues as a share of gross domestic product*, Scandinavian countries like Denmark and Sweden have relative large welfare states (55.6 and 54.4 respectively). In the U.S. the comparable figure is _____.

15. One major cluster of attitudes related to the *political spectrum* concerns _____ issues, while another concerns _____ issues.

16. In 1998, while 34.1 percent of the adult population identified with the *Republican Party*, _____ identified with the *Democratic Party*.

17. _____ _____ _____ are organizations formed by a special-interest group, independent of political parties, to pursue political aims by raising and spending money.

18. While conservatives suggest *voter apathy* amounts to an _____ to politics, liberals counter that most non-voters are _____ from politics.

19. The _____ *model*, closely allied with the *social-conflict paradigm*, is an analysis of politics that views power as concentrated among the rich.

20. The _____ _____ *model* is an analysis that explains politics in terms of the operation of a society's economic system.

21. Analysts claim *revolutions* share a number of traits, including: rising _____, _____ government, _____ leadership by intellectuals, and establishing a new _____.

22. According to Paul Johnson, *terrorism* has four distinguishing characteristics, including: terrorists try to paint violence as a _____ political tactic, terrorism is employed not just by groups, but also by _____ against their own people, democratic societies reject terrorism in principle, but they are especially _____ to terrorists because they afford extensive civil liberties to their people, and terrorism is always a matter of _____.

23. *Quincy Wright* cites five factors that promote *war*, including: perceived _____, social _____, _____ objectives, _____ imperatives, and the absence of _____.

24. The most recent approaches to *peace* include: _____, high-technology _____, _____ and disarmament, and resolving underlying _____.

<u>Definition and Short-Answer</u>

1. Differentiate between the concepts *power* and *authority*.
2. Differentiate between *Max Weber's* three types of *authority*.
3. Four types of *political systems* are reviewed in the text. Identify and describe each of these systems.
4. What are the general patterns in attitudes among U.S. citizens concerning *social* and *economic issues* as reviewed in the text?
5. What is the evidence that *voter apathy* is a problem in our society? What are its causes?
6. Discuss the *changing work place* using demographic data presented in the text. What are three changes that you think are positive? What are three changes you think are negative?
7. Differentiate between the *pluralist* and *power-elite* models concerning the distribution of power in the United States.
8. What are the five general patterns identified in the text concerning *revolutions*?
9. What are the five factors identified in the text as promoting *war*?
10. Several approaches to reducing the chances for *nuclear war* are addressed in the text. Identify these approaches.
11. In what three ways has politics gone global?
12. What are the five insights presented in the text concerning *terrorism*?
13. Discuss how the concepts of *democracy* and *freedom* are understood within the economic systems of *capitalism* and *socialism*.

PART VI: ANSWERS TO STUDY QUESTIONS

<u>True-False</u>

1.	T	(pp. 435-436)	12.	F	(p. 445)
2.	F	(p. 436)	13.	T	(p. 445)
3.	F	(p. 436)	14.	T	(p. 446)
4.	F	(p. 437)	15.	T	(p. 447)
5.	T	(p. 438)	16.	T	(p. 447)
6.	T	(p. 439)	17.	T	(p. 448)
7.	T	(p. 440)	18.	T	(p. 451)
8.	F	(p. 441)	19.	F	(p. 451)
9.	F	(p. 442)	20.	T	(p. 453)
10.	T	(p. 442)	21.	T	(p. 453)
11.	T	(p. 445)	22.	F	(p. 454)

Multiple Choice

1.	b	(p. 435)	14.	e	(p. 446)
2.	e	(pp. 435-436)	15.	d	(p. 447)
3.	d	(p. 436)	16.	a	(p. 447)
4.	a	(p. 436)	17.	b	(p. 448)
5.	c	(p. 436)	18.	c	(p. 448)
6.	c	(p. 438)	19.	c	(p. 450)
7.	c	(p. 439)	20.	e	(pp. 450-461)
8.	b	(p. 440)	21.	e	(pp. 451-452)
9.	e	(p. 442)	22.	a	(p. 453)
10.	d	(p. 442)	23.	c	(p. 453)
11.	a	(p. 442)	24.	d	(p. 451)
12.	b	(p. 443)	25.	e	(pp. 454-455)
13.	d	(p. 445)			

Matching

1.	h	(p. 435)	6.	f	(p. 445)
2.	d	(pp. 435-436)	7.	g	(p. 447)
3.	j	(p. 440)	8.	a	(p. 447)
4.	c	(p. 440)	9.	e	(p. 450)
5.	i	(p. 442)	10.	b	(p. 451)

Fill-In

1. Politics (p. 435)
2. Government (p. 435)
3. authority (pp. 435-436)
4. traditional, rational-legal, charismatic (p. 436)
5. charismatic (p. 436)
6. 191 (p. 437)
7. monarchy (p. 437)
8. bureaucracy, inequality (p. 438)
9. authoritarianism (p. 440)
10. Totalitarianism (p. 440)
11. Malaysia (p. 441)
12. welfare state (p. 442)
13. individualism (p. 442)
14. 31.7 (p. 442)
15. economic, social (p. 443)
16. 46.5 (p. 445)
17. Political Action Committees (p. 445)
18. indifference, alienation (p. 446)
19. power-elite (p. 447)
20. Marxist political-economy (p. 448)

21. expectations, unresponsive, radical, legitimacy (p. 450)
22. legitimate, governments, vulnerable, definition (pp. 450-451)
23. threats, problems, political, moral, alternatives (pp. 451-452)
24. deterrence, defense, diplomacy, conflict (pp. 454-455)

PART VII: IN FOCUS—IMPORTANT ISSUES

- Power and Authority

  How is *authority* different from *power?*

  Define and illustrate each of the following *types of authority*:

    traditional

    rational-legal

    charismatic

- Politics in Global Perspective

  Define and illustrate each of the following categories of *political systems*:

    monarchy

    democracy

  Discuss the differences in how capitalists and socialists understand the concepts of *democracy* and *freedom*.

318

authoritarianism

totalitarianism

- Politics in the United States

Describe the *political spectrum* in the United States. What strikes you most about the data presented in the text?

Generally discuss the evidence for *voter apathy* in the United States today. What are the two major explanations of voter apathy in the United States?

- Theoretical Analysis of Power in Society

Differentiate between the following competing models of power in the United States. What is the evidence being used in support of each model?

pluralist model

power-elite model

Marxist model

- Power Beyond the Rules

What are the four traits commonly shared by *revolutions?*

What are the four distinguishing characteristics of *terrorism?*

320

- War and Peace

  Identify and illustrate five factors that promote *war:*

  What are the four recent approaches to *peace* identified in the text? What are your thoughts on each in terms of promoting peace?

- Looking Ahead: Politics in the Twenty-First Century

  What are the four *global trends* being identified by the author?

PART VIII: ANALYSIS AND COMMENT

Global Sociology

"Soft Authoritarianism" or Planned Prosperity?: A Report From Singapore"

Key Points: Questions:

"Violence Beyond the Rules: A Report from the Former Yugoslavia"

Key Points: Questions:

Critical Thinking

"Information Warfare: Let Your Fingers Do the Fighting"

Key Points: Questions:

Controversy and Debate

"Online Democracy: Can Computers Increase Political Participation?"

Key Points: Questions:

Window on the World--Global Map 17-1

"Political Freedom in Global Perspective"

Key Points: Questions:

Seeing Ourselves--National Map 17-1

"Political Apathy among Young People across the United States"

Key Points: Questions:

18 | Family

PART I: CHAPTER OUTLINE

I.   The Family: Basic Concepts
II.   The Family: Global Variations
    A.   Marriage Patterns
    B.   Residential Patterns
    C.   Patterns of Descent
    D.   Patterns of Authority
III.   Theoretical Analysis of the Family
    A.   Functions of the Family: Structural-Functional Analysis
    B.   Inequality and the Family: Social-Conflict Analysis
    C.   Constructing Family Life: Micro-Level Analysis
        1.   Symbolic-Interaction Analysis
        2.   Social-Exchange Analysis
IV.   Stages of Family Life
    A.   Courtship
        1.   Romantic Love
    B.   Settling In: Ideal and Real Marriage
    C.   Child Rearing
    D.   The Family in Later Life
V.   U.S. Families: Class, Race, and Gender
    A.   Social Class
    B.   Ethnicity and Race
        1.   Hispanic Families
        2.   African American Families
        3.   Mixed Marriages
    C.   Gender
VI.   Transitions and Problems in Family Life
    A.   Divorce
        1.   Who Divorces?
    B.   Remarriage
    C.   Family Violence
        1.   Violence against Women
        2.   Violence against Children

VII.   Alternative Family Forms
   A.   One-Parent Families
   B.   Cohabitation
   C.   Gay and Lesbian Couples
   D.   Singlehood
VIII.   New Reproductive Technology and the Family
  IX.   Looking Ahead: Family in the Twenty-First Century
   X.   Summary
  XI.   Key Concepts
 XII.   Critical-Thinking Questions
XIII.   Applications and Exercises
 XIV.   Sites to See

PART II: LEARNING OBJECTIVES

1. To be able to define and illustrate basic concepts relating to the social institutions of kinship, family, and marriage.
2. To gain a cross-cultural perspective of the social institutions of kinship, family, and marriage.
3. To be able to analyze the social institutions of kinship, family, and marriage using the structural-functional, social-conflict, and symbolic-interaction perspectives.
4. To be able to describe the traditional life course of the U.S. family.
5. To be able to recognize the impact of social class, race, ethnicity, and gender socialization on the family.
6. To be able describe the problems and transitions that seriously affect family life.
7. To be able to describe the composition and prevalence of alternative family forms.
8. To become aware of the impact, both technologically and ethically, of new reproductive techniques on the family.
9. To be able to identify four sociological conclusions about the family as we enter the twenty-first century.

PART III: KEY CONCEPTS

bilateral descent

cohabitation

conjugal family

consanguine family

descent

endogamy

exogamy

extended family

family

family of affinity

family of orientation

family of procreation

family unit

family violence

homogamy

incest taboo

in vitro fertilization

kinship

marriage

matrilineal descent

matrilocality

monogamy

neolocality

nuclear family

patrilineal descent

patrilocality

polyandry

polygamy

polygyny

romantic love

PART IV: IMPORTANT RESEARCHERS

Lillian Rubin

Jessie Bernard

Paul Bohannan

PART V: STUDY QUESTIONS

True-False

1.   T   F   The family into which one is born is referred to as the *family of procreation*.
2.   T   F   Because it is based on marriage, the nuclear family is also known as the *conjugal family*.
3.   T   F   Norms of *endogamy* relate to marriage between people of the same social category.
4.   T   F   *Matrilocality* occurs more commonly in societies that engage in distant warfare or in which daughters have greater economic value.
5.   T   F   *Polyandry* is much more common around the world than is *polygyny*.
6.   T   F   *Neolocality* refers to a residential pattern in which a married couple lives apart from the parents of both spouses.
7.   T   F   Every known culture has some type of *incest taboo*.
8.   T   F   Our society places less of an emphasis on *romantic love* than most other cultures around the world.
9.   T   F   Economically speaking, industrialization transforms children from an asset to a *liability*.
10. T   F   While the actual number is smaller, the "ideal" number of children to have for most married U.S. adults is three or more.
11. T   F   Most children under the age of five whose parent(s) work outside of the home in paid employment attend organized *day care* or *preschool* programs.
12. T   F   Over forty-five percent of African American families are *headed by women*.
13. T   F   *Jessie Bernard's* research on marriage suggests that this institution is more beneficial for men than it is for women.
14. T   F   The *divorce rate* in the U.S. during the twentieth century has actually only increased by less than 30 percent.
15. T   F   While the *divorce rate* is in the U.S. high, relative to other industrialized societies it is fairly low.
16. T   F   *Blended families* are composed of children and some combination of biological parents and stepparents.

17.	T	F	According to the text, most *child abusers* are men.
18.	T	F	The percentage of households with *single adults* has actually been decreasing over the last two decades.
19.	T	F	Less than one-half of those couples who *cohabit* eventually marry.
20.	T	F	*Homosexual marriage* is illegal in all fifty states in the United States.
21.	T	F	*Test-tube babies* are, technically speaking, the result of the process of *in vitro fertilization*.
22.	T	F	Our author concludes that family life in the twenty-first century will be *highly variable*.

Multiple Choice

1. The family into which one is born and raised is referred to as the *family of*

    (a)   affinity.
    (b)   orientation.
    (c)   procreation.
    (d)   endogamy.

2. Which of the following refers to a social bond, based on blood, marriage or adoption, that joins individuals into families?

    (a)   descent group
    (b)   nuclear family
    (c)   family
    (d)   kinship

3. The *consanguine family* is also known as the

    (a)   conjugal family.
    (b)   family of orientation.
    (c)   nuclear family.
    (d)   family of procreation.
    (e)   extended family.

4. What is the family unit including parents and children, as well as other kin?

    (a)   a family
    (b)   a kinship group
    (c)   a nuclear family
    (d)   an extended family

5. Which of the following cultural norms promotes the pattern of marriage between people of the *same social category*?

   (a) endogamy
   (b) monogamy
   (c) exogamy
   (d) polygamy

6. Marriage between people of different social categories is called

   (a) polygamy.
   (b) monogamy.
   (c) exogamy.
   (d) endogamy.

7. What is a marriage that joins *one female* with *more than one male*?

   (a) polygamy
   (b) polyandry
   (c) endogamy
   (d) polygyny

8. What is the residential pattern in which a married couple lives apart from the parents of both spouses?

   (a) neolocality
   (b) patrilocality
   (c) matrilocality
   (d) avunculocality
   (e) bilateral descent

9. What is the system by which members of a society trace kinship over generations?

   (a) descent
   (b) family
   (c) marriage
   (d) extended family

10. In which of the following nations are couples *least likely* to marry?

   (a) Japan
   (b) the United States
   (c) Great Britain
   (d) Germany
   (e) Sweden

11. The type of sociological analysis of the family that holds that the family serves to perpetuate social inequality is:

    (a) social-exchange analysis.
    (b) structural-functional analysis.
    (c) social-conflict analysis.
    (d) symbolic-interaction analysis.

12. Which theory and theorist traced the origin of the family to the need for men to pass poverty on to their sons?

    (a) symbolic-interaction--George Herbert Mead
    (b) structural-functionalism--Talcott Parsons
    (c) structural functionalism--Emile Durkheim
    (d) social-conflict--Friedrich Engels

13. Which of the following is *not* one of the ways that families aid in the perpetuation of social inequality?

    (a) property and inheritance
    (b) bilineal descent
    (c) patriarchy
    (d) race and ethnicity

14. The depiction of courtship and marriage as forms of negotiation is found in the _____ *analysis*.

    (a) structural-functional
    (b) social-conflict
    (c) symbolic-interaction
    (d) social-exchange

15. Sociologists have noted that *romantic love* as a basis for marriage

    (a) is reinforced by cultural values.
    (b) acts as a strong incentive to leave one's original family of orientation to form a new family of procreation.
    (c) is not as stable a basis for marriage as social and economic bases.
    (d) all of the above

16. Most adults int he U.S. feel the *ideal number* of children is

    (a) one.
    (b) two.
    (c) three.
    (d) four.

17. Which of the following is *not* one of the familial adjustments made by parents in *later life*?

    (a) adjustment to retirement and spending more time together
    (b) helping to care for grandchildren
    (c) assumption of more household responsibilities
    (d) death of a spouse

18. What percentage of children with working mothers attend *day care centers or preschools*?

    (a) 29
    (b) 62
    (c) 16
    (d) 51

19. Lillian Rubin focused her research on the relationship between _____ and marriage.

    (a) social class
    (b) race
    (c) presence of children
    (d) age at marriage

20. Which group has the proportionately highest number of *single heads-of-households*?

    (a) African Americans
    (b) Hispanics
    (c) Asian Americans
    (d) whites

21. Which of the following is *not* a finding of Jessie Bernard's study of marriage?

    (a) married women have poorer mental health
    (b) married women have more passive attitudes toward life
    (c) married women report less personal happiness
    (d) married women are not generally required to participate in the labor force

22. The high U.S. *divorce rate* has many causes; which of the following is *not* identified in the text as being one of them?

    (a) Individualism is on the rise.
    (b) Women are more dependent on men.
    (c) Many marriages today are stressful.
    (d) Romantic love often subsides.
    (e) Divorce is easier to get and more socially acceptable.

23. Remarriage often creates families composed of both biological parents and stepparents and children. These are called

    (a) second families.
    (b) blended families.
    (c) focal families.
    (d) families of orientation.

24. In the U.S. annually, there are approximately _____ *reported cases* of child abuse.

    (a) 100,000
    (b) 6 million
    (c) 2 million
    (d) 300,000

25. Currently in the U.S., what percentage of children are living in *single-parent families*?

    (a) 16
    (b) 45
    (c) 9
    (d) 28

26. Which country, in 1989, became the first nation to legalize *same-sex marriages*?

    (a) Denmark
    (b) France
    (c) the United States
    (d) Japan

27. Which of the following statements is *not accurate* concerning *cohabitation*?

    (a) It is more popular today in the U.S. than it was in 1970.
    (b) Almost one-half of people between the ages twenty-five and forty-four have cohabited at some point in time.
    (c) Sixty percent of cohabiting couples eventually marry.
    (d) Over one-third of cohabiting couples have at least one child living with them.
    (e) Cohabiting tends to appeal to more independent minded individuals as well as those who favor gender equality.

28. Which of the following statements is *inaccurate*?

    (a) Homosexual marriages are not legal in the United States.
    (b) Seventy-six percent of women aged twenty to twenty-four in the United States are single.
    (c) One-in-four households in the United States contains a single person.
    (d) Thirty-three percent of births in the United States today are to unwed mothers.
    (e) The United States has a higher rate of births to unwed mothers than any other modern industrial nation.

Matching

1. ____ A family unit including parents, children, as well as other kin.
2. ____ People with or without legal or blood ties who feel they belong together and want to define themselves as a family.
3. ____ The system by which members of a society trace kinship over generations.
4. ____ Marriage between people of the same social category.
5. ____ A residential pattern in which a married couple lives apart from the parents of both spouses.
6. ____ A form of marriage uniting one female with more than one male.
7. ____ A system tracing kinship through both men and women.
8. ____ A form of marriage uniting one male with more than one female.
9. ____ The feeling of affection and sexual passion toward another person as the basis of marriage.
10. ____ Families composed of children and some combination of biological parents and stepparents.

a.	endogamy	f.	neolocality
b.	extended family	g.	family of affinity
c.	blended families	h.	polygyny
d.	bilateral decent	i.	polyandry
e.	descent	j.	romantic love

Fill-In

1. The _____ is a social institution found in all societies that unites individuals into cooperative groups that oversee the bearing and raising of children.
2. The family into which one is born is referred to as the *family of* _____.
3. The _____ *family* is based on blood ties.
4. _____ refers to a social bond, based on blood, marriage, or adoption, that joins individuals into families.
5. _____ refers to marriage between people of the same social group or category.
6. _____ is a marriage that joins one female with more than one male.
7. _____ refers to the system by which members of a society trace kinship over generations.
8. _____ *descent* is a system tracing kinship through both men and women.
9. Structural-functionalists identify several *vital tasks* performed by the family. These include: _____, _____ of sexual activity, social _____, and material and economic _____,
10. Cultural norms that forbid sexual relationships or marriage between specified kin are called _____ _____.
11. *Social-conflict* theorists argue that families perpetuate social inequality in several ways, including: Property and _____, _____, and _____ and _____.
12. Our culture celebrates _____ _____---the feeling of affection and sexual passion toward another person--as the basis for marriage.
13. _____ *percent* of U.S. children under the age of five whose mothers work outside the home in paid employment spend time in *organized child-care facilities*.
14. Women headed _____ *percent* of African American families in 1996.
15. Jessie Bernard suggests that every marriage is actually _____ different relationships.

333

16. The high U.S. *divorce rate* has many causes, including: _____ is on the rise, _____ _____ often subsides, women are now less _____ on men, many of today's marriages are _____, divorce is more socially _____, and from a legal standpoint, divorce is _____ to obtain.

17. Courts award *child support* in _____ percent of all divorces involving children.

18. Remarriage often creates _____ *families*, composed of children and some combination of biological parents and stepparents.

19. The FBI estimates that at least _____ women are victims of *domestic violence* each year in he United States.

20. Today, _____ states have enacted *marital rape laws*.

21. *Family violence* includes _____, _____, or _____ abuse of one family member by another.

22. _____ is the sharing of a household by an unmarried couple.

23. *Test-tube babies* are the result of _____ _____ _____.

24. Sociologists point out five probable *future trends* regarding the family. These include: _____ rates are likely to remain high, family life will be highly _____, men are likely to continue to play a limited role in _____ _____, we will continue to feel the effects of _____ changes in our families, and the importance of new _____ technology will increase.

Definition and Short-Answer

1. What are the four basic *functions* of the family according to structural-functionalists?
2. Define and describe the three patterns of *descent*.
3. Why has the *divorce rate* increased in recent decades in the United States? What are the basic demographic patterns involving divorce in our society today?
4. What are the four *stages* of the family life cycle outlined in the text? Describe the major events occurring during each of these stages.
5. In what ways are *middle-class* and *working-class* marriages different?
6. What are the arguments being made about the family by *social-conflict* theorists?
7. What are four important points made in the text concerning *family violence*?
8. Five *alternative family forms* are discussed in the text. Identify these and review the data concerning three of them. What are your opinions concerning these changes in the family?
9. What are the five conclusions being made about marriage and family life into the twenty-first century?
10. What are the dimensions of *family violence*? What are the demographic patterns concerning each of these?

PART V: ANSWERS TO STUDY QUESTIONS

True-False

1.	F	(p. 462)	12.	T	(p. 475)
2.	T	(p. 462)	13.	T	(p. 476)
3.	T	(p. 462)	14.	F	(p. 476)
4.	T	(p. 463)	15.	F	(p. 476)
5.	F	(p. 463)	16.	T	(p. 479)
6.	T	(p. 463)	17.	T	(p. 480)
7.	T	(p. 465)	18.	F	(p. 483)
8.	F	(p. 470)	19.	T	(pp. 481-484)
9.	T	(p. 471)	20.	T	(p. 482)
10.	F	(p. 471)	21.	T	(p. 482)
11.	F	(p. 472)	22.	T	(p. 483)

Multiple Choice

1.	b	(p. 462)	15.	d	(p. 470)
2.	d	(p. 462)	16.	b	(p. 471)
3.	e	(p. 462)	17.	c	(pp. 472-473)
4.	d	(p. 462)	18.	a	(p. 473)
5.	a	(p. 462)	19.	a	(p. 473)
6.	c	(p. 462)	20.	a	(pp. 474-475)
7.	b	(p. 463)	21.	d	(pp. 475-476)
8.	a	(p. 463)	22.	b	(pp. 476-477)
9.	a	(p. 463)	23.	b	(p. 479)
10.	e	(p. 464)	24.	c	(p. 480)
11.	c	(p. 467)	25.	d	(p. 480)
12.	d	(p. 467)	26.	a	(p. 481)
13.	b	(p. 467)	27.	c	(p. 481)
14.	d	(p. 468)	28.	e	(pp. 481-482)

Matching

1.	b	(p. 462)	6.	i	(p. 463)
2.	g	(p. 462)	7.	d	(p. 464)
3.	e	(p. 463)	8.	h	(p. 462)
4.	a	(p. 462)	9.	j	(p. 470)
5.	f	(p. 463)	10.	c	(p. 479)

Fill-In

1. family (p. 462)
2. orientation (p. 462)
3. consanguine (p. 462)
4. Kinship (p. 462)
5. endogamy (p. 462)

6. Polyandry (p. 463)
7. Descent (p. 463)
8. Bilateral (p. 464)
9. socialization, regulation, placement, security (pp. 465-466)
10. incest taboos (p. 467)
11. inheritance, patriarchy, race, ethnicity (p. 470)
12. romantic love (p. 472)
13. 29.4 (p. 472)
14. 47 (p. 474)
15. two (p. 475)
16. individualism, romantic love, dependent, stressful, acceptable, easier (pp. 476-477)
17. 58 (p. 478)
18. blended (p. 479)
19. 600,000 (p. 480)
20. all (p. 480)
21. emotional, physical, sexual (p. 480)
22. Cohabitation (p. 481)
23. in vitro fertilization (p. 482)
24. divorce, variable, child rearing, economic, reproductive (p. 483)

PART VII: IN FOCUS--IMPORTANT ISSUES

- The Family: Basic Concepts

  What does the author mean by saying that there is a trend toward a more *inclusive* definition of he family?

- The Family: Global Variations

  Identify and define or illustrate the different *patterns* found around the world for each of the following:

  marriage

  residence

descent

authority

- Theoretical Analysis of the Family

According to structural-functionalists, what are the *functions* performed by families? Provide one piece of evidence for each function.

In what ways do *conflict theorists* believe the family perpetuates inequality? Illustrate or define each of these.

Micro-level approaches explore how individuals shape and experience family life. Differentiate between the following two micro-level perspectives:

symbolic-interaction analysis

social-exchange analysis

- Stages of Family Life

  Briefly describe the content for each of the following stages in family life:

  courtship

  settling in

  child rearing

  the family in later life

- U.S. Families: Class, Race, and Gender

  Summarize the findings concerning Lillian Rubin's research on the relationship between *social class* and the family.

  Identify important demographic differences between white families and the following racial and ethnic minorities.

  African Americans

  Hispanics

Summarize the conclusions of Jessie Bernard concerning *gender* and the family.

- Transitions and Problems In Family Life

  Identify the major causes of *divorce* as listed in the text.

  What are the characteristics most associated with divorce?

  How common is *remarriage*?

  Identify three important facts concerning each of the following two types of *family violence*:

  > violence against women

  > violence against children

- Alternative Family Forms

  Identify two important demographic facts concerning *single-parent families* in our society today:

  How common is *cohabitation* in our society today?

  What are two important points being made about *gay and lesbian couples*?

  How common is *singlehood* in our society today?

- New Reproductive Technology and the Family

  What is *in vitro fertilization*?

- Looking Ahead: The Family In the Twenty-First Century

  What are the five likely trends for the family of the twenty-first century as identified by the author?

PART VIII: COMMENT AND ANALYSIS

Global Sociology

"The Weakest Families on Earth? A Report From Sweden"

Key Points: Questions:

"Early To Wed: A Report From Rural India"

Key Points: Questions:

Applying Sociology

"Who's Minding the Kids?"

Key Points: Questions:

Critical Thinking

"Which Will It Be: Real Marriage or Marriage "Lite"?"

Key Points: Questions:

Controversy and Debate

"Should We Save the Traditional Family?"

Key Points: Questions:

Window on the World--Global Map 18-1

"Marital Form in Global Perspective"

Key Points: Questions:

Seeing Ourselves--National Map 18-1

"Divorced People across the U.S."

Key Points: Questions:

19   Religion

PART I: CHAPTER OUTLINE

I.   Religion: Basic Concepts
    A.   Religion and Sociology
II.   Theoretical Analysis of Religion
    A.   Functions of Religion: Structural-Functional Analysis
    B.   Constructing the Sacred: Symbolic-Interaction Analysis
    C.   Inequality and Religion: Social-Conflict Analysis
III.   Religion and Social Change
    A.   Max Weber: Protestantism and Capitalism
    B.   Liberation Theology
IV.   Types of Religious Organization
    A.   Church
    B.   Sect
    C.   Cult
V.   Religion in History
    A.   Religion In Preindustrial Societies
    B.   Religion In Industrial Societies
VI.   World Religions
    A.   Christianity
    B.   Islam
    C.   Judaism
    D.   Hinduism
    E.   Buddhism
    F.   Confucianism
    G.   Religion: East and West
VIII.   Religion in the United States
    A.   Religious Affiliation
    B.   Religiosity
    C.   Religion and Social Stratification
        1.   Social Class
        2.   Ethnicity and Race

PART II: LEARNING OBJECTIVES

1.   To be able to define basic concepts relating to the sociological analysis of religion.
2.   To be able to identify and describe the three functions of religion as developed by Emile Durkheim.
3.   To be able to discuss the view that religion is socially constructed.
4.   To be able to discuss the role of religion in maintaining social inequality.
5.   To be able to describe how industrialization and science affect religious beliefs and practices.
6.   To be able to compare and contrast the basic types of religious organizations.
7.   To be able to distinguish between preindustrial and industrial societies in terms of religious beliefs and practices.
8.   To be able to identify and generally distinguish between the world's major religions.
9.   To be able to discuss the basic demographic patterns concerning religious affiliation, religiosity, secularization, and religious revival in the U.S. today.
10.   To begin to critically think about the role of religion in the world as it will unfold over the next generation, and to consider the relationship between religion and science.

PART III: KEY CONCEPTS

animism

bodhi

charisma

church

civil religion

conversion

creationism

344

creation science

cult

denomination

dhamma

dharma

faith

fundamentalism

karma

liberation theology

profane

religion

religiosity

ritual

sacred

sect

secularism

Torah

totem

PART IV: IMPORTANT RESEARCHERS

Emile Durkheim   Karl Marx

PART V: STUDY QUESTIONS

True-False

1. T F According to Emile Durkheim, the *profane* refers to that which is an ordinary element of everyday life.

2. T F Emile Durkheim defined a *totem* as an object in the natural world collectively defined as sacred.

3. T F According to Emile Durkheim, society has an existence and power of its own, beyond the lives of the people who collectively created it.

4. T F A major criticism of Emile Durkheim's analysis of religion is that he focuses too much attention on the *dysfunctions* of religious belief and practice.

5. T F The symbolic-interaction approach views religion as a *social construction*.

6. T F Social-conflict theory focuses on how religion promotes change and equality.

7. T F *Liberation theology* is a fusion of Christian principles with political activism, often Marxist in character.

8. T F Two types, or forms, of churches identified in the text are the *church formally aligned with the state* and the *denomination*.

9. T F Whereas a *cult* is a type of religious organization that stands apart from the larger society, a *sect* represents something almost entirely new and stands outside a society's cultural tradition.

10. T F *Animism* is the belief that natural objects are conscious life forms that affect humanity.

11. T F *Islam* is the most widespread religion in the world.

12. T F *Judaism* is the oldest of all the world religions.

13. T F Fewer than 40 percent of people in the United States identify with a religion.

14. T F *Religiosity* refers to the importance of religion in a person's life.

15. T F By global standards, *North Americans* are relatively nonreligious people.

16. T F *Ritualistic religiosity* describes an individual's degree of belief in religious doctrine.

17. T F A quasi-religious loyalty based in citizenship is called a *civil religion*.

18. T F In a recent national survey, almost one-third of U.S. adults described their religious upbringing as *fundamentalist*.

19. T F Science and new technologies are reducing the relevance of religion in modern society as many moral dilemmas and spiritual issues are resolved or are diminishing in significance.

20. T F The *Scopes Monkey Trial* of 1925 involved the prosecution of a science teacher who was teaching evolution in violation of Tennessee state law.

1. _____ refers to that which people set apart as extraordinary, inspiring a sense of awe and reverence.

   (a) Profane
   (b) Sacred
   (c) Animism
   (d) Religiosity

2. What is the term for the social institution involving beliefs and practices based upon a conception of the sacred?

   (a) faith
   (b) totem
   (c) religion
   (d) ritual

3. Emile Durkheim referred to the ordinary elements of everyday life as

   (a) religion.
   (b) faith.
   (c) ritual.
   (d) the profane.

4. Formal, ceremonial behavior refers to

   (a) the sacred.
   (b) ritual.
   (c) religion.
   (d) faith.

5. Which of the following is a function of religion according to *Emile Durkheim*?

   (a) social cohesion
   (b) social control
   (c) providing meaning and purpose
   (d) All are functions identified by Emile Durkheim.
   (e) None are functions, as he saw religion as having negative consequences for society.

6. The view that religion is completely *socially constructed* by a society's members is espoused by

   (a) Max Weber.
   (b) Peter Berger.
   (c) Karl Marx.
   (d) Emile Durkheim.

7.   Which of the following is an appropriate criticism of a *symbolic-interactionist* approach to religion:

      (a)   It ignores religion's link to inequality.
      (b)   It fails to consider the importance of rituals.
      (c)   It treats reality as objective.
      (d)   It ignores the social construction of religion.

8.   Who would be most likely to argue that religion motivates *capitalism*?

      (a)   a Marxist
      (b)   a symbolic interactionist
      (c)   a follower of Max Weber
      (d)   a person following the precepts of liberation theology

9.   *Liberation theology* advocates a blending of religion with

      (a)   the family.
      (b)   the economy.
      (c)   education.
      (d)   politics.

10.   A church, independent of the state, that accepts religious pluralism is a(n)

      (a)   denomination.
      (b)   sect.
      (c)   cult.
      (d)   civil religion.

11.   Which of the following is *not* a feature of a *sect*?

      (a)   charismatic leaders
      (b)   psychic intensity and informal structure
      (c)   membership through conversion
      (d)   proselytizing
      (e)   All of the above are features of a sect.

12.   A religious organization that is largely outside society's cultural traditions is called a

      (a)   totem.
      (b)   cult.
      (c)   ecclesia.
      (d)   sect.

13.   The belief that elements of the natural world are conscious life forms that affect humanity refers to

    (a)   animism.
    (b)   cults.
    (c)   a totem.
    (d)   sects.

14.   Which religion is the most *widespread* in the world?

    (a)   Islam
    (b)   Buddhism
    (c)   Christianity
    (d)   Judaism

15.   The followers of *Islam* are called

    (a)   Buddhists.
    (b)   animists.
    (c)   Hindus.
    (d)   Muslims.

16.   The *Qur'an* is sacred to

    (a)   Jews.
    (b)   Muslims.
    (c)   Buddhists.
    (d)   Confucians.

17.   A distinctive concept of *Judaism* is the _____, a special relationship with God by which Jews became the "chosen people."

    (a)   covenant
    (b)   Torah
    (c)   dharma
    (d)   Passover

18.   Which of the following is the *oldest* of all the world's religions?

    (a)   Christianity
    (b)   Judaism
    (c)   Hinduism
    (d)   Islam

19.   In which country did *Buddhisism* emerge?

        (a)   China
        (b)   Japan
        (c)   Iran
        (d)   Nepal
        (e)   India

20.   Which world religion is so intertwined with one nation that it cannot be diffused widely to other nations?

        (a)   Judaism
        (b)   Confucianism
        (c)   Hinduism
        (d)   Buddhism

21.   Approximately ____ percent of people in the U.S. identify with a religion.

        (a)   26
        (b)   49
        (c)   68
        (d)   86
        (e)   98

22.   The strength of a person's emotional ties to a religion is called

        (a)   ideological religiosity.
        (b)   ritualistic religiosity.
        (c)   experiential religiosity.
        (d)   intellectual religiosity.

23.   What percentage of U.S. adults consider themselves *Protestants*?

        (a)   24
        (b)   35
        (c)   56
        (d)   78

24.   Which of the following is the largest *Protestant denomination*?

        (a)   Baptist
        (b)   Presbyterian
        (c)   Methodist
        (d)   Episcopalian
        (e)   Lutheran

25. What is *secularization*?

    (a) the ecumenical movement
    (b) the historical decline in the importance of the supernatural and the sacred
    (c) the increase in religiosity in postindustrial society
    (d) fundamentalism

26. A quasi-religious loyalty binding individuals in a basically secular society is referred to as

    (a) a totem.
    (b) secularization.
    (c) religiosity.
    (d) fundamentalism.
    (e) civil religion.

27. Which of the following is *not* identified in the text as a distinction of *religious fundamentalism*?

    (a) Fundamentalists interpret sacred texts literally.
    (b) Fundamentalists promote religious pluralism.
    (c) Fundamentalists pursue the personal experience of God's presence.
    (d) Fundamentalism opposes "secular humanism."
    (e) Many fundamentalists endorse conservative political goals.

28. In the *Scopes trial* of 1925, the state of Tennessee prosecuted a man for

    (a) polygamy.
    (b) profanity.
    (c) cohabitation.
    (d) teaching evolution.

Matching

1. ____ That which is an ordinary element of everyday life.
2. ____ The social institution involving beliefs and practices based upon a conception of the sacred.
3. ____ Belief anchored in conviction rather than scientific evidence.
4. ____ An object in the natural world collectively defined as sacred.
5. ____ Suggested that the religious doctrine of Calvinism sparked the Industrial Revolution in Western Europe.
6. ____ A type of religious organization well integrated into the larger society.
7. ____ A church, independent of the state, that accepts religious pluralism.
8. ____ Extraordinary personal qualities that can turn an audience into followers.
9. ____ A type of religious organization that stands apart from the larger society.
10. ____ A religious organization that is largely outside a society's cultural traditions.
11. ____ The belief in many gods.
12. ____ The importance of religion in a person's life.
13. ____ The historical decline in the importance of the supernatural and the sacred.
14. ____ A conservative religious doctrine that opposes intellectualism and worldly accomodation in favor of restoring traditional, otherworldly spirituality.

a.	demonination	i.	church
b.	fundamentalism	j.	faith
c.	religiosity	k.	totem
d.	religion	l.	secularization
e.	charisma	m.	cult
f.	profane	n.	Max Weber
g.	polytheism	o.	Emile Durkheim
h.	sacred	p.	sect

Fill-In

1. *Emile Durkheim* labeled the ordinary elements of everyday life the _____.
2. A _____ is a natural object--or its representation--collectively defined as sacred.
3. _____ refers to belief anchored in conviction rather than scientific evidence.
4. According to Emile Durkheim, three major *functions of religion* include: social _____, social _____, and providing _____ and _____.
5. According to *Max Weber*, industrial capitalism developed in the wake of _____.
6. _____ *theology* is a fusion of Christian principles with political activism, often Marxist in character.
7. A _____ is a type of religious organization well integrated into the larger society.
8. _____ refers to extraordinary personal qualities that can turn audiences into followers.
9. _____ is the belief that natural objects are conscious forms of life that can affect humanity.
10. *Islam* has some 1.1 billion followers who are called _____.

11. Of special importance to Jewish people are the Bible's first five books, known as the _____.

12. The *Hindu principle* of _____ is a belief in the spiritual progress of the human soul.

13. _____ refers to the importance of religion in a person's life.

14. _____ *percent* of U.S. adults state no religious preference.

15. Charles Glock proposed five distinct *dimensions of religiosity*, including: _____, _____, _____, _____, and _____.

16. The historical decline in the importance of the supernatural and the sacred is referred to as _____.

17. A _____ religion is a quasi-religious loyalty based on citizenship.

18. _____ refers to a conservative religious doctrine that opposes intellectualism and worldly accommodation in favor of restoring traditional, otherworldly spirituality.

19. *Religious fundamentalism* is distinctive in five ways, including: interpreting sacred texts _____, rejecting religious _____, pursuing the personal experience of God's _____, opposition to secular _____, and endorsement of _____ political goals.

Definition and Short-Answer

1. According to *structural-functional* analysis, what are three major functions of religion? Provide an example for each from U.S. society.

2. Discuss *Max Weber's* points concerning the historical relationship between Protestantism and capitalism.

3. How do theorists operating from the *social conflict* perspective understand religion and how it operates in society? Provide two examples to illustrate.

4. In a one-page written discussion, debate the issue of whether science threatens or strengthens religion in society.

5. Discuss the issue concerning the extent of *religiosity* in the United States today.

6. Briefly describe the position of religious *fundamentalism* in our society today.

7. Discuss the relationship between *religion* and *social stratification* in the United States today.

8. What are the two major differences between *Eastern* and *Western* religions?

9. Briefly describe the history and dominant religious beliefs for two of the following religions: Christianity, Islam, Judaism, Hinduism, Buddhism, Confucianism.

10. Differentiate between the nature of religion in *preindustrial* and *industrial* societies.

11. Differentiate between *civil religion* and *religious fundamentalism*.

PART VI: ANSWERS TO STUDY QUESTIONS

True-False

1.	T	(p. 489)	11.	F	(p. 497)
2.	T	(p. 490)	12.	F	(p. 500)
3.	T	(p. 490)	13.	F	(p. 503)
4.	F	(p. 491)	14.	T	(p. 504)
5.	T	(p. 491)	15.	F	(p. 503)
6.	F	(p. 492)	16.	F	(p. 504)
7.	T	(p. 494)	17.	T	(p. 507)
8.	T	(p. 494)	18.	T	(p. 510)
9.	F	(p. 495)	19.	F	(p. 510)
10.	T	(p. 496)	20.	T	(p. 510)

Multiple Choice

1.	b	(p. 489)	15.	d	(p. 498)
2.	c	(p. 489)	16.	b	(p. 498)
3.	d	(p. 489)	17.	a	(p. 499)
4.	b	(p. 490)	18.	c	(p. 500)
5.	d	(p. 491)	19.	e	(p. 501)
6.	b	(p. 491)	20.	b	(p. 501)
7.	a	(p. 492)	21.	d	(p. 503)
8.	a	(p. 492)	22.	c	(p. 504)
9.	d	(p. 494)	23.	c	(p. 504)
10.	a	(p. 494)	24.	a	(p. 504)
11.	e	(p. 495)	25.	b	(p. 506)
12.	b	(p. 495)	26.	e	(p. 507)
13.	a	(p. 496)	27.	b	(p. 508)
14.	c	(p. 497)	28.	d	(p. 510)

Matching

1.	f	(p. 489)	8.	e	(p. 495)
2.	d	(p. 489)	9.	p	(p. 495)
3.	j	(p. 490)	10.	m	(p. 495)
4.	k	(p. 490)	11.	g	(p. 496)
5.	n	(p. 492)	12.	c	(p. 504)
6.	i	(p. 494)	13.	l	(p. 506)
7.	a	(p. 494)	14.	b	(p. 508)

1.   profane (p. 489)
2.   totem (p. 490)
3.   faith (p. 490)
4.   cohesion, control meaning, purpose (p. 491)
5.   Calvinism (p. 492)
6.   Liberation (p. 494)
7.   church (p. 494)
8.   charisma (p. 495)
9.   animism (p. 496)
10.   Muslims (p. 498)
11.   Torah (p. 499)
12.   karma (p. 501)
13.   Religiosity (p. 504)
14.   14.5 (p. 504)
15.   experimental, ritualistic, ideological, consequential, intellectual (p. 504)
16.   secularization (p. 506)
17.   civil (p. 507)
18.   fundamentalism (p. 508)
19.   literally, pluralism, presence, humanism, conservative (p. 508)

PART VII: IN FOCUS--IMPORTANT ISSUES

- Religion: Basic Concepts

  How do sociologists conceptualize and understand the place of *faith* and *ritual* in the institution of religion?

  Provide an illustration for Emile Durkheim's distinction between the *profane* and the *sacred*.

- Theoretical Analysis of Religion

  According to *structural-functionalist* Emile Durkheim, what are the three basic *functions of religion*?

  What points are being made by *symbolic-interactinist* Peter Berger concerning religion?

  How did *conflict theorist* Karl Marx understand religion?

- Religion and Social Change

  What is Max Weber's point concerning the relationship between *Protestantism* and *capitalism*?

- Types of Religious Organization

  Differentiate between each of the following:

  church

  sect

  cult

- Religion in History

  How is religion different in *preindustrial societies* as compared with industrial societies? What are the similarities?

- World Religions

  Identify three important points concerning each of the following religions.

    Christianity

    Islam

    Judaism

    Hinduism

    Buddhism

    Confucianism

What are the two basic distinctions between religion in the *East* and *West*?

- Religion in the United States

  How religious are we here in the United States? What is the evidence?

  What is the relationship between *social stratification* and religion?

    social class

    race and ethnicity

- Religion In a Changing Society

  Briefly discuss the place of each of the following patterns in the United States today:

    secularism

    civil religion

    religious revival

- Looking Ahead: Religion In the Twenty-First Century

  What conclusions are being made by the author concerning the place of religion in contemporary United States society?

PART VIII: COMMENT AND ANALYSIS

Social Diversity

"Religion and Patriarchy: Does God Favor Males?"

Key Points: Questions:

Critical Thinking

"Should Students Pray in School?"

Key Points: Questions:

Applying Sociology

"The Cyber-Church: Logging On to Religion"

Key Points: Questions:

Controversy and Debate

"Does Science Threaten Religion?"

Key Points: Questions:

Window on the World--Global Maps 19-1 Through 19-4

"Christianity, Islam, Hinduism, and Buddhism in Global Perspective"

"Key Points: Questions:

Seeing Ourselves--National Maps 19-1 and 19-2

"Membership in a Religious Organization, by County"

Key Points: Questions:

"Religious Diversity across the U.S."

Key Points: Questions:

20 Education

PART I: CHAPTER OUTLINE

I.   Education: A Global Survey
    A.   Schooling and Economic Development
    B.   Schooling in India
    C.   Schooling in Japan
    D   Schooling in Great Britain
    E.   Schooling in the United States

II.   The Functions of Schooling
    A.   Socialization
    B.   Cultural Innovation
    C.   Social Integration
    D.   Social Placement
    E.   Latent Functions of Schooling

III.   Schooling and Social Inequality
    A.   Social Control
    B.   Standardized Testing
    C.   School Tracking
    D.   Inequality Among Schools
        1.   Public and Private Schools
        2.   Inequality in Public Schooling
    E.   Access to Higher Education
    F.   Credentialism
    G   Privilege and Personal Merit

IV.   Problems in the Schools
    A.   Discipline and Violence
    B.   Student Passivity
        1.   Bureaucracy
        2.   College: The Silent Classroom
    C.   Dropping Out
    D.   Academic Standards

V.   Recent Issues in U.S. Education
    A.   School Choice
    B.   Schooling People with Disabilities
    C.   Adult Education

VII.   Looking Ahead: Schooling in the Twenty-First Century

362

PART II: LEARNING OBJECTIVES

1.   To be able to describe the different role of education in low-income and high-income countries.
2.   To compare education in India, Japan, and Great Britain to that provided in the United States.
3.   To be able to identify and describe the functions of schooling.
4.   To consider how education supports social inequality.
5.   To be able to discuss the major issues and problems facing contemporary education in the United States today.
6.   To be able to identify and evaluate alternatives to the current structure of the institution of education in our society.

PART III: KEY CONCEPTS

A Nation At Risk

charter schools

Coleman Report

credentialism

dropping out

education

functional illiteracy

hidden curriculum

mainstreaming

mandatory education laws

mass education

political correctness

progressive education

schooling

schooling for profit

silent classroom

student passivity

tracking

PART IV: IMPORTANT RESEARCHERS

David Karp and William Yoels   Randall Collins

James Coleman   Jonathan Kozol

Christopher Jencks   John Dewey

Theodore Sizer   Talcott Parsons

Samuel Bowles and Herbert Gintis

PART V: STUDY QUESTIONS

True-False

1.   T   F   Today, schooling in *low-income nations* is very diverse because it reflects the local culture.

2.   T   F   The United States actually has a *higher* illiteracy rate than most Latin American societies.

3.   T   F   Japan still does not have national *mandatory education laws.*

4.   T   F   The United States graduates a *smaller percentage* of its students from high school than does Japan.

5.   T   F   The United States was among the first nations to endorse the principle of *mass education.*

6.   T   F   The United States has a *smaller* percentage of its adult population holding a college degree than most other industrialized societies.

7.   T   F   About twenty-four percent of adults in the U.S. have a *college degree.*

8.   T   F   *John Dewey* was a foremost advocate of the idea that schooling should have *practical* consequences.

9.   T   F   Between the year 1985 and 1995, the percentage of students earning degrees in the social science and education *declined significantly.*

10.   T   F   *Social conflict* theorists support *tracking* in that they believe it gives students the kind of learning that fits their abilities and motivation.

11.   T   F   Roughly sixty-two percent of primary and secondary school children in the U.S. attend *public schools.*

12.   T   F   Most private school students in the United States attend *parochial schools.*

13.   T   F   The *Coleman Report* determined that the amount of educational funding was the most important factor in determining education achievement.

14.   T   F   About sixty-five percent of high-school graduates in the U.S. enroll in college the following fall.

15.   T   F   Male college graduates can expect to earn about forty percent more than female college graduates in their lifetime.

16.   T   F   The argument is being made that an emphasis on *credentialism* in our society leads to a condition of undereducation as people seek the status of a career and its earnings over the completion of degree programs at college.

17.   T   F   *Student passivity* in college tends to increase if instructors call students by name, and if they ask analytical rather than factual questions.

18.   T   F   The work *A Nation At Risk* focuses on the increasing violence in American schools.

19.   T   F   *Charter schools* refer to schools that operate with less state regulation so teachers and administrators can try new teaching strategies.

20.   T   F   *Mainstreaming* is a form of *inclusive education.*

1.   The social institution guiding a society's transmission of knowledge--including basic facts, job skills, and also cultural norms and values--to its members is the definition for

     (a)   schooling.
     (b)   teaching.
     (c)   education.
     (d)   curriculum.

2.   Formal instruction under the direction of specially trained teachers refers to

     (a)   curriculum.
     (b)   education.
     (c)   schooling.
     (d)   mainstreaming.

3.   Which of the following is *inaccurate* concerning India?

     (a)   People earn about five percent of the income standard in the United States, and poor families often depend on the earnings of children.
     (b)   Less than one-half of Indian children enter secondary school.
     (c)   About one-half of the Indian population is illiterate.
     (d)   More girls than boys in India reach secondary school.

4.   Which of the following is/are accurate concerning education and schooling in Japan?

     (a)   Industrialization brought mandatory education to Japan in 1872.
     (b)   In Japan, schooling reflects personal ability more than it does in the United States.
     (c)   The Japanese government pays much of the costs of higher education.
     (d)   More men and women graduate from high school in Japan than in the United States.
     (e)   All of the above are accurate.

5.   *Mandatory education* laws were found in every state in the United States by

     (a)   1781.
     (b)   1850.
     (c)   1822.
     (d)   1918.

6.   Who advocated the idea that schooling should have *practical* consequences and promoted *progressive education*?

     (a)   James Coleman
     (b)   John Dewey
     (c)   Daniel Moynihan
     (d)   Christopher Jencks

7. Which of the following nations has the highest percentage of adults with a *college degree*

   (a) the United States
   (b) Netherlands
   (c) Canada
   (d) Denmark
   (e) Sweden

8. The percentage of students receiving a bachelor's degree in which of the following areas showed the greatest *increase* during the period 1985-1995?

   (a) engineering
   (b) library and archival science
   (c) philosophy
   (d) pre-law
   (e) communications

9. According to *structural-functionalists*, which of the following functions of formal education helps forge a population into a single, unified society?

   (a) socialization
   (b) social placement
   (c) social integration
   (d) cultural innovation

10. Child care, establishing relationships and networks, and consuming the time and energy of teenagers are examples of

    (a) the latent functions of education.
    (b) school tracking.
    (c) social control.
    (d) mainstreaming.

11. *Structural-functionalists* overlook one core truth:

    (a) education serves as a form of social placement.
    (b) the quality of schooling is far greater for some than others.
    (c) schools serve several latent functions.
    (d) schooling helps forge a mass of people into a unified society.
    (e) education creates as well as transmits culture.

12. *Social-conflict* analysis associates formal education with:

    (a) student's skill enhancement.
    (b) the improvement of personal well-being.
    (c) patterns of social inequality.
    (d) global competitiveness.

13. *Compliance, punctuality,* and *discipline* are parts of the _____ of formal education.

    (a) hidden curriculum
    (b) manifest functions
    (c) residual schooling
    (d) tracking system

14. *Social conflict analysis* uses the term _____ to refer to the assignment of students to different types of educational programs.

    (a) hierarchical education
    (b) residual education
    (c) ability placement
    (d) competitive placement
    (e) tracking

15. The *Coleman Report* concluded that

    (a) social inequality is not a problem in public education within our society.
    (b) the simple answer to quality education is more funding for schools.
    (c) minority schools are actually better than schools that are predominately white schools in terms of their student achievement.
    (d) education is the great equalizer, and stressing the importance of differences between families is not particularly important for educational achievement.
    (e) schools alone cannot overcome social inequality.

16. Randell Collins calls the United States a(n) _____ *society* because people regard diplomas and degrees highly.

    (a) inclusive
    (b) elitist
    (c) credential
    (d) passive
    (e) bureaucratic

17. Theodore Sizer showed that bureaucratic schools are often insensitive to the cultural character of the community. He calls this

    (a) functional illiteracy.
    (b) specialization.
    (c) inclusiveness.
    (d) rigid conformity.
    (e) mainstreaming.

18.   Currently, what percentage of people between the ages of sixteen and twenty-four in the U.S. have *dropped out* of school?

    (a)   5
    (b)   11
    (c)   19
    (d)   25

19.   The National Commission on Excellence in Education (1983) issued a report called *A Nation At Risk*, in which it recommended

    (a)   ending student passivity.
    (b)   increasing credentialism.
    (c)   more stringent educational requirements.
    (d)   reducing the length of time students spend in school to allow more students to learn practical skills through employment.
    (e)   reducing our educational focus on reading, writing, and arithmetic.

20.   *Functional illiteracy* refers to

    (a)   an inability to read and write at all.
    (b)   an inability to read at the appropriate level of schooling based on one's age.
    (c)   an inability to write.
    (d)   reading and writing skills insufficient for everyday living.

21.   The *school choice* model focuses on the idea of

    (a)   competition.
    (b)   consensus.
    (c)   science.
    (d)   integration.

22.   One form of *school choice* involves a school providing special facilities and programs to promote educational excellence in a particular area. This is known as

    (a)   schooling for profit.
    (b)   magnet schools.
    (c)   charter schools.
    (d)   inclusion.

1. ___ The percentage of U.S. high-school graduates who attend college.
2. ___ Championed progressive education.
3. ___ Schooling in the U.S. reflects the value of _____.
4. ___ The percentage of U.S. adults aged 25-64 with a college degree.
5. ___ The assignment of students to different types of educational programs.
6. ___ The percentage of the 55 million primary and secondary school children attending state-funded public schools.
7. ___ The percentage of students bused outside their neighborhoods.
8. ___ Confirmed that predominately minority schools suffer problems, but cautioned that money alone will not magically improve academic quality.
9. ___ Evaluating people on the basis of education degrees.
10. ___ A 1983 study on the quality of schooling.

a.	tracking	f.	5
b.	65	g.	James Coleman
c.	equal opportunity	h.	John Dewey
d.	credentiaism	i.	A Nation at Risk
e.	24	j.	86

Fill-In

1. The social institution through which society provides its members with important knowledge, including basic facts, job skills, and cultural values and norms is termed _____.
2. In Japan, because of competitive exams, only _____ *percent* of high school graduates enter college.
3. By _____ all of the states in the U.S. had *mandatory education laws*.
4. Schooling in the United States attempts to promote _____ *education*, _____ *opportunity* and _____ *learning*.
5. *Functions* served by schooling include: _____, *cultural* _____, *social* _____, *social* _____, and several _____ *functions*.
6. The _____ *curriculum* refers to subtle presentation of political or cultural ideas in the classroom.
7. The assignment of students to different types of educational programs is referred to as _____.
8. Although only _____ percent of U.S. school children are *bused to schools outside their neighborhoods for racial balance purposes*, this policy has generated heated controversy.
9. The *Coleman Report* suggests that even if school funding were exactly the same everywhere, students whose _____ value and encourage education would still perform better.
10. The most crucial factor affecting access to U.S. higher education is _____.
11. _____ is evaluating a person on the basis of educational degrees.
12. The average *annual earnings* for a male with a college education is about $ _____, while the average earnings for a woman with a college education is about $ _____.

13.   *Theodore Sizer* identified through his research five ways in which large, _____ schools undermine education, including rigid conformity, numerical rating, rigid expectations, specialization, and little individual responsibility.

14.   Recent studies have linked higher levels of *student participation* to four teaching strategies, including: calling students by _____ when they volunteer, positively _____ student participation, asking _____ rather than factual questions and giving students time to answer, and asking for students' _____ even when they do not volunteer.

15.   The 1983 report by the National Commission on Excellence in Education was entitled _____.

16.   Four alternative approaches to increasing *school choice* include giving _____ to families with school-aged children and allowing them to spend that money on any school they wanted, _____ schools, schooling for _____, and _____ schools.

17.   _____ refers to the integrating of special students into the overall educational program.

18.   About _____ million adults in the U.S. are now enrolled in college.

Definition and Short-Answer

1.   Describe the four basic *functions* of education as reviewed in the text.
2.   What were the basic findings of the *Coleman Report*?
3.   How do *annual earnings* differ for men and women given the same levels of education achievement?
4.   What are the five serious problems with the *bureaucratic* nature of our educational system?
5.   What recommendations were made in the report *A Nation At Risk*?
6.   Differentiate between the educational systems of the U.S., India, Great Britain, and Japan.
7.   What are the major *problems* in U.S. education? Identify the specific factors involved in each problem identified. What is one recommendation you have to solving each of the problems?
8.   What are the three alternative approaches identified as ways of increasing *school choice*? What are your opinion of each of these?

PART VII: ANSWERS TO STUDY QUESTIONS

True-False

1.	T	(p. 524)	11.	F	(p. 531)
2.	F	(p. 524)	12.	T	(p. 531)
3.	F	(p. 524)	13.	F	(p. 533)
4.	F	(p. 526)	14.	T	(p. 534)
5.	T	(p. 527)	15.	T	(p. 534)
6.	F	(p. 527)	16.	F	(p. 534)
7.	T	(p. 527)	17.	F	(p. 538)
8.	T	(p. 527)	18.	F	(p. 539)
9.	F	(p. 528)	19.	T	(p. 541)
10.	F	(p. 530)	20.	t	(P. 541)

Multiple Choice

1.	c	(p. 523)	12.	c	(p. 530)
2.	c	(p. 523)	13.	a	(p. 530)
3.	d	(p. 523)	14.	e	(p. 530)
4.	e	(pp. 524-525)	15.	e	(p. 533)
5.	d	(p. 527)	16.	c	(p. 534)
6.	b	(p. 527)	17.	d	(p. 537)
7.	a	(p. 527)	18.	b	(p. 538)
8.	d	(p. 528)	19.	c	(p. 539)
9.	c	(p. 529)	20.	d	(p. 539)
10.	a	(pp. 529-530)	21.	a	(p. 540)
11.	b	(p. 530)	22.	b	(p. 540)

Matching

1.	b	(p. 526)	6.	j	(p. 531)
2.	h	(p. 527)	7.	f	(p. 533)
3.	c	(p. 527)	8.	g	(p. 533)
4.	e	(p. 527)	9.	d	(p. 534)
5.	a	(p. 530)	10.	i	(p. 539)

Fill-In

1. education (p. 523)
2. 30 (p. 526)
3. 1918 (p. 527)
4. mandatory, equal, practical (p. 527)
5. socialization, innovation, integration, placement, latent (p. 528-529)
6. hidden (p. 530)
7. tracking (p. 530)
8. 5 (p. 533)
9. families (p. 533)
10. money (p. 534)
11. Credentialism (p. 534)
12. 48,616; 35,379 (p. 535)
13. bureaucratic (pp. 536-537)
14. name, reinforcing, analytical, opinions (p. 538)
15. A Nation at Risk (p. 539)
16. vouchers, magnet, profit, charter (pp. 540-541)
17. mainstreaming (p. 541)
18. 25 (p. 541)

PART VII: IN FOCUS--IMPORTANT ISSUES

- Education: A Global Survey

  Briefly characterize *schooling* in each of the following countries:

    India

    Japan

    Great Britain

    United States

- The Functions of Schooling

  Illustrate each of the following *functions of schooling*:

    socialization

    cultural innovation

    social integration

    social placement

  Identify three *latent functions* of schooling:

- Schooling and Social Inequality

  In what ways do social-conflict theorists believe each of the following lead to social inequality in schooling?

  social control

  standardized testing

  school tracking

  Briefly summarize the findings of the *Coleman Report*:

- Problems In the Schools

  What is the evidence that schools have problems in the following areas?

  discipline and violence

  student passivity

  dropping out

  academic standards

374

What were the findings and conclusions of the study *A Nation At Risk*?

- Recent Issues In U.S. Education

    Describe each of the following alternatives for *school choice*:

    vouchers

    magnet schools

    schooling for profit

    charter schools

    What are the arguments for and against these *school choice* alternatives?

- Looking Ahead: Schooling In the Twenty-First Century

    What are three important issues confronting schools over the next generation?

PART VIII: ANALYSIS AND COMMENT

Applying Sociology

"Following the Jobs: Trends in Bachelor's Degrees"

Key Points: Questions:

Social Diversity

"Schooling in the United States: Savage Inequality"

Key Points: Questions:

""Cooling Out" the Poor: Transforming Disadvantage into Deficiency"

Key Points: Questions:

Controversy and Debate

"Political Correctness: Improving or Undermining Education?"

Key Points: Questions:

Window on the World--Global Maps 20-1

"Illiteracy in Global Perspective"

Key Points: Questions:

Seeing Ourselves--National Maps 20-1 and 20-2

"College Attendance across the United States"

Key Points: Questions:

"High School Dropouts across the United States"

Key Points: Questions:

21 Health and Medicine

PART I: CHAPTER OUTLINE

I. What is Health?
   A. Health and Society
II. Health: A Global Survey
   A. Health In History
   B. Health In Low-Income Countries
   C. Health In High-Income Countries
III. Health in the United States
   A. Social Epidemiology: Who Is Healthy?
      1. Age and Sex
      2. Social Class and Race
   B. Cigarette Smoking
   C. Eating Disorders
   D. Sexually Transmitted Diseases
      1. Gonorrhea and Syphilis
      2. Genital Herpes
      3. AIDS
   E. Ethical Issues Surrounding Death
      1. When Does Death Occur?
      2. Do People Have a Right to Die?
      3. What about Mercy Killing?
IV. The Medical Establishment
   A. The Rise of Scientific Medicine
   B. Holistic Medicine
   C. Paying for Health: A Global Survey
      1. Medicine in Socialist Societies
      2. Medicine in Capitalist Societies
   D. Medicine in the United States

378

PART II: LEARNING OBJECTIVES

1. To become aware of the ways in which the health of a population is shaped by society.
2. To develop a global and historical perspective on health and illness.
3. To recognize how race, social class, and age affect the health of individuals in our society.
4. To be able to discuss cigarette smoking, eating disorders, and sexually transmitted diseases as serious health problems in our society.
5. To be able to recognize and evaluate ethical issues surrounding dying and death.
6. To be able to compare and evaluate the relative effectiveness of scientific medicine and holistic medicine.
7. To be able to compare and evaluate the relative effectiveness of medicine in socialist and capitalists societies.
8. To be able to differentiate between the viewpoints being provided by the three major sociological perspectives.

PART III: KEY CONCEPTS

AIDS

direct-fee system

eating disorder

euthanasia

health

health care

HIV

HMO

holistic medicine

living will

medicine

physician's role

psychosomatic disorder

scientific medicine

sick role

social epidemiology

socialized medicine

WHO

PART IV: IMPORTANT RESEARCHERS

Erving Goffman   Talcott Parsons

PART V: STUDY QUESTIONS

True-False

1.	T	F	The World Health Organization defines *health* as simply the absence of disease.
2.	T	F	*Kwashiorkor* is a negative health condition found in West Africa caused by protein deficiency.
3.	T	F	The top five *causes of death* in the U.S. have changed very little since 1900.
4.	T	F	Sex is a stronger predictor of health than race.
5.	T	F	The leading cause of death among African American males age fifteen to twenty-four is *homicide*.
6.	T	F	Generally speaking, the less schooling people have the greater their chances of *smoking*.

7.	T	F	An *eating disorder* is defined as an intense form of dieting or other kind of weight control in pursuit of being very thin.
8.	T	F	Most cases of *syphilis* in the U.S. involve African Americans.
9.	T	F	Almost seventy percent of all global *HIV cases* are recorded in sub-Saharan Africa.
10.	T	F	HIV is both *infectious* and *contagious*.
11.	T	F	In 1997, the Supreme Court decided that under the U.S. Constitution, there is no "right to die."
12.	T	F	The *American Medical Association* was founded in 1945.
13.	T	F	*Holistic medicine* stresses that physicians have to take the primary responsibility for health care in society.
14.	T	F	Approximately 70 percent of *physicians* in the new Russian Federation are women.
15.	T	F	The U.S. is unique among industrialized societies in lacking government programs that ensure basic medical care to every citizen.
16.	T	F	Only about 25 percent of the U.S. population has some private or company-paid medical insurance coverage.
17.	T	F	Over one-half of the people in the U.S. are members of *HMOs*.
18.	T	F	One criticism of the *symbolic-interaction* paradigm is that this approach seems to deny that there are any objective standards of well-being.
19.	T	F	Most surgery in the U.S. is *elective*, or not prompted by a medical emergency.
20.	T	F	The most common objection to the *conflict approach* is that it minimizes the gains in U.S. health brought about by scientific medicine and higher living standards.

Multiple Choice

1. The *health* of any population is shaped by

    (a)   the society's cultural standards.
    (b)   the society's technology.
    (c)   the society's social inequality.
    (d)   all of the above

2. The *World Health organization* reports that _____ people around the world suffer from serious illness due to poverty.

    (a)   100,000
    (b)   500,000
    (c)   750,000
    (d)   1 billion
    (e)   2.5 billion

3. During the first half of the nineteenth century in Europe and the United states, the improvement in health was primarily due to

    (a) the rising standard of living.
    (b) medical advances.
    (c) changes in cultural values toward medicine.
    (d) immigration.

4. In 1900, _____ caused one-fourth of deaths in the U.S. Today, however, most deaths are caused by

    (a) chronic diseases/infectious diseases.
    (b) accidents/crime.
    (c) infectious diseases/chronic diseases.
    (d) cancer/accidents.
    (e) crime/accidents.

5. _____ is the study of how health and disease are distributed throughout a society's population.

    (a) Demography
    (b) Social epidemiology
    (c) Epistomolgy
    (d) Medicalization

6. Which of the following were the *leading causes of death* in the U.S. in 1900?

    (a) accidents and heart disease
    (b) cancer and diphtheria
    (c) influenza and pneumonia
    (d) lung disease and kidney disease
    (e) homicide and diabetes

7. Which of the following is *true* concerning age, sex, and health in the United States?

    (a) Across the life course, men are healthier than women.
    (b) Males have a slight biological advantage that renders them less likely than females to die before or immediately after birth.
    (c) Socialization aids men's health to a greater degree than it does women's health.
    (d) Young women are more likely to die than young men.
    (e) Across the life course, women are healthier than men.

8. While seventy-six percent of white males born in 1997 are expected to live to age *sixty-five*, only _____ percent of African American males are expected to live that long.

    (a) 40
    (b) 46
    (c) 51
    (d) 58
    (e) 65

9. According to medical experts, about how many people die prematurely in the U.S. each year as a direct result of *smoking*?

    (a) 100,000
    (b)   50,000
    (c) 200,000
    (d) 1 million
    (e) 450,000

10. Which of the following statements is *inaccurate*?

    (a) Ninety-five percent of people who suffer from anorexia nervosa and bulimia (eating disorders) are female.
    (b) Research shows that college-age women believe that being thin is critical to physical attractiveness.
    (c) Research shows that college-age women believe guys like thin girls.
    (d) Most men, like women, think that their body shape is not close to what they want it to be.
    (e) Our idealized image of beauty leads many young women to diet to the point of risking their health.

11. Of the reported cases of *gonorrhea* and *syphilis* in the U.S., the vast majority involved

    (a) whites.
    (b) African Americans.
    (c) Hispanics.
    (d) Asians.

12. By 1997, the total number of people in the U.S. who had been diagnosed with HIV was

    (a) 100,000.
    (b) 900,000.
    (c) 650,000.
    (d) 1,700,000.

13. North and South America account for _____ percent of all known *HIV infection cases.*

    (a)   8
    (b)   20
    (c)   34
    (d)   53

14. Homosexual sexual activity accounts for about _____ percent of transmited cases of *AIDS.*

    (a)   less than 5
    (b)   11
    (c)   27
    (d)   48
    (e)   72

15. Assisting in the death of a person suffering from an incurable disease is known as

    (a)   annihilation.
    (b)   amniocentesis.
    (c)   genocide.
    (d)   euthanasia.

16. The institutionalization of *scientific medicine* by the AMA resulted in:

    (a)   expensive medical education.
    (b)   domination of medicine by white males.
    (c)   an inadequate supply of physicians in rural areas.
    (d)   all of the above

17. *Holistic medicine* is a reaction to scientific medicine. Which of the following is *not* an emphasis advocates of holistic medicine share?

    (a)   an emphasis upon the environment in which the person exists
    (b)   an emphasis upon the responsibility of society for health promotion and care
    (c)   an emphasis upon optimum health for all
    (d)   an emphasis upon the home setting for medical treatment

18. _____ refers to a health-care system in which the government owns and operates most medical facilities and employs most physicians.

    (a)   A health maintenance organization
    (b)   Socialized medicine
    (c)   A direct-fee system
    (d)   Holistic medicine

19.   *European* governments pay about ____ percent of medical costs, whereas in the *United States*, the government pays about ____ percent of medical costs.

(a)   80/less than half
(b)   100/10
(c)   25/50
(d)   40/60
(e)   less than half/more than half

20.   Which country does not offer a comprehensive health program to the entire population?

(a)   Sweden
(b)   Great Britain
(c)   the United States
(d)   Canada

21.   An association that provides comprehensive medical care for a fixed fee is termed a(n)

(a)   WHO.
(b)   DFS.
(c)   AMA.
(d)   HMO.

22.   Medical expenditures in the U.S. today amount to more than _____ per person annually, more than any other nation in the world.

(a) $3,300
(b) $1,200
(c) $9,350
(d) $2,450
(e) $5,100

23.   Which of the following *theoretical paradigms* in sociology utilizes concepts like *sick role* and *physician's role* to help explain health behavior?

(a)   social-conflict
(b)   social-exchange
(c)   symbolic-interaction
(d)   cultural materialism
(e)   structural-functional

24. Critics fault the _____ *approach* for implying that there are no objective standards of well-being.

   (a) social-conflict
   (b) structural-functional
   (c) symbolic-interactionist
   (d) cultural materialist

25. Which of the following *theoretical paradigms* in sociology focuses on the issues of *access* and *profits* in the study of health care?

   (a) social-conflict
   (b) structural-functional
   (c) symbolic-interaction
   (d) social-exchange

26. What percentage of surgical operations in the U.S. each year are *elective*?

   (a) one-fifth
   (b) one-fourth
   (c) one-half
   (d) three-quarters

Matching

1. ___ The number one cause of death in the U.S. today.
2. ___ The number two cause of death in the U.S. today.
3. ___ The study of how health and disease are distributed throughout a society's population.
4. ___ The percentage of eating disorder victims who are women.
5. ___ The social institution that focuses on combating disease and improving health.
6. ___ An approach to health care that emphasizes prevention of illness and takes account of the person's entire physical and social environment.
7. ___ A medical-care system in which the government owns most facilities and employs most physicians.
8. ___ Percentage of physicians in Russia who are women.
9. ___ The percentage of health expenditures paid by European governments today.
10. ___ Patterns of behavior defined as appropriate for those who are ill.

a.	sick role	f.	80
b.	cancer	g.	medicine
c.	socialized medicine	h.	heart disease
d.	70	i.	95
e.	social epidemiology	j.	holistic medicine

1. Society shapes the *health* of people in five major ways. These include: cultural patterns define _____. What is "healthy" is often the same as what people define as _____ good. Cultural _____ of health change over time. A society's _____ affects people's health. And, social _____ affects people's health.

2. After 1850, *medical advances* began to improve health, primarily by controlling _____ *diseases*.

3. In 1900, _____ and _____ caused one-fourth of all *deaths* in the United States.

4. *Social* _____ is the study of how health and disease are distributed throughout a society's population.

5. The leading cause of death today in the U.S. is _____.

6. Death is now rare among young people, with two notable exceptions: a rise in mortality resulting from _____ and, more recently, from _____.

7. Consumption of *cigarettes* has fallen since 1960, when almost _____ percent of U.S. adults smoked. Today, only about _____ percent of U.S. adults are smokers.

8. _____ percent of people who suffer from *anorexia nervosa* or *bulimia* are women.

9. AIDS, acquired immune deficiency syndrome, is caused by _____, or the human immunodeficiency virus.

10. *HIV* is *infectious* but not _____.

11. Specific behaviors put people at high risk for *HIV* infection. These include _____ sex, sharing _____, and using any kind of _____.

12. _____ is assisting in the death of a person suffering from an incurable disease.

13. _____ is a social institution concerned with combating disease and improving health.

14. _____ *medicine* is an approach to health care that emphasizes prevention of illness and takes account of the person's entire physical and social environment.

15. About _____ percent of U.S. physicians are *women*.

16. While the U.S. government pays for less than one-half of its people's medical costs, *European* governments pay for about _____ percent of their people's medical costs.

17. Expenditures for medical care in the United States has increased dramatically since 1950. The medical care bill of the U.S. in 1996 was over _____ *dollars* or about _____ *dollars* per person.

18. The _____ refers to patterns of behavior defined as appropriate for those who are ill.

19. One strength of the _____ *paradigm* lies in revealing that what people view as healthful or harmful depends on numerous factors, many of which are not, strictly speaking, medical.

20. *Social-conflict* analysis focuses attention on the _____ issue, the _____ motive, and medicine as _____ in helping us understand health and medical care in our society.

1. It is pointed out in the text that the *health* of any population is shaped by important characteristics of the society as a whole. What are three general characteristics and an example of each?
2. How have the *causes of death* changed in the U.S. over the last century?
3. What is *social epidemiology*? Provide two illustrations of patterns found in the United States.
4. What is *HIV*? What is *AIDS*? How is it transmitted?
5. What is meant by the *sick role*?
6. Describe the three basic characteristics of *holistic medicine*.
7. How does the health-care system of the U.S. differ from those in other capitalist systems?
8. What are *social-conflict* analysts' arguments about the health care system in the United States?
9. What factors are identified for why the U.S. does not have a *national health-care system*?
10. What do *symbolic-interactionists* mean by *socially constructing illness* and *socially constructing treatment*?

PART VI: ANSWERS TO STUDY QUESTIONS

True-False

1.	F	(p. 539)	11.	T	(p. 551)
2.	T	(p. 541)	12.	F	(p. 552)
3.	F	(p. 543)	13.	F	(p. 552)
4.	T	(p. 544)	14.	T	(p. 553)
5.	T	(p. 545)	15.	T	(p. 555)
6.	T	(p. 546)	16.	F	(p. 555)
7.	T	(p. 547)	17.	F	(p. 556)
8.	T	(p. 548)	18.	T	(p. 558)
9.	T	(p. 549)	19.	T	(p. 559)
10.	F	(p. 549)	20.	T	(p. 559)

Multiple Choice

1.	d	(pp. 539-540)	14.	d	(p. 550)
2.	d	(p. 541)	15.	d	(p. 551)
3.	a	(p. 542)	16.	d	(p. 552)
4.	c	(p. 543)	17.	c	(p. 552)
5.	b	(p. 543)	18.	a	(p. 553)
6.	c	(p. 543)	19.	b	(p. 555)
7.	e	(p. 544)	20.	d	(p. 555)
8.	d	(p. 546)	21.	d	(p. 556)
9.	e	(p. 546)	22.	a	(p. 555)
10.	d	(p. 547)	23.	e	(pp. 556-557)
11.	b	(p. 548)	24.	c	(p. 558)
12.	c	(p. 548)	25.	a	(p. 558)
13.	a	(p. 549)	26.	d	(p. 559)

1.	h	(p. 543)	6.	j	(p. 552)
2.	b	(p. 543)	7.	c	(p. 553)
3.	e	(p. 543)	8.	d	(p. 553)
4.	i	(p. 547)	9.	f	(p. 555)
5.	g	(p. 551)	10.	a	(p. 556)

Fill-In

1. health, morally, standards, technology, inequality (pp. 539-540)
2. infectious (p. 543)
3. influenza, pneumonia (p. 543)
4. epidemiology (p. 543)
5. heart disease (p. 543)
6. accidents, AIDS (p. 544)
7. 45, 25 (p. 546)
8. 95 (p. 547)
9. HIV (p. 548)
10. contagious (p. 549)
11. anal, needles, drugs (p. 550)
12. Euthanasia (p. 551)
13. Medicine (p. 561)
14. Holistic (p. 552)
15. 27 (p. 553)
16. 80, 44 (p. 553)
17. trillion, 3,300 (p. 555)
18. sick role (p. 556)
19. symbolic-interaction (p. 558)
20. access, profit, politics (pp. 558-559)

PART VII: IN FOCUS--IMPORTANT ISSUES

- What is Health?

What are the five major ways in which society shapes people's *health*?

1.

2.

3.

4.

5.

- Health: A Global Survey

  Generally describe the health of people living in *low-income countries*.

  What was the impact of *industrialization* on health in the U.S. and Europe?

- Health in the United States

  Briefly discuss the health patterns found in the United States using the following variables:

  age and sex

  social class and race

  How significant a health problem are the each of the following? Provide demographic evidence of illness and disease each as discussed in the text.

  cigarette smoking

  eating disorders

  sexually transmitted diseases

According to legal and medical experts, how is *death* defined?

Do people have the *right to die*?

What are the laws in the United States concerning *euthanasia*? What are your opinion on this issue?

- The Medical Establishment

Describe impact of the rise of *scientific medicine* on health care in the United States.

What are the components of *holistic medicine*?

Briefly summarize how medical care is paid for in the following *socialist societies*:

the People's Republic of China

the Russian Federation

Briefly summarize how medical care is paid for in the following *capitalist societies*:

Sweden

Great Britain

Canada

Japan

How expensive is medical care in the United States? How do we pay for this medical care?

- Theoretical Analysis of Health and Medicine

    According to structural-functionalist analysis, what are the components of the *sick role*?

    What is the *physician's role*?

What do symbolic-interactionist's mean by the *social construction of illness*?

According to social-conflict analysts, what are the three ways in which health care is related to *social inequality*? Describe and illustrate each of these.

- Looking Ahead: Health and Medicine In the Twenty-First Century

Identify and describe the four *trends* identified by the author concerning health and health care in the U.S. over the next several decades.

PART VIII: ANALYSIS AND COMMENT

Global Sociology

"Killer Poverty: A Report from Africa"

Key Points: Questions:

"When Health Fails: A Report from Russia"

Key Points: Questions:

Applying Sociology

"Masculinity: A Threat to Health?"

Key Points: Questions:

Controversy and Debate

"The Genetic Crystal Ball: Do We Really Want to Look?"

Key Points: Questions:

Window on the World--Global Maps 21-1 and 21-2

"The Availability of Physicians in Global Perspective"

Key Points: Questions:

"HIV Infection of Adults in Global Perspective"

Key Points: Questions:

Seeing Ourselves--National Map 21-1

"Life Expectancy Across the United States"

Key Points: Questions:

22

Population, Urbanization, and Environment

PART I: CHAPTER OUTLINE

I.   Demography: The Study of Population
    A.   Fertility
    B.   Mortality
    C.   Migration
    D.   Population Growth
    E.   Population Composition

II. History and Theory of Population Growth
    A.   Malthusian Theory
    B.   Demographic Transition Theory
    C.   Global Population Today: A Brief Survey
        1.   The Low-Growth North
        2.   The High-Growth South

III. Urbanization: The Growth of Cities
    A.   The Evolution of Cities
        1.   The First Cities
        2.   Preindustrial European Cities
        3.   Industrial European Cities
    B.   The Growth of U.S. Cities
        1.   Colonial Settlement: 1565-1800
        2.   Urban Expansion: 1800-1860
        3.   The Metropolitan Era: 1860-1950
        4.   Urban Decentralization: 1950-Present
    C.   Suburbs and Urban Decline
    D.   Postindustrial Sunbelt Cities
    E.   Megalopolis: Regional Cities
    F.   Edge Cities

IV.   Urbanism As A Way of Life
A.   Ferdinand Toennies: Gemeinschaft and Gesellschaft
B.   Emile Durkheim: Mechanical and Organic Solidarity
C.   Georg Simmel: The Blase' Urbanite
D.   The Chicago School: Robert Park and Louis Wirth
E.   Urban Ecology
F.   Urban Political Economy
V.   Urbanization In Poor Societies
VI.   Environment and Society
A.   The Global Dimension
B.   Technology and the Environmental Deficit
C   Culture: Growth and Limits
1.   The Logic of Growth
2.   The Limits to Growth
C.   Solid Waste: The Disposable Society
D.   Water and Air
1.   Water Supply
2.   Water Pollution
3.   Air Pollution
E.   The Rain Forests
1.   Global Warming
2.   Declining Biodiversity
F.   Environmental Racism
IV.   Looking Ahead: Toward a Sustainable World
V.   Summary
VI.   Key Concepts
VII.   Critical-Thinking Questions
VIII.   Applications and Exercises
XIV.   Sites to See

PART II: LEARNING OBJECTIVES

1.   To learn the basic concepts used by demographers to study populations.
2.   To be able to compare Malthusian theory and demographic transition theory.
3.   To be able to recognize how populations differ in industrial and nonindustrial societies.
4.   To gain an understanding of the worldwide urbanization process, and to be able to put it into historical perspective.
5.   To be able to describe demographic changes in the U.S. throughout its history.
7.   To consider urbanism as a way of life as viewed by several historical figures in sociology.
8.   To consider the idea of urban ecology.
9.   To gain an appreciation for the global dimension of the natural environment.
10.   To develop an understanding of how sociology can help us confront environmental issues.
11.   To be able to discuss the dimensions of the "logic of growth" and the "limits to growth" as issues and realities confronting our world.
12.   To be able to identify and discuss major environmental issues confronting our world today.
13.   To begin to develop a sense about the ingredients for a sustainable society and world in the century to come.

PART III: KEY CONCEPTS

Population:

age-sex pyramid

crude birth rate

crude death rate

demographic transition theory

demography

emigration

fecundity

fertility

immigration

infant mortality rate

life expectancy

Malthusian theory

migration

mortality

natural growth rate

net-migration

sex ratio

zero population growth

Urbanization:

Gemeinschaft

Gesellschaft

metropolis

megalopolis

suburbs

urbanization

urban ecology

urban renewal

Environment:

ecologically sustainable culture

ecology

ecosystem

environmental deficit

environmental racism

greenhouse effect

natural environment

rain forests

PART IV: IMPORTANT RESEARCHERS

Ferdinand Tonnies   Emile Durkheim

Robert Park   Louis Wirth

Georg Simmel   Thomas Malthus

Donella Meadows

PART V: STUDY QUESTIONS

True-False--Population and Urbanization

1. T F Demographers using what is known as the *crude birth rate* only take into account women of childbearing age in the calculation for this figure.
2. T F The U.S., using the demographer's *natural growth rate* measure, is experiencing a significant decline in population.
3. T F Population growth in the United States and other industrialized nations is well below the world average of 1.4 percent.
4. T F A significantly larger percentage of the U.S. population over the next two decades will be comprised of *childbearing aged women* than at any other period in our nation's history.
5   T F The world's population reached 1 billion in 1800, 2 billion in 1930, 3 billion in 1963, 4 billion in 1974, 5 billion in 1987, and 6 billion in 1999.
6. T F *Malthusian theory* predicted that while population would increase in a *geometric progression*, food supplies would increase only by an *arithmetic progression*.
7. T F According to *demographic transition theory*, population patterns are linked to a society's level of technological development.
8. T F In poor countries throughout the world, birth rates have *fallen* since 1950.
9. T F In the mid-eighteenth century, the *Industrial Revolution* triggered a *second urban revolution*.
10. T F Most of the ten *largest cities* in the U.S. (by population) are in the *Sunbelt*.
11. T F Compared to *Louis Wirth, Robert Park* had a relatively negative view of urban life.
12. T F The *third urban revolution* began during the middle of the twentieth century in poor societies and continues to this day.

True-False--Environment

1.	T	F	The *natural environment* includes the air, water, and soil, but not living organisms.
2.	T	F	The cultural values of material comfort, progress, and science form the foundation for the *logic of growth* thesis.
3.	T	F	The *limits of growth* thesis, stated simply, is that humanity must implement policies to restrain the growth of population, cut back on production, and use fewer natural resources in order to head off environmental collapse.
4.	T	F	The limits to growth theorists are also referred to as *neo-Malthusians*.
5.	T	F	The United States is being characterized in the text as a *disposable society*.
6.	T	F	Over fifty percent of solid waste in the U.S. is either *burned* or *recycled*.
7.	T	F	Almost one-half of all household trash in the U.S. is composed of plastic, glass, and food waste.
8.	T	F	According to what scientists call the *hydrological cycle*, the earth naturally recycles water and refreshes the land.
9.	T	F	The global consumption of *water* has tripled since 1950 and is expanding faster than the world's population.
10.	T	F	Households around the world account for more *water use* than does industry.
11.	T	F	*Biodiversity* tends to be relatively low in rain forest environments.
12.	T	F	The *greenhouse effect* is the result of too little carbon dioxide in the atmosphere.

Multiple-Choice--Population and Urbanization

1. How many people are added to the planet *each year*?

   (a) 5 million
   (b) 20 million
   (c) 50 million
   (d) 80 million

2. In the 1999, the world population stood at approximately

   (a) 2 billion.
   (b) 4 billion.
   (c) 6 billion.
   (d) 8 billion.

3. The incidence of childbearing in a country's population refers to

   (a) fertility.
   (b) fecundity.
   (c) demography.
   (d) sex ratio.
   (e) life expectancy.

4.   *Fecundity,* or maximum possible childbearing is sharply reduced in practice by

    (a)   cultural norms.
    (b)   finances.
    (c)   personal choice.
    (d)   all of the above

5.   Which region of the world has both the *highest* birth rate, death rate, and infant mortality rate?

    (a)   Latin America
    (b)   Asia
    (c)   Europe
    (d)   Oceania
    (e)   Africa

6.   The movement of people into and out of a specified territory is

    (a)   demographic transition.
    (b)   migration.
    (c)   fecundity.
    (d)   mortality.
    (e)   fertility.

7.   The *sex ratio* in the U.S. is:

    (a)   85.
    (b)   100.
    (c)   90.
    (d)   105.
    (e)   96.

8.   During the twentieth century, the world's population has increased _____-fold.

    (a)   two
    (b)   three
    (c)   four
    (d)   five
    (e)   six

9.   *Demographic transition theory* links population patterns to a society's

    (a)   religious beliefs and practices.
    (b)   technological development.
    (c)   natural resources.
    (d)   sexual norms.

10. *Stage 3* of the demographic transition theory is characterized by

    (a)   increasing death rates.
    (b)   increasing birth rates.
    (c)   decreasing death rates.
    (d)   none of the above

11. The *first city* to have ever existed is argued to be

    (a)   Athens.
    (b)   Cairo.
    (c)   Tikal.
    (d)   Jericho.
    (e)   Rome

12. According to the text, the *second urban revolution* was triggered by

    (a)   the fall of Rome.
    (b)   the post-World War II baby boom.
    (c)   the Industrial Revolution.
    (d)   the discovery of the New World.
    (e)   the fall of Greece.

13. The period called *the metropolitan era* occurred between

    (a)   1624-1800.
    (b)   1860-1950.
    (c)   1950-1970.
    (d)   1970 to the present.

14. The period of *1950 to the present* is described in the text as

    (a)   urban decentralization.
    (b)   the metropolitan era.
    (c)   urban expansion.
    (d)   the second urban revolution.

15. A vast urban region containing a number of cities and their surrounding suburbs is known as a

    (a)   metropolis.
    (b)   suburb.
    (c)   Gemeinschaft.
    (d)   megalopolis.

16.   *Ferdinand Tonnies'* concept referring to the type of social organization by which people stand apart based on self-interest is

(a)   megalopolis.
(b)   sector model.
(c)   Gesellschaft.
(d)   multi-nuclei model.
(e)   Gemeinschaft.

17.   The link between the *physical* and *social* dimensions of cities is known as

(a)   Gesellschaft.
(b)   urban ecology.
(c)   organic solidarity.
(d)   mechanical solidarity.
(e)   demography.

18.   _____ *analysis* is a branch of urban ecology that investigates what people in particular neighborhoods have in common.

(a)   Wedge-shaped
(b)   Concentric zones
(c)   Multicentered model
(d)   Social area

19.   This model of urbanization claims that city life is defined by people with power, and that capitalism turns cities into real estate to be traded for profit.

(a)   concentric zone
(b)   ecological
(c)   urban political economy
(d)   urban renewal strategy

20.   Approximately what percentage of people living in *poor societies* currently reside in *urban areas*?

(a)   82
(b)   50
(c)   25
(d)   67
(e)   42

1.   _____ is the study of the interaction of living organisms and the natural environment.

     (a)   Environmentalism
     (b)   Sociobiology
     (c)   Ecosystem
     (d)   Ecology

2.   The Greek meaning of the word *eco* is

     (a)   weather.
     (b)   satisfaction.
     (c)   house.
     (d)   work.
     (e)   material.

3.   _____ is a system composed of the interaction of all living organisms and their natural environment.

     (a)   Ecosystem
     (b)   Environment
     (c)   Biosphere
     (d)   Ecology

4.   People in rich nations represent fifteen percent of the world's population, but consume ____ percent of the world's *energy*.

     (a)   twenty-five
     (b)   fifty
     (c)   sixty-five
     (d)   eighty
     (e)   ninety-eight

5.   Which of the following cultural values form the foundation of the *logic of growth* perspective?

     (a)   material comfort
     (b)   progress
     (c)   science
     (d)   all of the above
     (e)   none of the above

6.	Which of the following is *not* a projection for the next century using the *limits of growth thesis*?

	(a)	a stabilizing, then declining population
	(b)	declining industrial output per capita
	(c)	declining resources
	(d)	increasing, then declining pollution
	(e)	increasing food per capita

7.	How many pounds of *solid waste* are generated in the U.S. each day?

	(a)	15 million
	(b)	1 billion
	(c)	100 million
	(d)	8 billion
	(e)	250 million

8.	Which type of solid waste represents about *one-half* of all household trash in the U.S?

	(a)	metal products
	(b)	yard waste
	(c)	paper
	(d)	plastic
	(e)	glass

9.	What percentage of the solid waste in the U.S. is either *recycled* or *burned*?

	(a)	10
	(b)	30
	(c)	2
	(d)	50

10.	While industry accounts for 25 percent of water usage globally, individuals account for _____ percent of usage.

	(a)	90
	(b)	65
	(c)	50
	(d)	25
	(e)	10

11.	*Rain forests* cover approximately _____ percent of the earth's land surface.

	(a)	1
	(b)	7
	(c)	2
	(d)	11

12.   Rain forests are home to almost _____ *percent* of our planet's species.

        (a)   90
        (b)   75
        (c)   50
        (d)   30
        (e)   10

13.   A way of life that meets the needs of the present generation without threatening the environmental legacy of future generations refers to

        (a)   ecologically sustainable culture.
        (b)   the Green Revolution.
        (c)   environmental racism.
        (d)   the greenhouse effect.

14.   Strategies recommended for creating a sustainable ecosystem include

        (a)   conservation of finite resources.
        (b)   bringing population under control.
        (c)   reducing waste.
        (d)   all of the above

Matching--Population and Urbanization

1.   ____   The incidence of childbearing in a society's population.
2.   ____   Maximum possible childbearing.
3.   ____   A theory claiming that population would soon rise out of control.
4.   ____   A thesis linking population patterns to a society's level of technological development.
5.   ____   The concentration of humanity into cities.
6.   ____   1860-1950.
7.   ____   Developed the concepts Gemeinschaft and Gesellschaft.
8.   ____   Developed the concepts of mechanical and organic solidarity.
9.   ____   A type of social organization by which people stand apart from one another in pursuit of self-interest.
10.   ____   Social bonds based on common sentiments and shared moral values.
11.   ____   Argued that urbanites develop a blase' attitude, selectively tuning out much of what goes on around them.
12.   ____   Saw the city as a living organism, truly a human kaleidoscope.

        a.   Ferdinand Tonnies   g.   Robert Parks
        b.   mechanical solidarity   h.   Malthusian theory
        c.   fertility   i.   Emile Durkheim
        d.   Gesellschaft   j.   fecundity
        e.   demographic transition theory   k.   urbanization
        f.   great metropolis era   l.   Georg Simmel

408

Matching-Environment

1. ____ The earth's surface and atmosphere, including living organisms as well as the air, soil, and other resources necessary to sustain life.
2. ____ The study of the interaction of living organisms and the natural environment.
3. ____ The system composed of the interaction of all living organisms and their natural environment.
4. ____ Profound and negative long-term harm to the natural environment caused by humanity's focus on short-term material affluence.
5. ____ The number of gallons of water consumed by a person in the U.S. over a lifetime.
6. ____ Regions of dense forestation most of which circle the globe close to the equator.
7. ____ A rise in the earth's average temperature due to an increasing concentration of carbon dioxide in the atmosphere.
8. ____ The pattern by which environmental hazards are greatest in proximity to poor people and especially minorities.
9. ____ The number of people added to the world's population each year (net gain).
10. ____ The number of people added to the world each year in poor societies.

a.	natural environment	f.	ecology
b.	greenhouse effect	g.	environmental deficit
c.	10 million	h.	rain forests
d.	75 million	i.	environmental racism
e.	80 million	j.	ecosystem

Fill-In--Population and Urbanization

1. _____ is the incidence of childbearing in a society's population.
2. _____ refers to the incidence of death in a country's population.
3. The *crude death rate* in Africa in 1999 was _____.
4. Movement out of a territory--or _____--is measured in terms of an *out-migration rate*.
5. The _____ _____ refers to the number of males for every hundred females in a given population.
6. *Thomas Malthus* saw population increasing according to _____ progression, and food production increasing in _____ progression.
7. _____ *theory* is the thesis that population patterns are linked to a society's level of technological development.
8. _____ _____ refers to the level of reproduction that maintains population at a steady state.
9. The term _____ is from the Greek meaning "mother city."
10. The *Bureau of the Census* recognizes 256 urban areas in the U.S. which they call MSAs, or _____.
11. Urban decentralization has created _____ _____, business centers some distance from the old downtowns.
12. _____ refers to a type of social organization by which people are bound closely together by kinship and tradition.

13. _____ _____ is the study of the link between the physical and social dimensions of cities.

14. In 1950, only seven cities in the world had populations over five million, and only two of these were in low-income countries. By 1995, _____ cities has passed this mark, and _____ were in low-income countries.

Fill-In--Environment

1. The _____ _____ refers to the earth's surface and atmosphere, including living organisms, air, water, soil, and other resources necessary to sustain life.

2. An _____ is defined as the system composed of the interaction of all living organisms and their natural environment.

3. The concept of *environmental deficit* implies three important ideas. First, the state of the environment is a _____ _____. Second, much environmental damage is _____. And third, in some respects environmental damage is _____.

4. Core values that underlie cultural patterns in the U.S. include progress, material comfort, and science. Such values form the foundation for the _____ *thesis*.

5. The _____ *thesis* states that humanity must implement policies to control the growth of population, material production, and the use of resources in order to avoid environmental collapse.

6. It is estimated that fifty percent of household trash is _____.

7. In the U.S. only about _____ percent of *solid waste* is recycled.

8. The earth naturally recycles water and refreshes the land through what scientists call the _____ *cycle*.

9. We need to curb *water consumption* by industry, which uses _____ percent of the global total, and by farming, which consumes _____ of the total for irrigation.

10. Strategies for creating an *ecologically sustainable culture* include bringing _____ _____ under control, _____ of finite resources, and reducing _____.

Definition and Short-Answer--Population and Urbanization

1. What are the three basic factors which determine the *size* and *growth rate* of a population? Define each of these concepts.

2. Differentiate between *Malthusian theory* and *demographic transition theory* as perspectives on population growth.

3. What are the three stages in the *demographic transition theory*? Describe each.

4. Identify and describe the five *periods of growth* of U.S. cities.

5. Differentiate between the concepts *metropolis* and *megalopolis*.

6. Differentiate between the perspectives of *Louis Wirth* and *Robert Park* concerning urbanization.

7. Describe how *urbanization* patterns are changing around the world.

8. Compare the views of *Ferdinand Tonnies* and *Emile Durkheim* concerning urbanization.

9. What are three factors that are causing *urban growth* in poor societies?

10. What is *urban ecology*? What are two criticism of this approach?
11. Briefly review the *evolution of cities* as described in the text.
12. Discuss significant points made in the text about the *low-growth north* and the *high-growth south*.
13. What is the perspective offered by *Georg Simmel* urbanism?
14. What are the three *urban revolutions*? Briefly describe each.

Definition and Short-Answer--Environment

1. Differentiate between the concepts *ecology* and *natural environment*.
2. What three important ideas are implied by the concept *environmental deficit*?
3. Briefly describe the pattern of word *population growth* prior to and after the Industrial Revolution.
4. Critically differentiate between the *logic of growth* and the *limits to growth* views concerning the relationship between human technology and the natural environment.
5. What is meant by the term *disposable society*? What evidence is being presented to support this view of the U.S?
6. Review the global research concerning either *water pollution* or *air pollution*.
7. Discuss the connection between the depletion of the rain forest and global warming and declining biodiversity.
8. What is the *biodiversity crisis* and why is it so significant?

PART VI: ANSWERS TO STUDY QUESTIONS

True-False--Population and Urbanization

1.	F	(p. 567)	7.	T	(p. 573)
2.	F	(p. 569)	8.	F	(p. 574)
3.	T	(p. 569)	9.	T	(p. 576)
4.	F	(p. 571)	10.	T	(p. 578)
5.	T	(p. 572)	11.	F	(p. 581)
6.	T	(p. 572)	12.	T	(p. 583)

True-False--Environment

1.	F	(p. 583)	7.	F	(p. 587)
2.	T	(p. 585)	8.	T	(p. 587)
3.	T	(p. 585)	9.	T	(p. 589)
4.	T	(p. 586)	10.	F	(p. 589)
5.	T	(p. 586)	11.	F	(p. 591)
6.	F	(p. 586)	12.	F	(p. 591)

Multiple-Choice--Population and Urbanization

1.	d	(p. 567)	11.	d	(p. 576)
2.	c	(p. 567)	12.	c	(p. 576)
3.	a	(p. 567)	13.	b	(p. 577)
4.	d	(p. 567)	14.	a	(p. 577)
5.	e	(p. 569)	15.	a	(p. 578)
6.	b	(p. 569)	16.	c	(p. 579)
7.	e	(p. 571)	17.	b	(p. 581)
8.	c	(p. 572)	18.	d	(p. 581)
9.	b	(p. 572)	19.	c	(p. 582)
10.	c	(p. 573)	20.	b	(p. 583)

Multiple-Choice--Environment

1.	d	(p. 583)	8.	c	(p. 587)
2.	c	(p. 584)	9.	b	(p. 587)
3.	a	(p. 584)	10.	e	(p. 588)
4.	d	(p. 584)	11.	b	(p. 590)
5.	d	(p. 585)	12.	c	(p. 590)
6.	e	(p. 586)	13.	a	(p. 594)
7.	b	(p. 586)	14.	d	(p. 594)

Matching--Population and Urbanization

1.	c	(p. 567)	7.	a	(p. 579)
2.	j	(p. 567)	8.	i	(p. 579)
3.	h	(p. 572)	9.	d	(p. 579)
4.	e	(p. 572)	10.	b	(p. 579)
5.	k	(p. 576)	11.	l	(p. 580)
6.	f	(p. 577)	12.	g	(p. 581)

Matching--Environment

1.	a	(p. 583)	6.	h	(p. 590)
2.	f	(p. 583)	7.	b	(p. 591)
3.	j	(p. 584)	8.	i	(p. 592)
4.	g	(p. 584)	9.	e	(p. 594)
5.	c	(p. 599)	10.	d	(p. 594)

Fill-In--Population and Urbanization

1. Fertility (p. 567)
2. Mortality (p. 568)
3. 14 (p. 568)

4. emigration (p. 569)
5. sex ratio (p. 571)
6. geometric, arithmetic (p. 572)
7. demographic transition (pp. 572-573)
8. Zero population growth (p. 574)
9. megalopolis (p. 578)
10. metropolitan statistical areas (MSAs) (p. 578)
11. edge cities (p. 578)
12. Gemeinschaft (p. 579)
13. Urban ecology (p. 581)
14. 33, 25 (p. 583)

Fill-In--Environment

1. natural environment (p. 583)
2. ecosystem (p. 584)
3. social issue, unintended, reversible (p. 584)
4. logic of growth (p. 584)
5. limits of growth (p. 585)
6. paper (p. 586)
7. 30 (p. 586)
8. hydological (p. 587)
9. 25, two-thirds (p. 589)
10. population growth, conservation, waste (p. 589)

PART VII: IN FOCUS--IMPORTANT ISSUES

- Demography: The Study of Population

  Define each of the following factors that affects *population size*:

    fertility

        crude birth rate
        fecundity

    mortality

        crude death rate
        life expectancy

    migration

        immigration
        emigration

What is the *natural growth rate* of the United States? How doe it compare to the comparable rate in other parts of the world like Asia and Africa? Explain.

In what ways is the *age-sex pyramid* an important measure of population growth?

- History and Theory of Population growth

  Briefly describe the components of each of the following theories of population growth:

  Malthusian theory

  demographic transition theory

  What is meant by the *low-growth North*?

  What is meant by the *high-growth South*?

414

- Urbanization: The Growth of Cities

Identify and describe the three *urban revolutions*:

first

second

third

Describe each of the following periods in the *growth of cities* in the United States:

colonial settlement

urban expansion

the metropolitan era

urban decentralization

415

- Urbanization As a Way of Life

  How did each of the following theorists characterize cities and the process of *urbanization*?

  Ferdinand Tonnies

  Emile Durkheim

  Georg Simmel

  the Chicago School

  Robert Park

  Louis Wirth

  What is *urban ecology*?

  How is the *urban political economy model* different than the ecological model in term of understanding urban issues?

- Urbanization in Poor Societies

  Briefly describe the *third urban revolution*:

- Environment and Society

  Differentiate between each of the following views concerning environmental issues:

  the logic of growth

  the limits to growth

  What are two important points being made in the text concerning each of the following:

  solid waste

  water

  air

Why are the *rain forests* so important to the world and all living things?

- Looking Ahead: Toward a Sustainable World

  What are the three recommendations being made for establishing an *ecologically sustainable culture*?

  What specific ideas would you recommend implementing to encourage each of these?

PART VIII: ANALYSIS AND COMMENT

Global Sociology

"Empowering Women: The Key to Controlling Population Growth"

Key Points: Questions:

Applying Sociology

"Why Grandmother Had No Trash"

Key Points: Questions:

Controversy and Debate

"Apocalypse: Will People Overwhelm the Earth?"

Key Points: Questions:

Seeing Ourselves--National Map 20-1

"Population Change across the United States"

Key Points: Questions:

Window on the World--Global Maps 22-1 and 22-2

"Population Growth in Global Perspective"

Key Points: Questions:

"Water Consumption in Global Perspective"

Key Points: Questions:

23

Collective Behavior and Social Movements

PART II: LEARNING OBJECTIVES

1. To be able to identify and discuss the specific problems associated with studying collective behavior from a sociological perspective.
2. To be able to identify and describe the basic characteristics of collectivities, and to be able to distinguish them from groups.
3. To be able to differentiate between localized and dispersed collectivities, and to be able to provide examples for each.
4. To be able to identify and distinguish between the different theories used to explain the nature of collectivities.
5. To be able to identify and describe the four basic types of social movements.
6. To be able to compare and critique the six different theories used to describe the nature of social movements.
7. To be able to identify and illustrate the four stages of a social movement.
8. To be able to discuss the relationship between social movements and social change from a sociological perspective.

PART IV: KEY CONCEPTS

acting crowd

alternative social movements

casual crowd

collective behavior

collectivity

conspicuous consumption

contagion theory

conventional crowd

convergence theory

crowd

deprivation theory

dispersed collectivities

emergent-norm theory

expressive crowd

fad

fashion

gossip

localized collectivities

mass behavior

mass hysteria

mass-society theory

mob

panic

propaganda

public opinion

redemptive social movements

reformative social movement

relative deprivation

resource-mobilization theory

revolutionary social movement

riot

rumor

social movement

structural-strain theory

PART IV: IMPORTANT RESEARCHERS

Gustave Le Bon   Ralph Turner and Lewis Killian

Charles Horton Cooley   Thorstein Veblen

Herbert Blumer   Alexis de Tocqueville

William Kornhauser   Neil Smelser

Fredrick Miller

PART V: STUDY QUESTIONS

True-False

1. T   F   *Collective behavior* is difficult to study because it is wide-ranging, complex, and transitory.
2. T   F   People gathered at a beach or observing an automobile accident are used in the text to illustrate *conventional crowds*.
3. T   F   A *mob* is defined as a highly emotional crowd that pursues a violent or destructive goal.
4. T   F   Using *contagion theory*, it is argued that people lose their individual identities and surrender personal will and responsibility to a collective mind.
5. T   F   *Emergent-norm theory* is linked to the social-conflict perspective.
6. T   F   *Mass behavior* refers to collective behavior among people dispersed over a wide geographic area.
7. T   F   *Propaganda* refers to information presented with the intention of shaping public opinion.

8.	T	F	*Mass hysteria* is a form of localized collective behavior by which people react to a threat or other stimulus with irrational, frantic, and often self-destructive behavior.
9.	T	F	Sociologist Thorstein Veblen argued that while fads often involve *conspicuous conception*, fashion does not.
10.	T	F	According to the text, *social movements* are rare in preindustrial societies.
11.	T	F	*Reformative social movements* have greater depth, but less scope than *redemptive social movements*.
12.	T	F	The rise of the Ku Klux Klan and passage of Jim Crow laws by whites intent on enforcing segregation in the South after the Civil War illustrate *deprivation theory*.
13.	T	F	Using *mass-society theory*, social movements are *personal* as well as *political*.
14.	T	F	*Mass-society theory* argues that social movements attract socially isolated people who feel personally insignificant.
15.	T	F	According to *structural-strain theory*,. people form social movements because of a shared concern about the inability of society to operate as they believe it should.
16.	T	F	*Resource-mobilization theory* suggests that "discontent" is the most significant resource in determining the success of a social movement.
17.	T	F	One clear strength of *new social movements theory* is its recognition that social movements have increased in scale in response to the development of a global economy and international political connections.
18.	T	F	As social movements unfold, the stage of *bureaucratization* precedes the stage of *coalescence*.
19.	T	F	Perhaps the most important reason that people in the United States avoid joining in social movements may have to do with *cultural norms* about how change should occur.
20.	T	F	The scope of social movements is likely to *decrease* in the next century as women and other historically excluded categories gain political voice.

Multiple-Choice

1. Which of the following is *not* identified as a difficulty in researching *collective behavior* using the sociological perspective?

    (a) the concept of collective behavior is wide-ranging
    (b) collective behavior is complex
    (c) collective behavior is often transitory
    (d) collective behavior tends to be localized to historical context

2. A large number of people whose minimal interaction occurs in the absence of well-defined and conventional norms refers to a

    (a) collectivity.
    (b) group.
    (c) secondary group.
    (d) category.

3. Herbert Blumer identified several *types of crowds* based on their level of emotional intensity. Which of the following is *not* a type of crowd identified by Blumer?

    (a) casual
    (b) conventional
    (c) expressive
    (d) acting
    (e) emergent

4. A _____ is a temporary gathering of people who share a common focus of attention and who influence one another.

    (a) group
    (b) crowd
    (c) dispersed collectivity
    (d) category

5. A _____ is a highly emotional crowd that pursues a violent or destructive goal.

    (a) riot
    (b) protest
    (c) mob
    (d) aggregate

6. A *theory of crowds* which claims that the motives that drive collective action do not originate within a crowd, but rather are carried into the crowd by particular individuals is called _____ *theory*.

    (a) contagion
    (b) reactive
    (c) convergence
    (d) subversive

7. One of the first theories of *crowds*, developed by French sociologist Gustave Le Bon, is called _____ *theory*, which focuses on how anonymity in a crowd causes people to lose their identities and surrender personal will and responsibility to a collective mind.

    (a) mob
    (b) convergence
    (c) retreative
    (d) contagion

8. A theory which argues that crowds are not merely irrational collectivities, nor are they always deliberately arranged and organized is _____ *theory*

    (a) consensual
    (b) emergent-norm
    (c) structural
    (d) reactive

425

9.   *Emergent-norm theory* represents a _____ approach to crowd dynamics.

        (a)   social-conflict
        (b)   symbolic-interaction
        (c)   structural-functional
        (d)   functionalism

10.   Which of the following is *not* an example of a *dispersed collectivity*?

        (a)   rumor
        (b)   gossip
        (c)   propaganda
        (d)   public opinion
        (e)   riots

11.   Which of the following is *not* an essential characteristic of *rumor*?

        (a)   It thrives in a climate of ambiguity.
        (b)   It is unstable.
        (c)   It is difficult to stop.
        (d)   All are characteristics of rumor.

12.   The radio broadcast by H.G. Wells "War of the Worlds" is used to illustrate:

        (a)   gossip.
        (b)   rumor.
        (c)   mass hysteria.
        (d)   panic.

13.   An unconventional social pattern that people embrace briefly but enthusiastically refers to

        (a)   a fad.
        (b)   gossip.
        (c)   fashion.
        (d)   mass hysteria.
        (e)   rumor.

14.   What *type* of social movement seeks limited social change for the entire society?

        (a)   revolutionary
        (b)   redemptive
        (c)   deprivation
        (d)   alternative
        (e)   reformative

15. The following points--people join social movements as a result of experiencing relative deprivation; social movements are a means of seeking change that brings participants greater benefits; social movements are especially likely when rising expectations are frustrated, best fit which *theory of social movements*?

    (a)   deprivation
    (b)   resource-mobilization
    (c)   structural-strain
    (d)   mass-society

16. _____ *theory* suggests social movements attract socially isolated people who feel personally insignificant.

    (a)   Mass-society
    (b)   Structural-strain
    (c)   Resource-mobilization
    (d)   New social movements

17. _____ *theory* identifies six factors that encourage the development of a social movement, including structural conductiveness, structural strain, growth and spread of an explanation, precipitating factors, mobilization for action, and lack of social control.

    (a)   Resource-mobilization
    (b)   Deprivation
    (c)   Structural-strain
    (d)   Conductive order

18. Addressing the changing character of social movements, this theory focuses on the globalization of social movements and a focus on cultural change for the improvement of social and physical surroundings.

    (a)   global-resource theory
    (b)   new social movements theory
    (c)   mass-society theory
    (d)   modernization theory

19. *Emergence* is identified as *stage 1* of a social movement. Which of the following is *not* identified as a stage in the evolution of a social movement?

    (a)   bureaucratization
    (b)   coalescence
    (c)   decline
    (d)   realignment

20. It is being argued that the most important reason that people in the United States avoid joining in social movements may have to do with

    (a)   money.
    (b)   cultural norms.
    (c)   time.
    (d)   political orientation.

Matching

1. _____ Activity involving a large number of people, often spontaneous, and sometimes controversial.
2. _____ A crowd that forms around an event with emotional appeal.
3. _____ A collectivity motivated by an intense, single-minded purpose.
4. _____ A theory that suggests crowds exert hypnotic influence over their members.
5. _____ Holds that crowd behavior is not a product of the crowd itself, but is carried into the crowd by particular individuals.
6. _____ Collective behavior among people dispersed over a wide geographic area.
7. _____ Ambiguous, unstable, and difficult to stop.
8. _____ A form of localized collective behavior by which people react to a threat or other stimulus with irrational, frantic, and often self-destructive behavior.
9. _____ A form of dispersed collective behavior by which people react to a real or imagined event with irrational, frantic, and often self-destructive behavior.
10. _____ A social movement with selective focus, but seeks radical change in those it engages.
11. _____ A social movement seeking limited change in only part of a population.
12. _____ A perceived disadvantage arising from some specific comparisons.
13. _____ A theory that sees social movements as personal and political.
14. _____ A theory of social movements that emphasizes the distinctive features of recent social movements in postindustrial societies.

    a.   acting crowd   h.   rumor
    b.   panic   i.   mass hysteria
    c.   mass-society theory   j.   mass behavior
    d.   contagion theory   k.   collective behavior
    e.   redemptive social movement   l.   new social movements theory
    f.   expressive crowd   m.   convergence theory
    g.   alternative social movement   n.   relative deprivation

Fill-In

1. *Collective behavior* is difficult for sociologists to study for the following reasons: it is _____, _____, and _____.
2. Collectivities are of two kinds: a _____ collectivity, referring to people in physical proximity to one another, and a _____ collectivity, or mass behavior.
3. A _____ is a large number of people whose minimal interaction occurs in the absence of well-defined conventional norms.
4. Three key *differences* between *social groups* and *collectivities* are that the latter are based on _____ social interaction, have no clear _____ _____, and generate weak and unconventional _____.

428

5. Five types of *crowds* are identified in the text, including _____, _____, _____, _____, and _____.

6. A _____ is a highly emotional crowd that pursues a violent or destructive goal.

7. _____ *theory* holds that crowd behavior is not a product of the crowd itself, but is carried into the crowd by particular individuals.

8. Representing a symbolic-interaction approach, _____ *theory* suggests that crowd behavior reflects the desires of participants, but is also guided by norms that emerge as the situation unfolds.

9. *Rumor* has three essential characteristics, including: thriving on _____, being _____, and _____ to stop.

10. While a _____ is a form of localized collective behavior by which people react to a threat or other stimulus with irrational, frantic, and often self-destructive behavior, _____ _____ is a form of dispersed collective behavior by which people react to a real or imagined event with irrational, frantic, and often self-destructive behavior.

11. Thorstein Veblen defined _____ _____ as the practice of spending money with the intention of displaying one's wealth to others.

12. Four *types of social movements* are identified in the text. The least threatening is termed an _____ social movement. There is also _____ social movements which are selective, but seek radical change. _____ social movements aim for only limited social change--but target everyone. Finally, _____ social movements are the most extreme.

13. _____ _____ is a perceived disadvantage arising from some specific comparison.

14. Using *mass-society theory*, social movements are viewed as _____ as well as _____.

15. According to Neil Smelser's *structural-strain theory* there are six factors that foster social movements, including: structural _____, structural _____, growth and spread of an _____, precipitating _____, mobilization for _____, and lack of social _____.

16. _____ _____ *theory* points out that no social movement is likely to succeed--or even get off the ground--without substantial resources.

17. _____ *theory* reminds us that not just material resources but also cultural symbols form the foundation of social movements.

18. One clear strength of _____ _____ _____ *theory* is its recognition that social movements are increasing in scale in response to the growing power of the state and the development of a global political system.

19. The *third stage* of a social movement after emergence and coalescence is _____.

20. There are three reasons why the scope of social movements is likely to increase. First, protest should increase as _____, _____, and other historically excluded categories gain a greater political voice. Second, the _____ is increasing awareness of global issues. Third, new technology and the emerging global _____ means social movements are now uniting people around the world.

Definition and Short-Answer

1.   What are the basic characteristics of *dispersed collectivities*?
2.   What are the four *types of crowds* identified by Herbert Blumer? Briefly describe each of these. What is the fifth type of crowd identified by our author?
3.   Differentiate between *contagion theory, convergence theory,* and *emergent-norm theory* in terms of how each explains crowd behavior.
4.   Differentiate between the concepts *rumor* and *gossip*.
5.   Identify and describe the six characteristics that foster social movements according to *structural-strain theory*.
6.   What are the six theories of social movements? Discuss how each of these helps us explain social movements. What is one criticism of each theory?
7.   What are the four *stages* of a social movement? Describe each. Identify a social movement in U.S. history and explain how it fits these stages.
8.   Differentiate between the concepts *mass hysteria* and *panic*.
9.   Identify and describe the four *types* of social movements, providing an illustration for each.
10. Why are social movements expected to increase in *scope* over the next few decades? Do you agree? Why?

PART VII: ANSWERS TO STUDY QUESTIONS

True-False

1.	T	(pp. 599-600)	11.	F	(p. 610)
2.	F	(p. 601)	12.	T	(p. 610)
3.	T	(p. 601)	13.	T	(p. 611)
4.	T	(p. 603)	14.	T	(p. 611)
5.	F	(p. 605)	15.	T	(p. 612)
6.	T	(p. 605)	16.	F	(p. 615)
7.	T	(p. 606)	17.	T	(p. 615)
8.	F	(p. 606)	18.	F	(p. 616)
9.	F	(p. 608)	19.	T	(p. 618)
10.	T	(p. 609)	20.	F	(p. 619)

Multiple-Choice

1.	d	(pp. 599-600)	11.	d	(pp. 605-606)
2.	a	(p. 599)	12.	c	(p. 607)
3.	e	(p. 600)	13.	e	(p. 609)
4.	b	(p. 600)	14.	a	(p. 610)
5.	c	(p. 601)	15.	a	(p. 610)
6.	c	(p. 604)	16.	d	(p. 611)
7.	d	(p. 603)	17.	b	(pp. 612-613)
8.	b	(pp. 604-605)	18.	b	(pp. 612-613)
9.	b	(pp. 604-605)	19.	d	(p. 616)
10.	e	(pp. 605-606)	20.	b	(p. 618)

Matching

1.	k	(p. 599)	8.	b	(p. 606)
2.	f	(p. 601)	9.	i	(p. 606)
3.	a	(p. 601)	10.	e	(p. 610)
4.	d	(p. 603)	11.	g	(p. 610)
5.	m	(p. 604)	12.	n	(p. 610)
6.	j	(p. 605)	13.	c	(p. 611)
7.	h	(p. 605)	14.	l	(p. 615)

Fill-In

1. wide-ranging, complex, transitory (p. 599)
2. localized, dispersed (p. 599)
3. collectivity (p. 600)
4. limited, social boundaries, norms (p. 600)
5. casual, conventional, expressive, acting, protest (pp. 600-601)
6. mob (p. 601)
7. Convergence (p. 604)
8. emergent-norm (p. 605)
9. ambiguity, unstable, difficult (pp. 605-606)
10. panic, mass hysteria (p. 606)
11. conspicuous consumption (p. 607)
12. alternative, redemptive, reformative, revolutionary (p. 610)
13. Relative deprivation (p. 611)
14. personal, political (p. 612)
15. conduciveness, strain, explanation, factors, action, control (pp. 612-613)
16. resource-mobilization (p. 613)
17. Cultural (p. 614)
18. new social movements (p. 615)
19. bureaucratization (p. 616)
20. women, African Americans, Information Revolution, economy (p. 619)

PART VII: IN FOCUS--IMPORTANT ISSUES

• Studying Collective Behavior

What are three reasons why *collective behavior* is difficult for sociologists to study?

1.

2.

3.

What are the three important ways that collectivities are distinguished from social groups?

    1.

    2.

    3.

- Localized Collectivities: Crowds

Differentiate between the following types of crowds as identified by Herbert Blumer.

    casual crowd

    conventional crowd

    expressive crowd

    acting crowd

Briefly describe the following explanations of *crowd behavior*:

    contagion theory

        What is a criticism of this theory?

    convergence theory

        What is a criticism of this theory?

    emergent-norm theory

        What is a criticism of this theory?

- Dispersed Collectivities: Mass Behavior

  Provide an illustration for each of the following:

  rumor

  gossip

  public opinion

  propaganda

  panic

  mass hysteria

  fashions

  fads

- Social Movements

  Describe each of the following theories of *social movements*:

  deprivation theory

  What is one criticism of this theory?

  mass-society theory

  What is one criticism of this theory?

structural-strain theory

What is one criticism of this theory?

resource-mobilization theory

What is one criticism of this theory?

cultural theory

What is one criticism of this theory?

new social movements theory

What is one criticism of this theory?

- Looking Ahead: Social Movements In the Twenty-First Century

  What is the future of social movements as projected by the author?

PART VIII: ANALYSIS AND COMMENT

Critical Thinking

"The Rumor Mill: Paul Is Dead!"

Key Points: Questions:

Controversy and Debate

"Are You Willing to Take a Stand"

Key Points: Questions:

Seeing Ourselves--National Map 23-1

"Support for Public Broadcasting across the United States"

Key Points: Questions:

Social Change: Traditional, Modern, and Postmodern Societies

24

PART I: CHAPTER OUTLINE

I. What is Social Change?
II. Causes of Social Change
    A. Culture and Change
    B. Conflict and Change
    C. Ideas and Change
    D. Demographic Change
III. Modernity
    A. Four Dimensions of Modernization
    B. Ferdinand Tonnies: The Loss of Community
    C. Emile Durkheim: The Division of Labor
    D. Max Weber: Rationalization
    E. Karl Marx: Capitalism
IV. Theoretical Analysis of Modernity
    A. Structural-Functional Theory: Modernity As Mass Society
        1. The Mass Scale of Modern Life
        2. The Ever-Expanding State
    B. Social Conflict Theory: Modernity As Class Society
        1. Capitalism
        2. Persistent Inequality
    C. Modernity and the Individual
        1. Mass Society: Problems of Identity
        2. Class Society: Problems of Powerlessness
    D. Modernity and Progress
    E. Modernity: Global Variation
V. Postmodernity
VI. Looking Ahead: Modernization and Our Global Future
VII. Summary
VIII. Key Concepts
IX: Critical-Thinking Questions
X. Applications and Exercises
XI. Sites to See

PART II: LEARNING OBJECTIVES

1. To be able to identify and describe the four general characteristics of social change.
2. To be able to identify and illustrate the different sources of social change.
3. To be able to discuss the perspectives on social change as offered by Ferdinand Tonnies, Emile Durkheim, Max Weber, and Karl Marx.
4. To be able to identify and describe the general characteristics of modernization.
5. To be able to identify the key ideas of two major interpretations of modern society: mass society and class society.
6. To be able to discuss the ideas of postmodernist thinkers and critically consider their relevance for our society.

PART III: KEY CONCEPTS

anomie

class society

diffusion

discovery

division of labor

Gemeinschaft

Gesellschaft

individualism

invention

mass society

mechanical solidarity

modernity

modernization

organic solidarity

other-directedness

postmodernity

progress

relative deprivation

social change

social character

social movement

tradition-directedness

PART IV: IMPORTANT RESEARCHERS

Karl Marx   Max Weber

Emile Durkheim   Ferdinand Tonnies

William Ogburn   David Reisman

Herbert Marcuse   William Bennett

PART V: STUDY QUESTIONS

True-False

1.	T	F	Three pivotal *sources* of social change are *diffusion, invention,* and *discovery*.
2.	T	F	*Max Weber* argued that technology and conflict are more important than ideas in transforming society.
3.	T	F	Overall, only about 9 percent of U.S. residents have not moved during the last thirty years.
4.	T	F	*Modernity* is defined as social patterns resulting from industrialization.
5.	T	F	According to *Peter Berger*, a characteristic of modernization is the expression of personal choice.
6.	T	F	The concepts of *Gemeinschaft* and *Gesellschaft* were developed by *Ferdinand Tonnies*.
7.	T	F	According to our author, *Emile Durkheim's* view of modernity is both more complex and more positive than that of *Ferdinand Tonnies*.
8.	T	F	Compared to *Emile Durkheim, Max Weber* was more critical of modern society, believing that the rationalization of bureaucracies would cause people to become alienated.
9.	T	F	A *mass society* is one in which industry and bureaucracy have enhanced social ties.
10.	T	F	*Class society theory* maintains that persistent social inequality undermines modern society's promise of individual freedom.
11.	T	F	According to *David Reisman*, a type of social character he labels *other-directedness* represents rapidly changing industrial societies.
12.	T	F	People in the U.S. are less likely than people in other industrialized societies to see *scientific advances* as helping mankind.
13.	T	F	*Postmodernity* refers to the recent trend in industrialized societies of a return to tradition values and practices.
14.	T	F	The *communitarianism movement* rests on the simple premise the "strong rights presume strong responsibilities."

Multiple Choice

1.   The transformation of culture and social institutions over time refers to

   (a)   social statics.
   (b)   social change.
   (c)   cultural lag.
   (d)   modernity.

2. *William Ogburn's* theory of _____ states that material culture changes faster than nonmaterial culture.

   (a)   modernity
   (b)   cultural lag
   (c)   modernization
   (d)   anomie
   (e)   rationalization

3. _____ is the process of social change begun by industrialization.

   (a)   Postmodernity
   (b)   Anomie
   (c)   Mass society
   (d)   Modernization
   (e)   Modernity

4. He developed the theory of *Gemeinschaft* and *Gesellschaft*, arguing that the Industrial Revolution weakened the social fabric of family and tradition by introducing a business-like emphasis on facts, efficiency, and money.

   (a)   Karl Marx
   (b)   Emile Durkheim'
   (c)   Max Weber
   (d)   Ferdinand Tonnies

5. For *Emile Durkheim*, modernization is defined by the increasing _____ of a society.

   (a)   mechanical solidarity
   (b)   alienation
   (c)   division of labor
   (d)   conspicuous consumption

6. In contrast to Ferdinand Tonnies, who saw industrialization as amounting to a loss of solidarity, _____ viewed modernization not as a loss of community but as a change from community based on bonds of likeness to community based on economic interdependence.

   (a)   Emile Durkheim
   (b)   Karl Marx
   (c)   Max Weber
   (d)   Peter Berger

7. For *Max Weber*, modernity means replacing a traditional world view with a(n) _____ way of thinking.

    (a) alienated
    (b) marginal
    (c) mechanical
    (d) organic
    (e) rational

8. *Karl Marx's* theory underestimated the dominance of _____ in modern society.

    (a) inequality
    (b) alienation
    (c) power
    (d) bureaucracy
    (e) false consciousness

9. Which of the following is most *accurate?*

    (a) Emile Durkheim's concept of organic solidarity refers to social bonds of mutual dependency based on specialization.
    (b) Ferdinand Tonnies saw societies as changing from the social organization based on Gesellschaft to the social organization based on Gemeinschaft.
    (c) Peter Berger argued that modern society offers less autonomy than is found in preindustrial societies.
    (d) Emile Durkheim's concept of mechanical solidarity is very similar in meaning to Ferdinand Tonnies' concept of Gesellschaft.

10. *Emile Durkheim's* concepts of *mechanical solidarity* and *organic solidarity* are similar in meaning to the concepts

    (a) mass society and class society.
    (b) tradition-directedness and other-directedness.
    (c) anomie and progress.
    (d) Gemeinschaft and Gesellschaft.
    (e) none of the above

11. _____ *theory* focuses on the expanding scale of social life and the rise of the state in the study of modernization.

    (a) Dependency
    (b) Modernization
    (c) Social class
    (d) Rationalization
    (e) Mass-society

442

12.	_____ *theory* views the process of modernization as being linked to the rise of capitalism, and sees its effects as involving the persistence of social inequality.

(a)	Mass-society
(b)	Class-society
(c)	Modernity
(d)	Cultural lag

13.	Which social scientist described *modernization* in terms of its affects on *social character*?

(a)	Peter Berger
(b)	William Ogburn
(c)	David Reisman
(d)	Herbert Marcuse
(e)	David Klein

14.	_____ refers to personality patterns common to members of a particular society.

(a)	Mass-society
(b)	Class-society
(c)	Traditionalism
(d)	Social character
(e)	Autonomy

15.	David Reisman suggests that _____ is representative of modern societies.

(a)	other-diectedness
(b)	self-directedness
(c)	mechanical-directedness
(d)	anomic-directedness

16.	_____ *theory* argues that persistent social inequality undermines modern society's promise of individual freedom.

(a)	Mass-society
(b)	Modernization
(c)	Traditional-rational
(d)	Mechanical
(e)	Class-society

17.	_____ suggested that we be critical of *Max Weber's* view that modern society is rational because technological advances rarely empower people; instead, we should focus on the issue of how technology tends to reduce people's control over their own lives.

(a)	Emile Durkheim
(b)	Herbert Spencer
(c)	David Reisman
(d)	Herbert Marcuse
(e)	Ferdinand Tonnies

18.	The *Kaiapo*

(a)	is a small society in Brazil.
(b)	is a ritual among the Mbuti of the Ituri forest.
(c)	is a sacred tradition involving animal sacrifices which has been made illegal by the Canadian government.
(d)	are a people of Asia who represent the Gesellschaft concept developed by Ferdinand Tonnies.
(e)	is a ritualistic war pattern of the Maring, a New Guinea culture of horticulturalists.

19.	According to public opinion polls, in which of the following modern societies does the largest percentage of the population believe that *scientific advances* are helping society?

(a)	Great Britain
(b)	Japan
(c)	the United States
(d)	Canada
(e)	Mexico

20.	The bright light of "progress" is fading; science no longer holds the answers; cultural debates are intensifying; in important respects, modernity has failed; and social institutions are changing--are all themes running through _____ *thinking*.

(a)	class society
(b)	postmodern
(c)	mass society
(d)	social movements

Matching

1. ___ The transformation of culture and social institutions over time.
2. ___ Social patterns resulting from industrialization.
3. ___ Developed the concepts of Gemeinschaft and Gesellschaft.
4. ___ Developed the concepts of mechanical and organic solidarity.
5. ___ Argued that modern society was dominated by rationality.
6. ___ Understood modern society as being synonymous with capitalism.
7. ___ A society in which industry and bureaucracy have eroded traditional social ties.
8. ___ A capitalist society with pronounced social stratification.
9. ___ Personality patterns common to members of a particular society.
10. ___ The premise that strong rights presume strong responsibilities.

a.	mass society	f.	social character
b.	social change	g.	Emile Durkheim
c.	Max Weber	h.	communitarian
d.	Ferdinand Tonnies	i.	class society
e.	modernity	j.	Karl Marx

Fill-In

1. _____ refers to the transformation of culture and social institutions over time.

2. The process of *social change* has four major characteristics, including: social change is _____, social change is sometimes _____ but often _____, social change is _____, and some changes matter more than _____.

3. Focusing on culture as a source, *social change* results from three basic processes: _____, _____, and _____.

4. _____ refers to social patterns linked to industrialization.

5. According to Peter Berger, four major characteristics of *modernization* include: the decline of small, _____ communities, the _____ of personal choice, increasing social _____, and future orientation and growing awareness of _____.

6. *Emile Durkheim's* concept of *organic solidarity* is closely related to *Ferdinand Tonnies'* concept of _____.

7. _____ is a condition in which society provides little moral guidance to individuals.

8. For *Max Weber*, modernity amounts to the progressive replacement of a traditional world-view with a _____ way of thinking.

9. *Mass society theory* draws upon the ideas of _____, _____, and _____.

10. A _____ *society* is a society in which industry and expanding bureaucracy have eroded traditional social ties.

11. _____ *society* is a capitalist society with pronounced social stratification.

12.   _____ _____ refers to personality patterns common to members of a particular society.

13.   *David Reisman* argues that preindustrial societies promote _____-directedness, or rigid personalities based on conformity to time-honored ways of living.

14.   Five themes have emerged as part of *postmodern thinking*. These include that in important respects, _____ has failed; The bright promise of " _____ " is fading; _____ no longer holds the answers; Cultural debates are fading; and, social institutions are _____.

Definition and Short-Answer

1.   What are four characteristics of *social change*?

2.   Five general domains which are involved in *causing* social change are identified and discussed in the text. List these and provide an example for each.

3.   *Peter Berger* identifies four general characteristics of *modern societies*. What are these characteristics?

4.   Differentiate between *Ferdinand Tonnies, Emile Durkheim, Max Weber,* and *Karl Marx's* perspective on modernization.

5.   What factors of *modernization* do theorists operating from the *mass society* theory focus upon?

6.   What are the two types of *social character* identified by *David Reisman*? Define each of these.

7.   What are the arguments being made by *postmodernists* concerning social change in modern society? What do critics of this view say?

8.   Referring to *Table 24-1*, select a nonindustrialized society and compare it to the U.S. on four elements of society identified in the table. Provide a specific illustration representing a relative comparison for each element.

9.   Four general types of *social movements* are discussed in the text. Identify, define, and illustrate each of these.

10.   Four explanations of *social movements* are discussed in the text. Identify and describe each of these.

11.   *Peter Berger* has identified four major characteristics of modernization. What are these? Provide an illustration for each of these.

PART VI: ANSWERS TO STUDY QUESTIONS

True-False

1.	T	(pp. 624-625)	8.	T	(p. 630)
2.	F	(p. 625)	9.	F	(p. 632)
3.	T	(p. 626)	10.	T	(p. 633)
4.	T	(p. 626)	11.	T	(p. 635)
5.	T	(p. 627)	12.	F	(p. 638)
6.	T	(p. 628)	13.	F	(p. 638)
7.	T	(p. 629)	14.	T	(p. 642)

Multiple Choice

1.	b	(p. 624)	11.	e	(p. 632)
2.	b	(p. 624)	12.	b	(p. 634)
3.	d	(p. 626)	13.	c	(pp. 635)
4.	d	(p. 628)	14.	d	(p. 635)
5.	c	(p. 629)	15.	a	(p. 635)
6.	a	(p. 629)	16.	e	(p. 637)
7.	e	(p. 639)	17.	d	(p. 637)
8.	d	(p. 630)	18.	a	(p. 636)
9.	a	(pp. 627-628)	19.	c	(p. 638)
10.	d	(p. 629)	20.	b	(pp. 638-639)

Matching

1.	b	(p. 624)	6.	j	(p. 630)
2.	e	(p. 626)	7.	a	(p. 632)
3.	d	(p. 628)	8.	i	(p. 633)
4.	g	(p. 629)	9.	f	(p. 635)
5.	c	(p. 629)	10.	h	(p. 642)

Fill-In

1. social change (p. 624)
2. inevitable, intentional, unplanned, controversial, others (p. 624)
3. invention, discovery, diffusion (pp. 624-625)
4. modernity (p. 626)
5. traditional, expansion, diversity, time (pp. 626-627)
6. Gesellschaft (p. 628)
7. anomie (p. 629)
8. rational (p. 629)
9. Tonnies, Durkheim, Weber (p. 631)
10. mass (p. 632)
11. class (p. 633)
12. social character (p. 635)
13. tradition (p. 635)
14. modernity, progress, science, intensifying, changing (pp. 638-639)

PART VII: IN FOCUS--IMPORTANT ISSUES

- What Is Social Change?

  What are the four major characteristics of the process of *social change*?

- Causes of Social Change

  Provide an illustration for each of the following *causes of social change*:

  culture and change

  > invention

  > discovery

  > diffusion

  conflict and change

  ideas and change

  demographic change

- Modernity

  What are the four major characteristics of *modernization*?

448

Briefly summarize the view of modernity as expressed by each of the following theorists:

Ferdinand Tonnies

Emile Durkheim

Max Weber

Karl Marx

- Theoretical Analysis of Modernity

According to structural-functionalists, what are the essential characteristics of *mass-society*?

What is the major problem associated with mass-society? Illustrate:

According to conflict theorists, what are the essential characteristics of *class-society*?

What is the major problem associated with class-society? Illustrate:

- Postmodernity

  What are the five themes shared by *postmodern* thinkers?

  Provide evidence for two of these themes.

- Looking Ahead: Modernization and Our Global Future

  How do *modernization theory* and *dependency theory* shed light on issues raised in this chapter concerning modernization?

PART VIII: COMMENT AND ANALYSIS

Global Sociology

"Does "Modern" Mean "Progress"? The Case of Brazil's Kaiapo"

Key Points: Questions:

Critical Thinking

"Tracking Change: Is Life in the United States Getting Better or Worse?"

Key Points: Questions:

Controversy and Debate

"Personal Freedom and Social Responsibility: Can We Have It Both Ways?"

Key Points: Questions:

Seeing Ourselves--National Map 24-1

"Who Stays Put? Residential Stability across the United States"

Key Points: Questions: